AF470325

An olo.éditions production
www.oloeditions.com

Original title:
Crazy Photography
© 2012 olo.éditions

Concept & selection:
Nicolas Marçais, Philippe Marchand
Author: Diane Routex
Editing: Nicolas Marçais
Layout: Justine Jacquot-Haméon
Graphic design: Philippe Marchand

Published by Vivays Publishing Ltd
www.vivays-publishing.com
This edition © 2012 Vivays Publishing Ltd

English translation: Carol Gullidge
in association with First Edition
Translations Ltd, Cambridge, UK
Edited by Andrew Whittaker
Typesetting: Ute Conin, Cologne
Printed in China by Imago

ISBN 978-1-908126-41-2

CRAZY PHOTOGRAPHY

Vivays Publishing

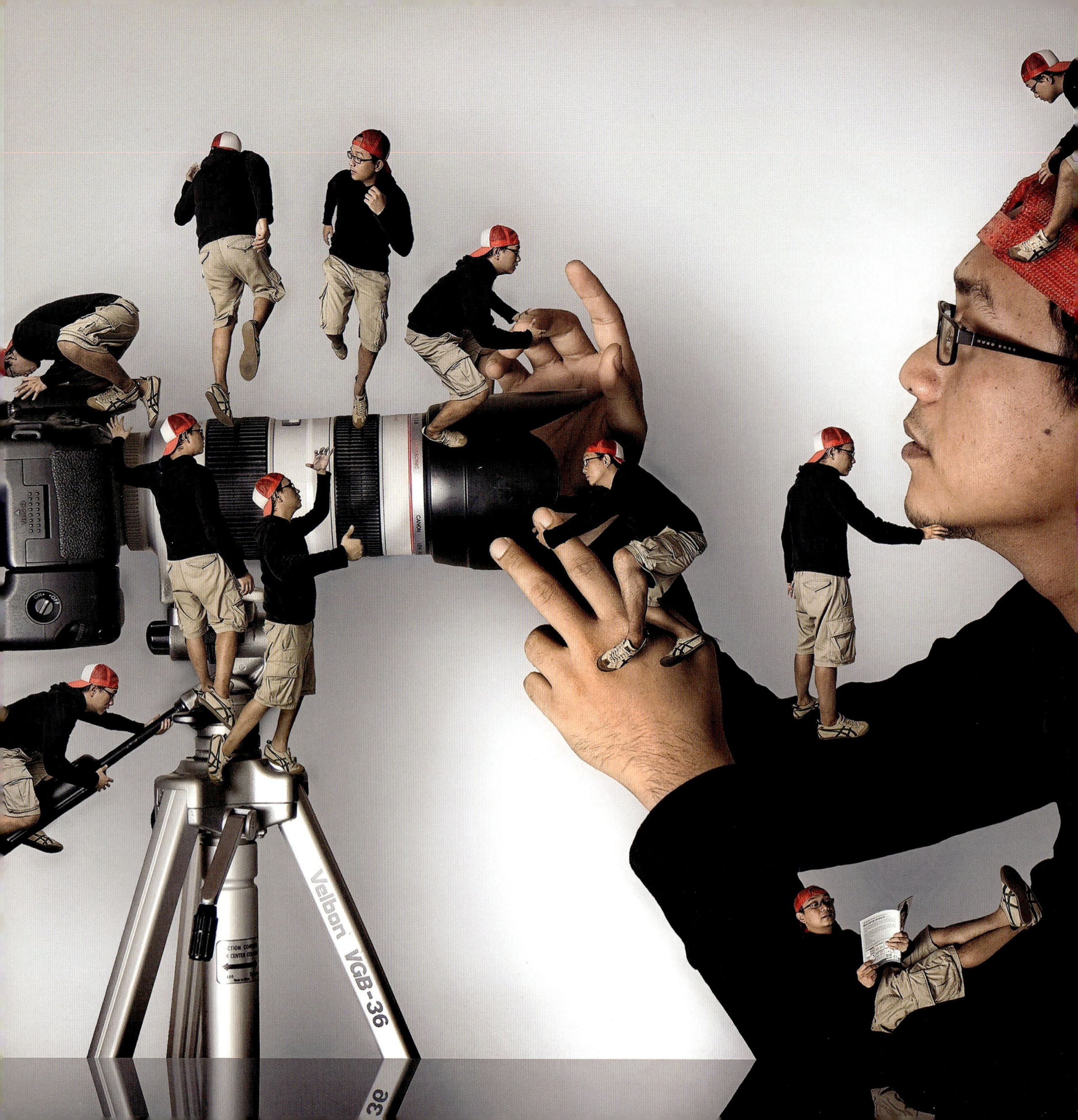
Velbon VGB-36

When Joseph Nicéphore Niépce showed the world its first photograph in the 1820s people were astonished by the image, a simple rooftop scene in Burgundy. They were amazed at this recreation of reality – the snapshot of a place in time. Even today, so many years on, the humble photograph can still shock and inspire. Of course, digital technology has breathed new life into the medium, making photography more accessible but also vastly expanding the bounds of what can be achieved. The fertile imagination has never had a more adaptable ally, capable of creating extraordinary fantasy worlds or dark, twisted interpretations of reality. Equally, the ability of more traditional photographers from Beijing to New York to compose challenging, rationale-defying images, often without the use of digital manipulation, continues to inspire.

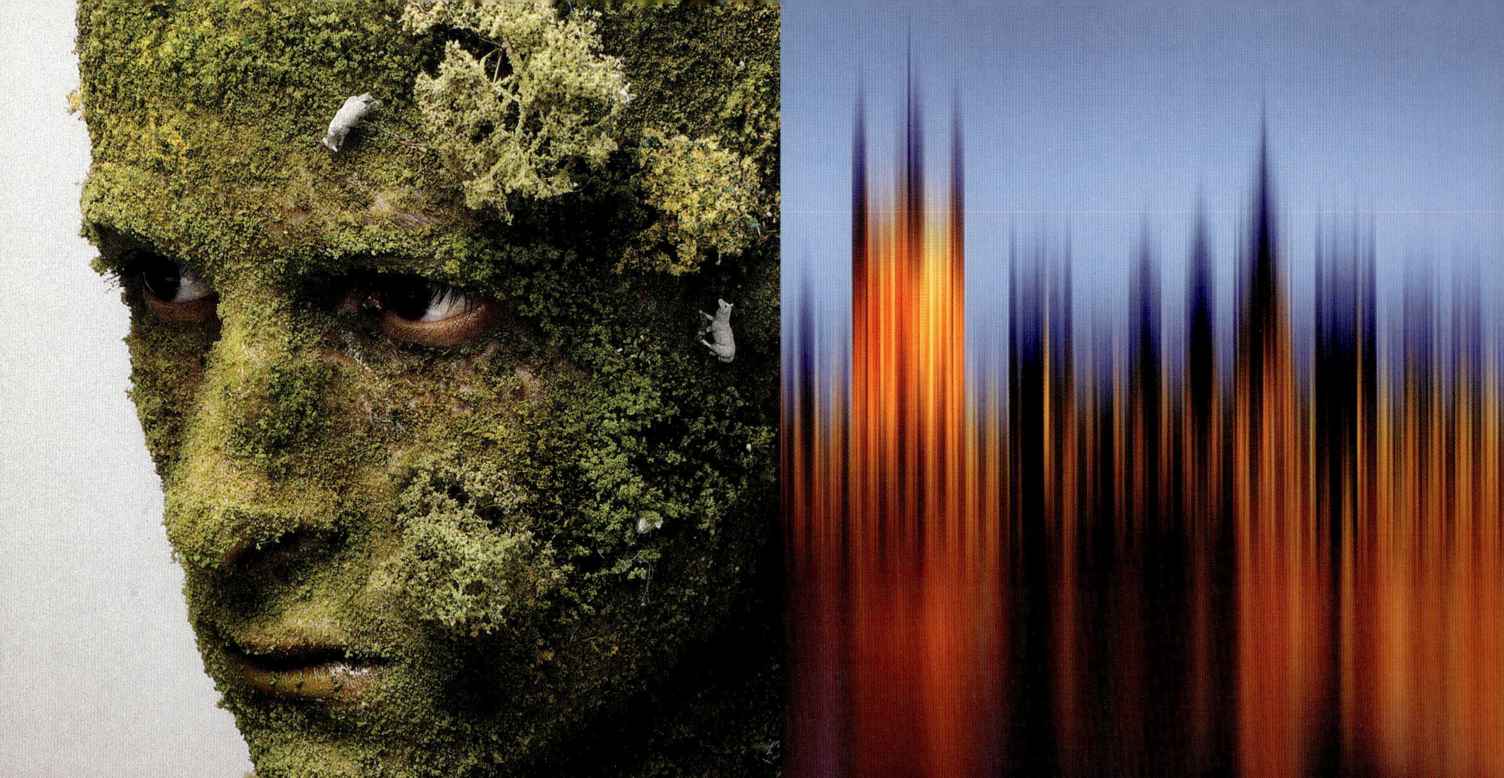

1

Body

Iain Crawford
Ari Mahardhika
Alex Castro
Levi van Veluw
Alberto Seveso
Bernard Demenge
Mr Toledano
Giuseppe Mastromatteo
Romain Laurent
Jens Sage
Liu Bolin
Mohammed Amine Nasseri

2

Scenery

Carl Warner
Michael Hughes
Studio Parris Wakefield
Todd McLellan
Jack Ambridge
Yang Yi
Alexandre Orion
Pep Ventosa
Barry Underwood
Michael Paul Smith
Pierre Javelle & Akiko Ida

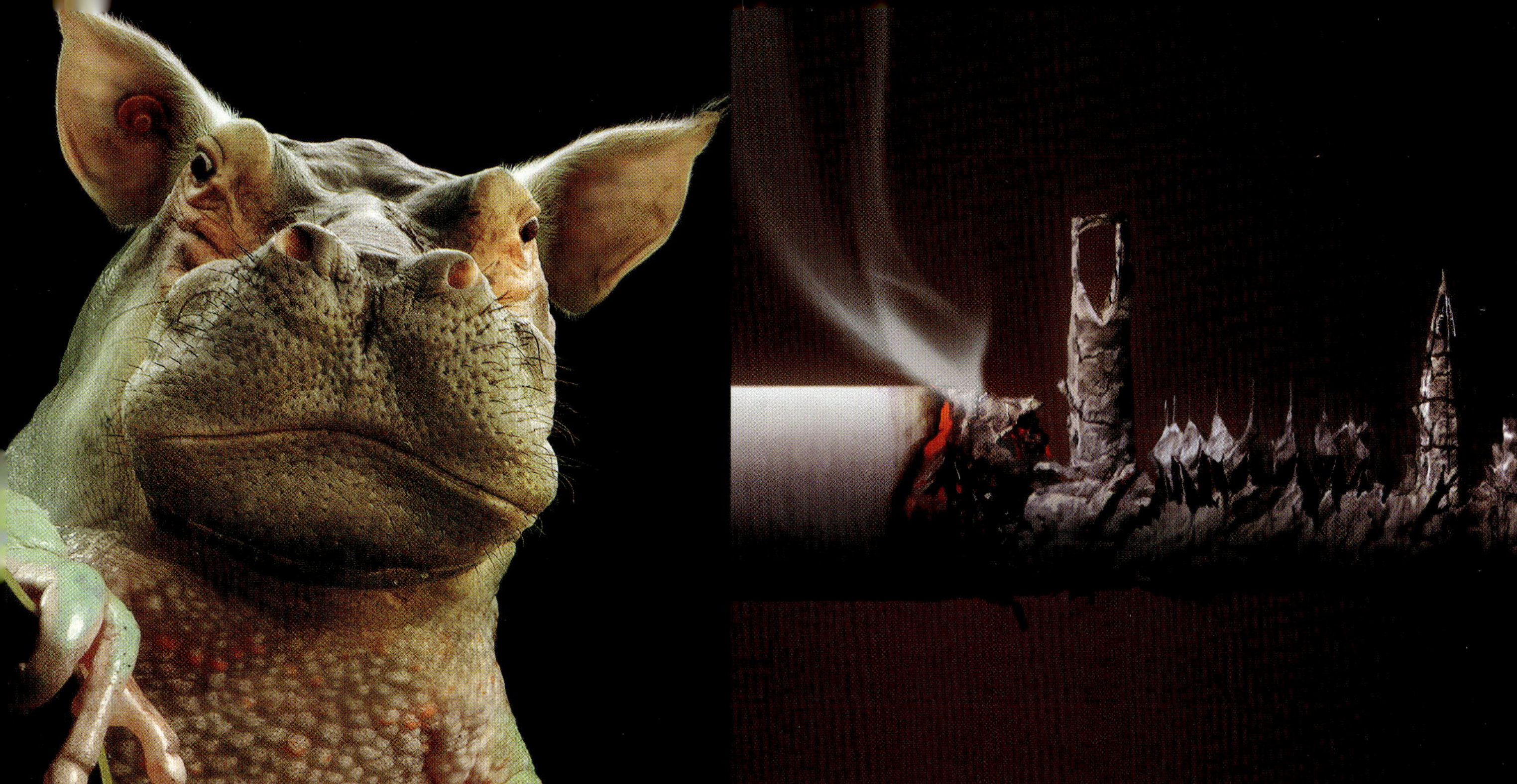

3

Fears

Jan Oliehoek
Jonathan Hobin
Laurence Demaison
Liu Di
Lucas C. Simões
Anton Semenov
Anthony Hibbert
Taylor James
Jérôme Abramovitch
Hilary Pecis
Cristian Crisis
Marc Da Cunha Lopes

4

Dreams

Anton Marrast
Aled Lewis
Michael Bosanko
Robert Overweg
Jaime Jasso
Li Wei
Erik Johansson
Thomas Edwards
Cecelia Webber
Lori Nix

BODY

Portrait photography gained momentum in the mid 19th century with the development of the daguerreotype, and for more than a century afterwards the human figure was depicted in print from every conceivable angle and in every possible setting, from the battlefield to the boudoir. In more recent years, the advent of digital photography has spawned myriad new possibilities. The body can be cloned, torn apart, deluged, spliced and concealed via the wonders of post-production manipulation. And yet, in an era where so much can be achieved with technology, some photographers still rely simply on costumes, props and tricks of the light to create dramatic images of the human figure.

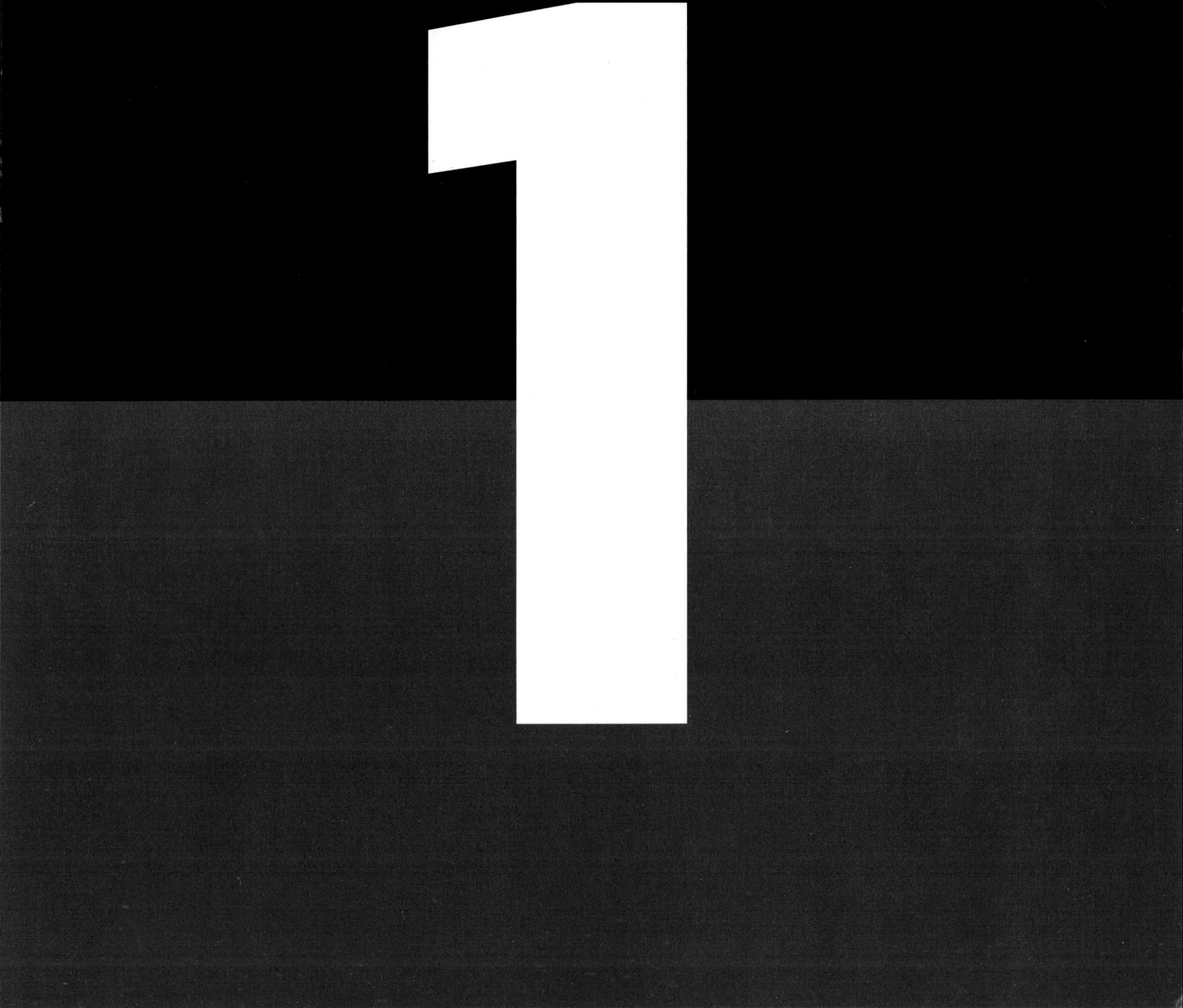

10

IAIN CRAWFORD

BODY

www.iaincrawford.com

Iain Crawford's photography reveals a world that we know well but which is rarely seen with such clarity. He stops the clocks, freezes time, capturing the minute details of movement and colour that are too small or too quick to comprehend with the naked eye.

Iain, an esteemed London-based fashion photographer, plays with colours, textures and fluid materials, from paint to powder, water to fabric. He captures the split second at which those materials impact on the human form, when the model is splashed, sprayed or splattered, the figure draped as if by flowing cloth. Moments that are otherwise lost can be pored over, dissected in all their beauty. Iain uses the techniques of high-speed photography to achieve the remarkable images. Exposure, shutter and flash are all precisely synchronised to capture the briefest instant in all its minute detail. 'I love the fusion between paint and model,' says Iain, discussing the images in which models are engulfed by coloured liquid. 'The resulting shapes are as opulent as any piece of bespoke couture. The excitement and anticipation as we waited to see the next piece of unpredictable chaos was electric. There was something magical about how random chance materialised into beautiful images in front of our eyes.'

HOCKEY
BLUE PAINT (Overleaf, left)
GREEN PAINT (Overleaf, right)

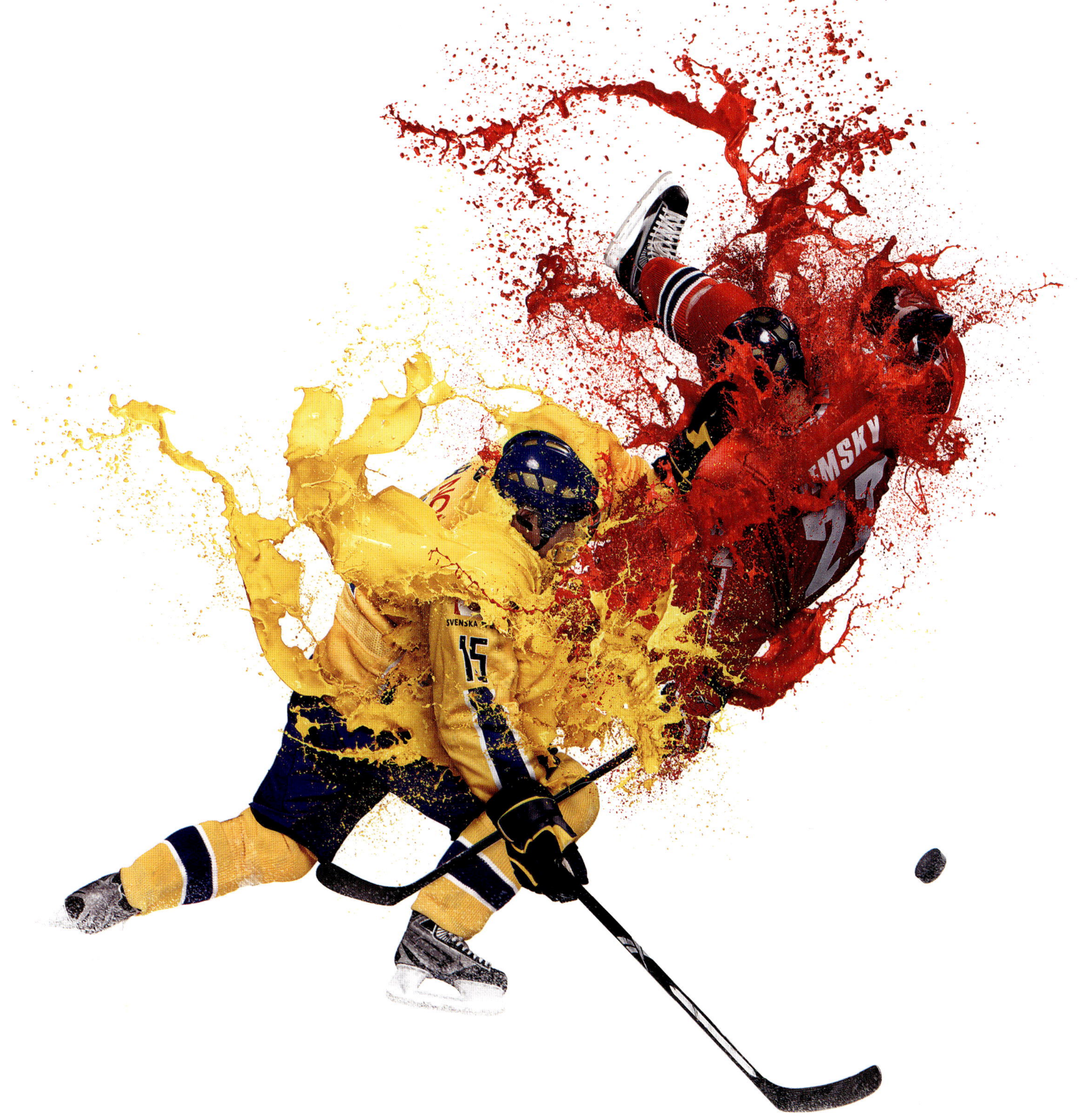
EMSKY
SVENSKA
15

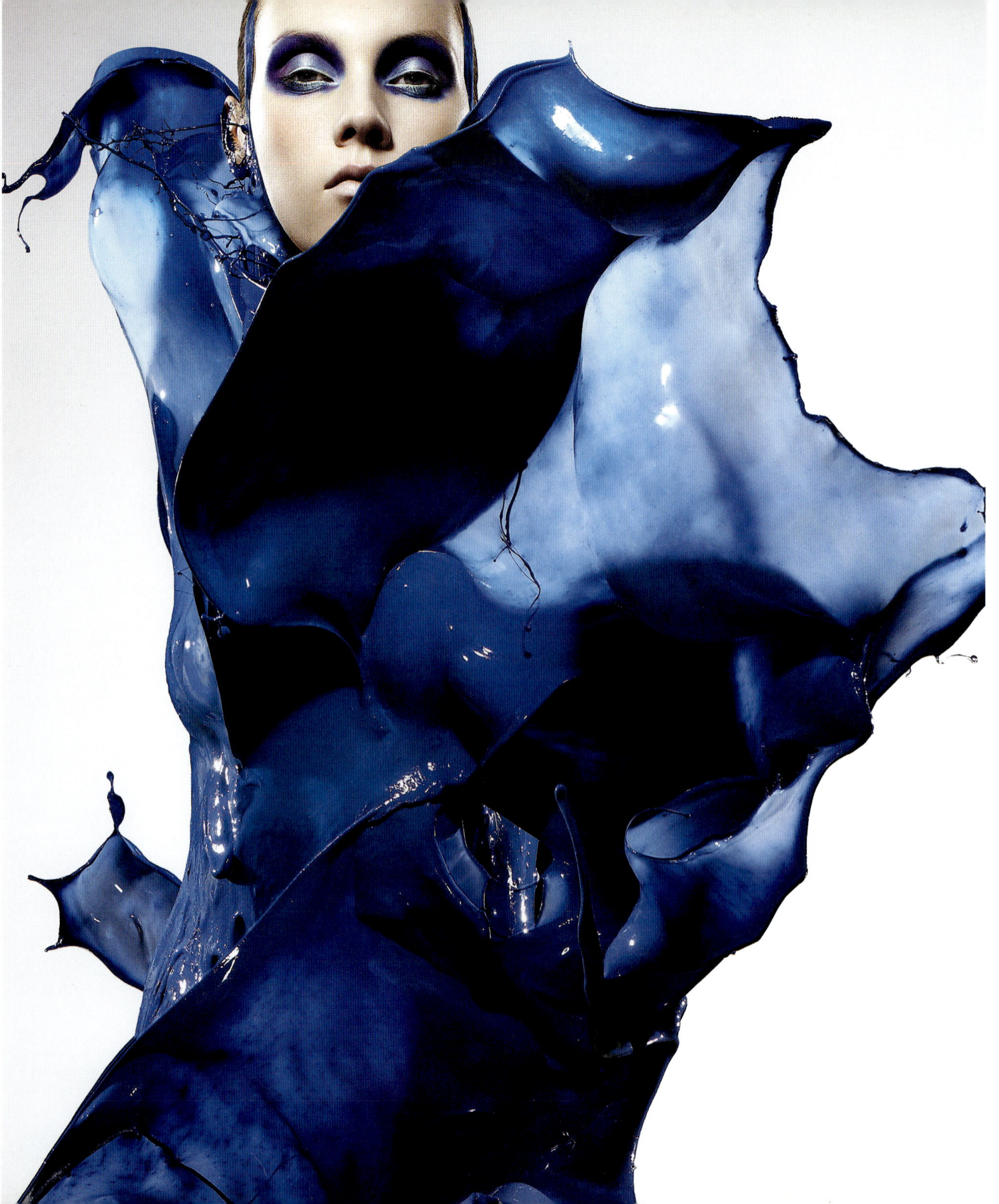

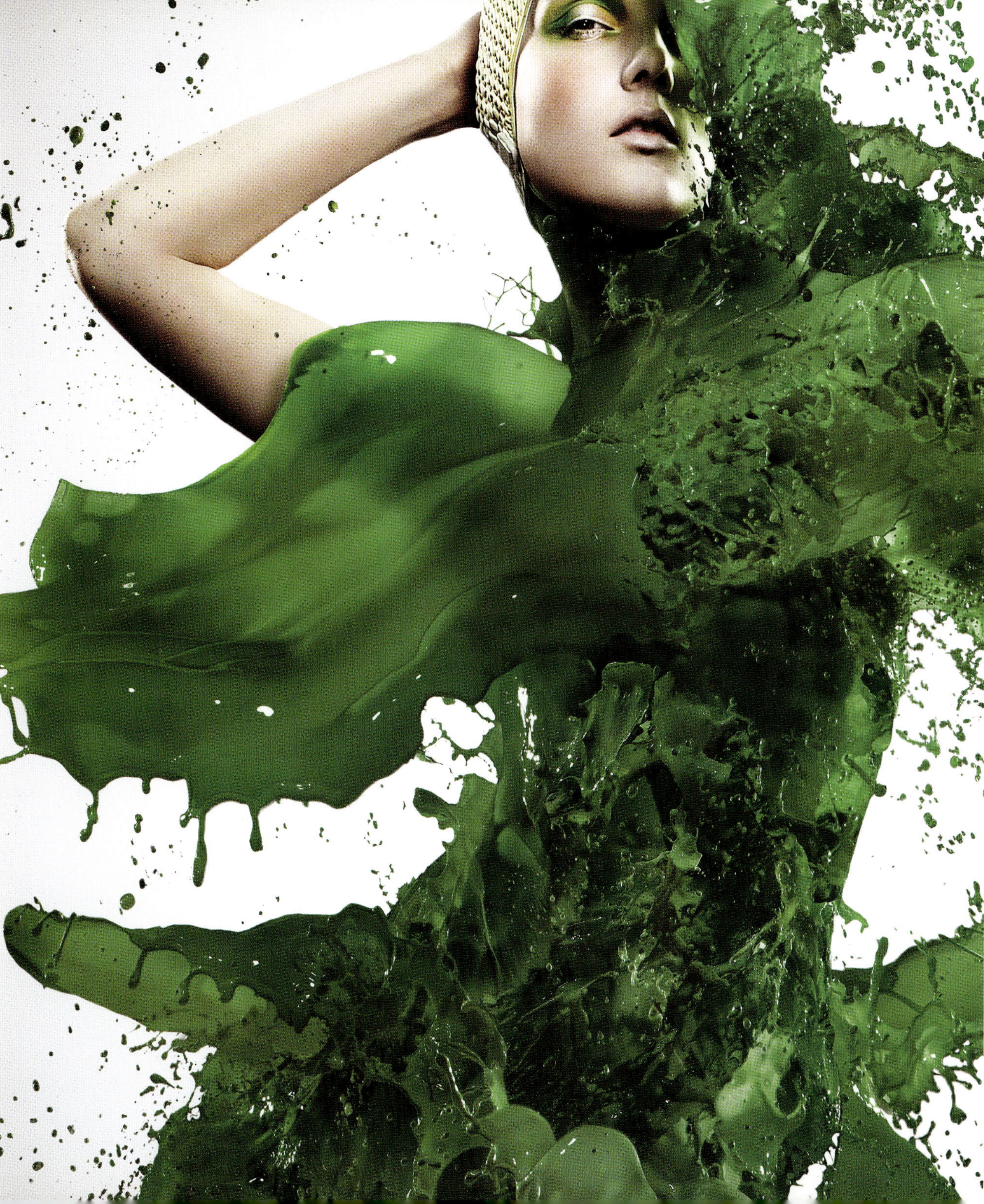

14

BODY

ARI MAHARDHIKA

www.flickr.com/photos/31488305@N04/sets

Who doesn't talk to themselves once in a while? Sometimes it's the only interesting conversation on offer. Photographer Ari Mahardhika takes those conversations to a new level, using the techniques of photomontage and digital cloning to play with notions of scale and the self.

Ari, native to Indonesia, has devoted the past six years to teaching himself photography. As you can see he takes an unconventional approach, crowding a full-scale image of himself or his friend, Audy, with tiny clones of that same figure. Each montage begins as a drawing, with Ari's latest Lilliputian vision set down on paper. This can take a week, after which he spends several hours with a tripod and a self-timer, shooting the relevant photographs. Each photograph is taken in front of a white wall at Ari's home, the blank background allowing for the image to be manipulated further on in the creative process that unfurls on his computer. Once the multiple miniature images have been assembled, Ari adds light, shadow and reflection for realism. In some montages Ari is beset with mini-me characters climbing all over his body; in others his full-scale representation watches as multiple miniatures busy themselves with some task. 'My montages are like a mixture of thoughts that I express in the form of fractions of me,' acknowledges the artist.

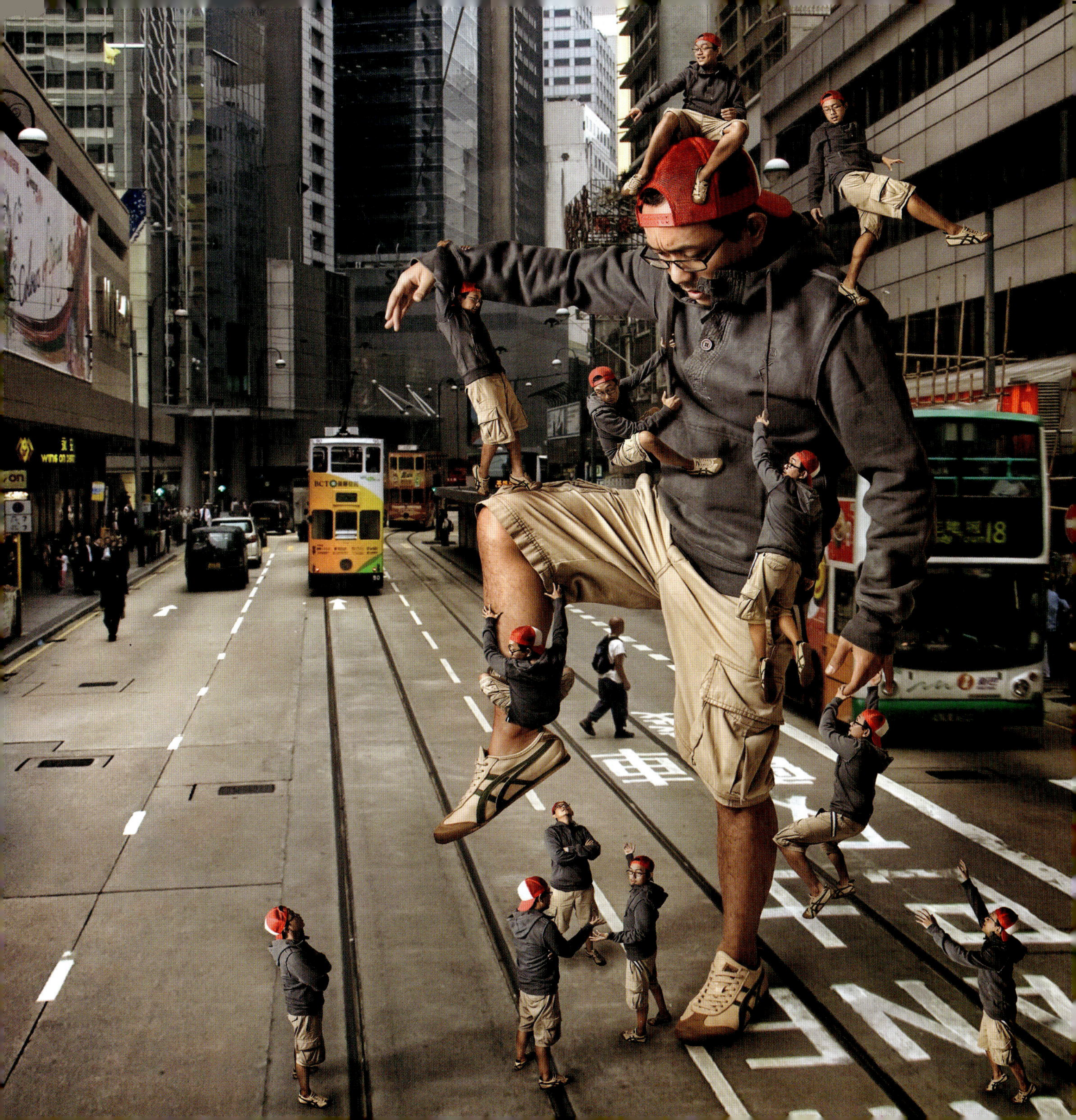

16

ALEX CASTRO

BODY

alexcastro.com.mx

Alex Castro has created a bestiary for the Photoshop age, jumbling up the species and awakening the animal inside all of us.

In his *Regresiones* series, Mexican designer Alex seamlessly blends animal heads with human torsos. The images are credible, natural and mildly disturbing. Frequently featured on the cover of the edgy *Picnic* magazine, the photos depict such characters as a monkey clad in a sweatshirt, a crow resplendent in a suit and even an elegant ostrich adorned with bead necklaces. Here and there, a human hand or arm is exposed. Alex demonstrates an impressive mastery of both classical portraiture (framing, lighting, tones, expression – it's all in there) and contemporary digital manipulation. In fusing the monkeys, birds, deer et al with human busts, he endows the beasts with emotions that would doubtless pass unnoticed in traditional animal photography. Subtly, beautifully, Alex reminds us that we're not so far removed from the natural world and, indeed, that we might not be the only species capable of contemplative thought.

REGRESIÓN #006A
REGRESIÓN #004M (Overleaf, left)
REGRESIÓN #002V (Overleaf, right)

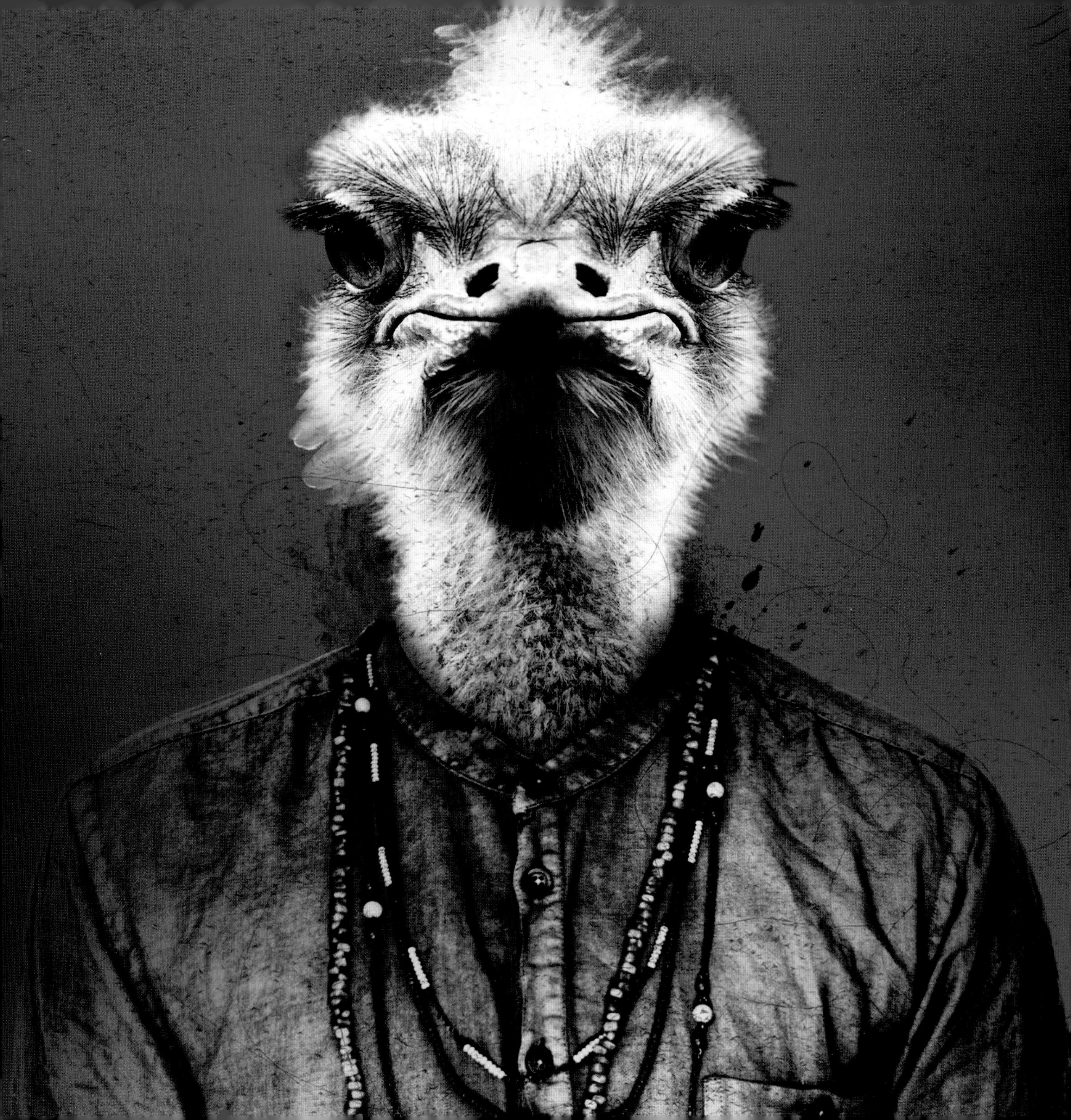

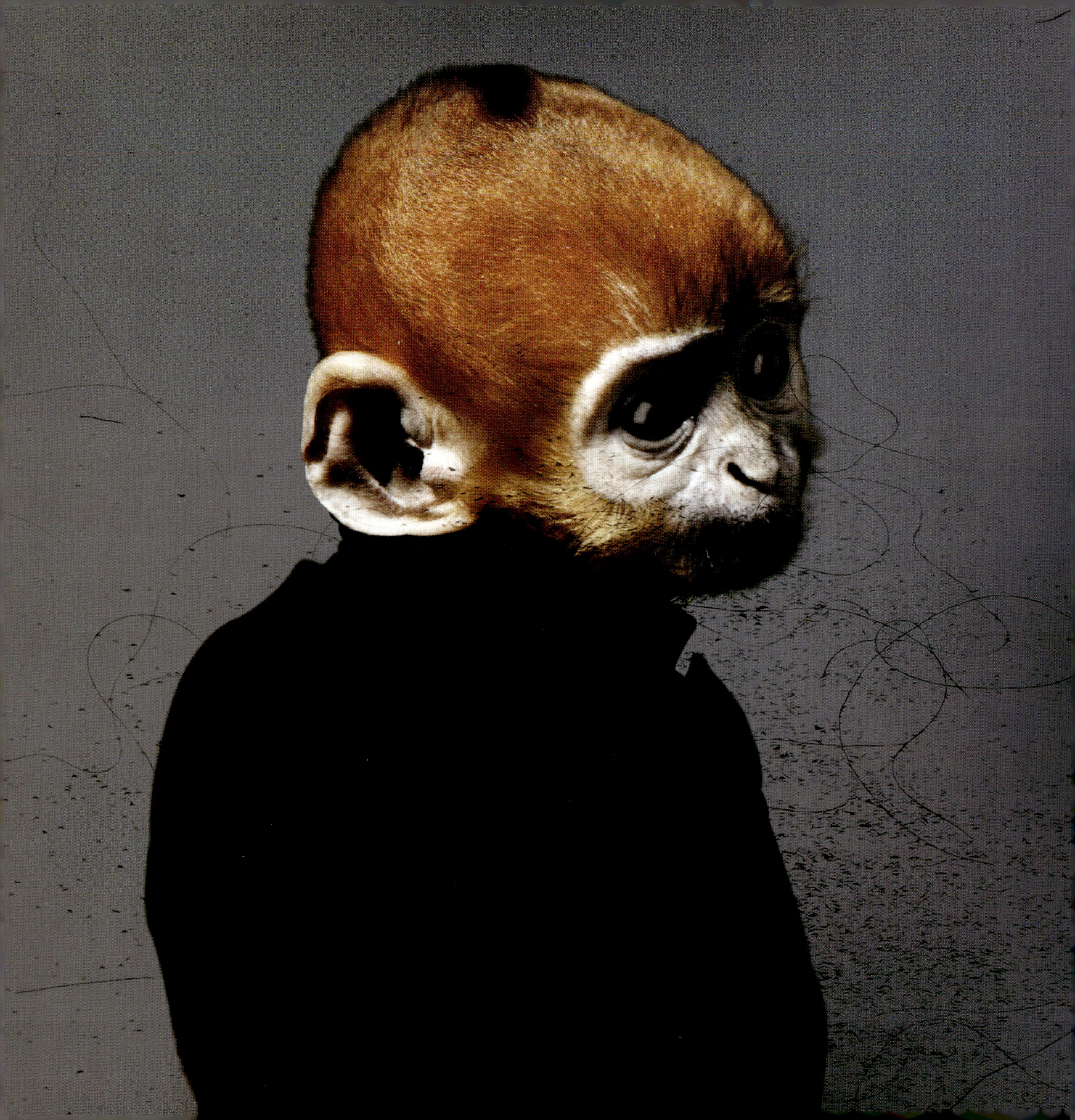

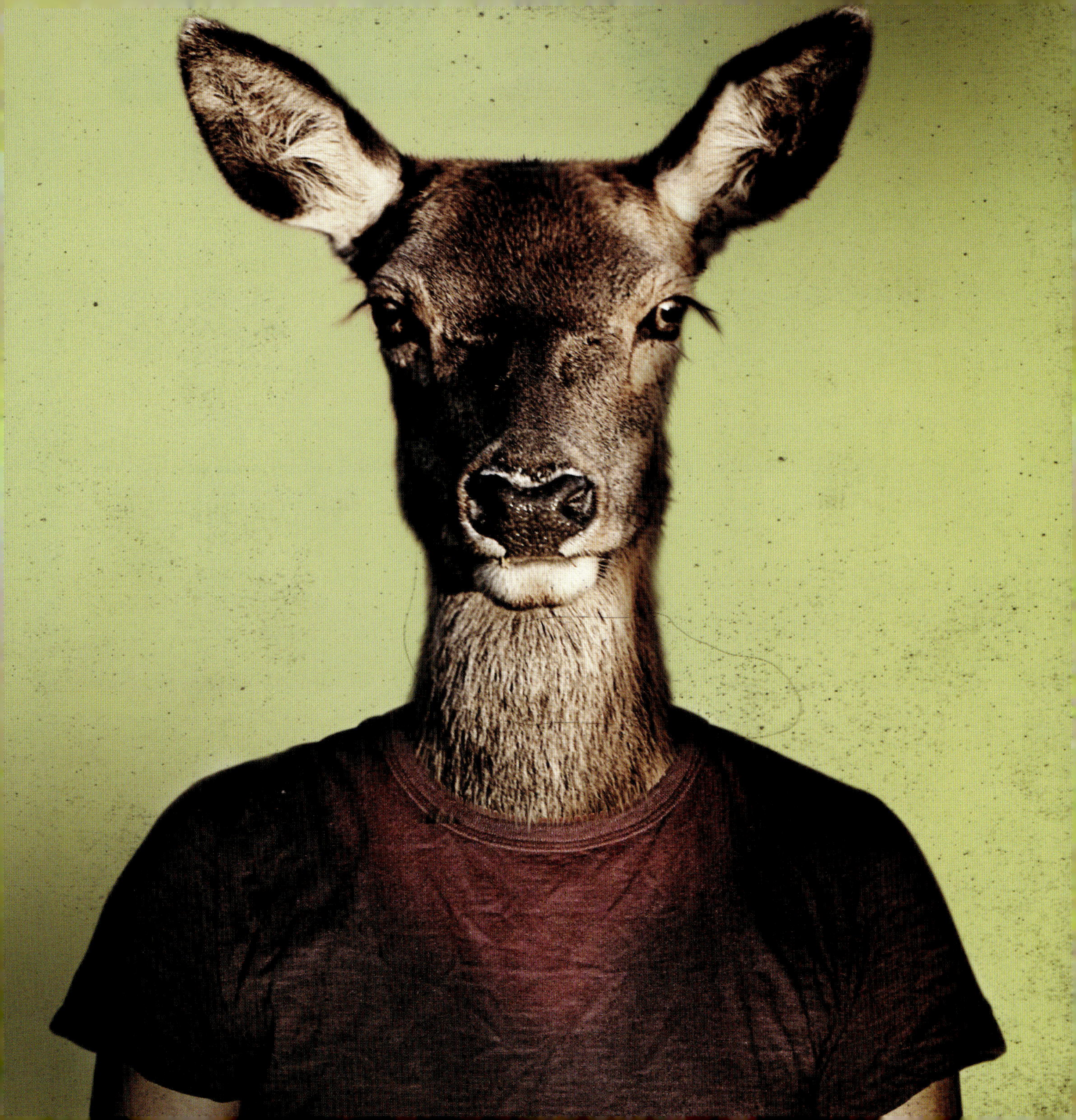

20

LEVI VAN VELUW

BODY

www.levivanveluw.com

Dutch photographer Levi van Veluw has reinvented self-portraiture. Where others see the face as the image, he views it as the canvas or the frame on which to mount materials and objects. The photographic record of each work, shot by Levi himself, is an integral part of the process

The head in Levi's photographs is usually his own. He layers it with carpet, gravel, wooden blocks, moss and even miniature cows, hoping to bring new contexts to the materials used and, in doing so, to interrogate the attributes of daily life. In his *Material Transfer* series, Levi completed three portraits within twenty-four hours, one with his head clad in cheap grey carpet, another in pebbles and the third in shards of wood. The series revealed a preoccupation with materiality, patterns and textures. 'The work you see is not a portrait,' he explains. 'But an information-rich image of colour, form, texture and content.' In *Landscapes* Levi radically reinterpreted the traditional landscape painting. He took grass, trees, babbling brooks and animals, lifted them from the two-dimensional canvas and transposed them onto the three-dimensional contours of his own head. He was literally 'in the landscape'. In large part, he suggests, the process is about control: 'Taking control of my environment and therefore taking control of life.'

ORIGIN OF THE BEGINNING 1.3
MATERIAL TRANSFERS, GRAVEL (Overleaf, left)
LANDSCAPES, LANDSCAPE I (Overleaf, right)

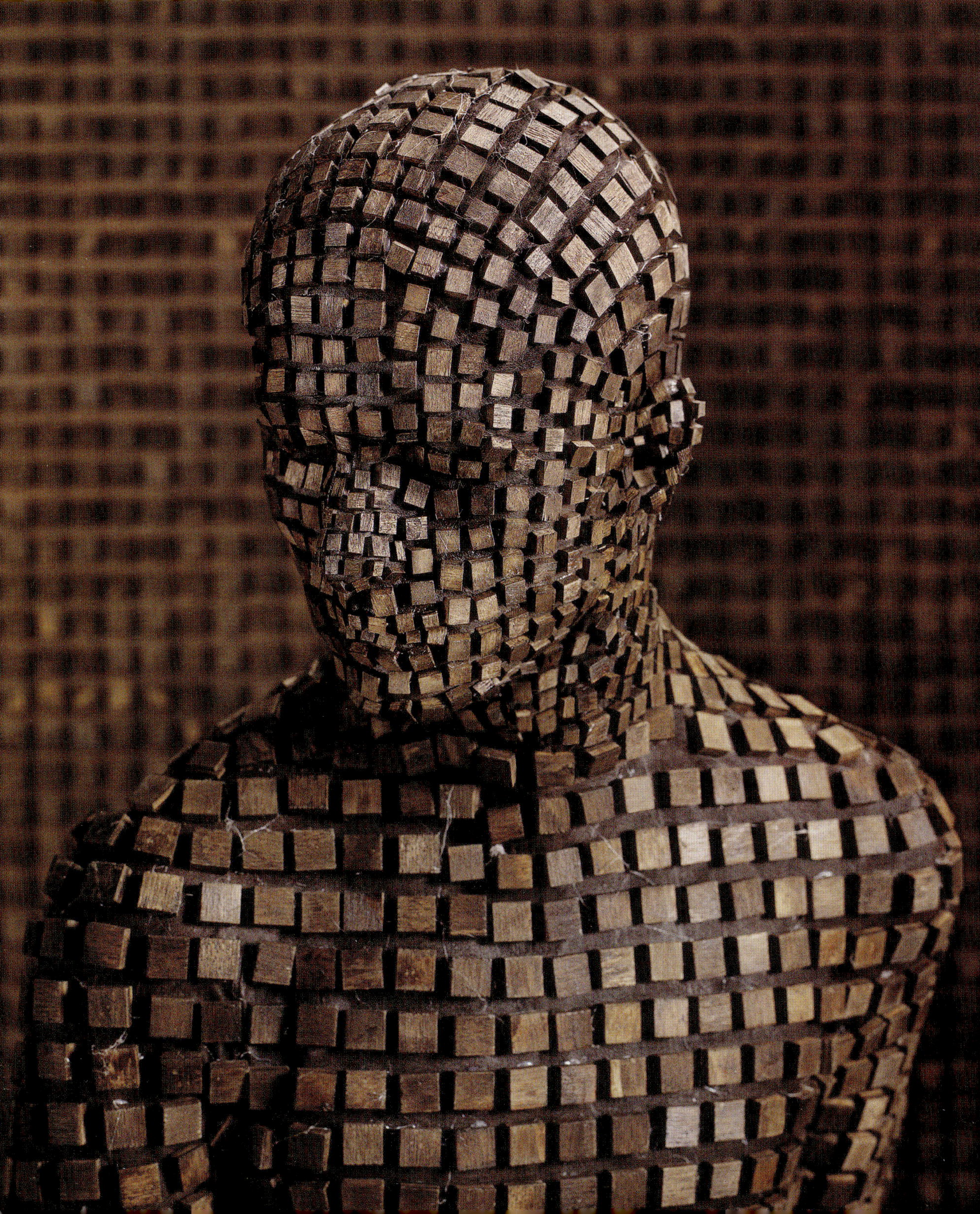

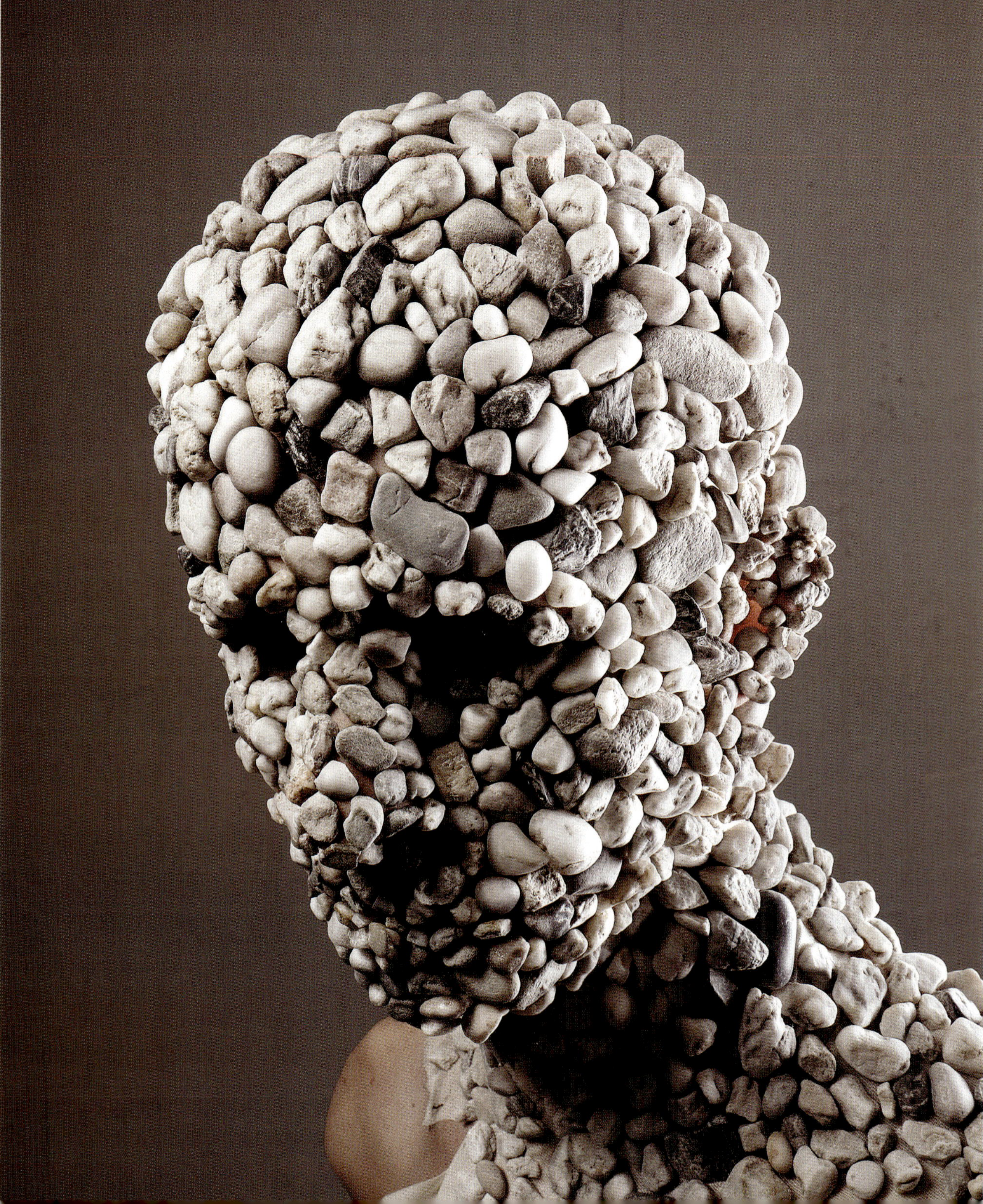

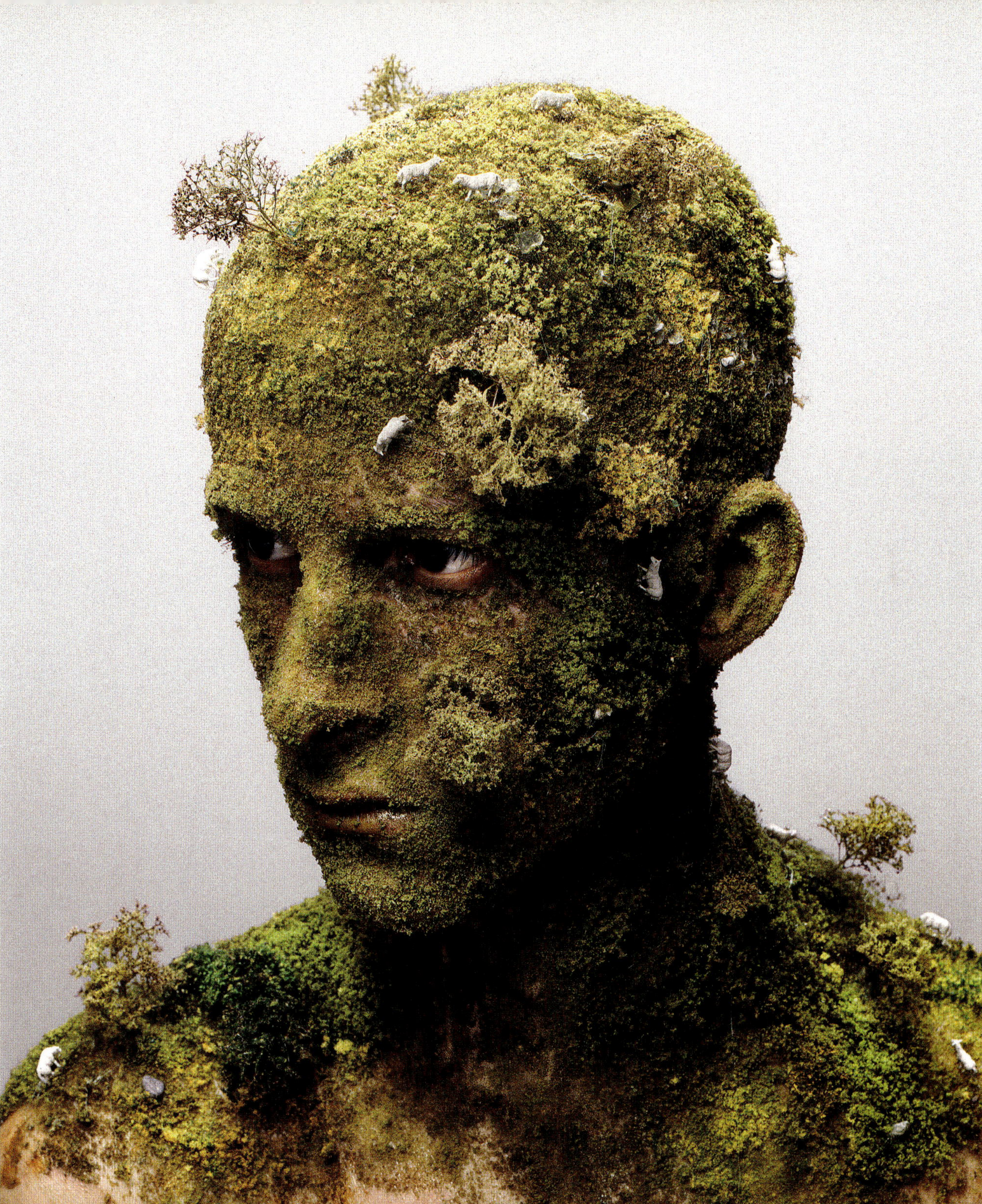

ALBERTO SEVESO

www.burdu976.com

Italian illustrator and designer Alberto Seveso creates vector images, manipulating his subjects into a collage of irregular shapes. In doing so, he turns the human body into a convoluted puzzle; part flesh and part abstract pattern.

Alberto made an online name for himself with a technique dubbed 'sperm-shaping'. He took photographs of models, which he then blended with colourful swirling forms not dissimilar to the shape of sperm. The title of one series of portraits, *A me mi piace la gnocca!* ('I love the pussy!'), offers some indication of where Alberto's creative oeuvre draws its inspiration from. The organic shapes and patterns in Alberto's work have become increasingly complex as they manipulate the contours of the human body. The artist has also brought his talents to bear on photographs of the great and good of popular culture, from David Lynch to Ice Cube and Kelly Slater. Rather than theorise about his work, Alberto prefers to let audiences generate their own impression. As he explains: '(It) does not really matter who I am or where I come from, the world has no borders. My illustrations speak for me.'

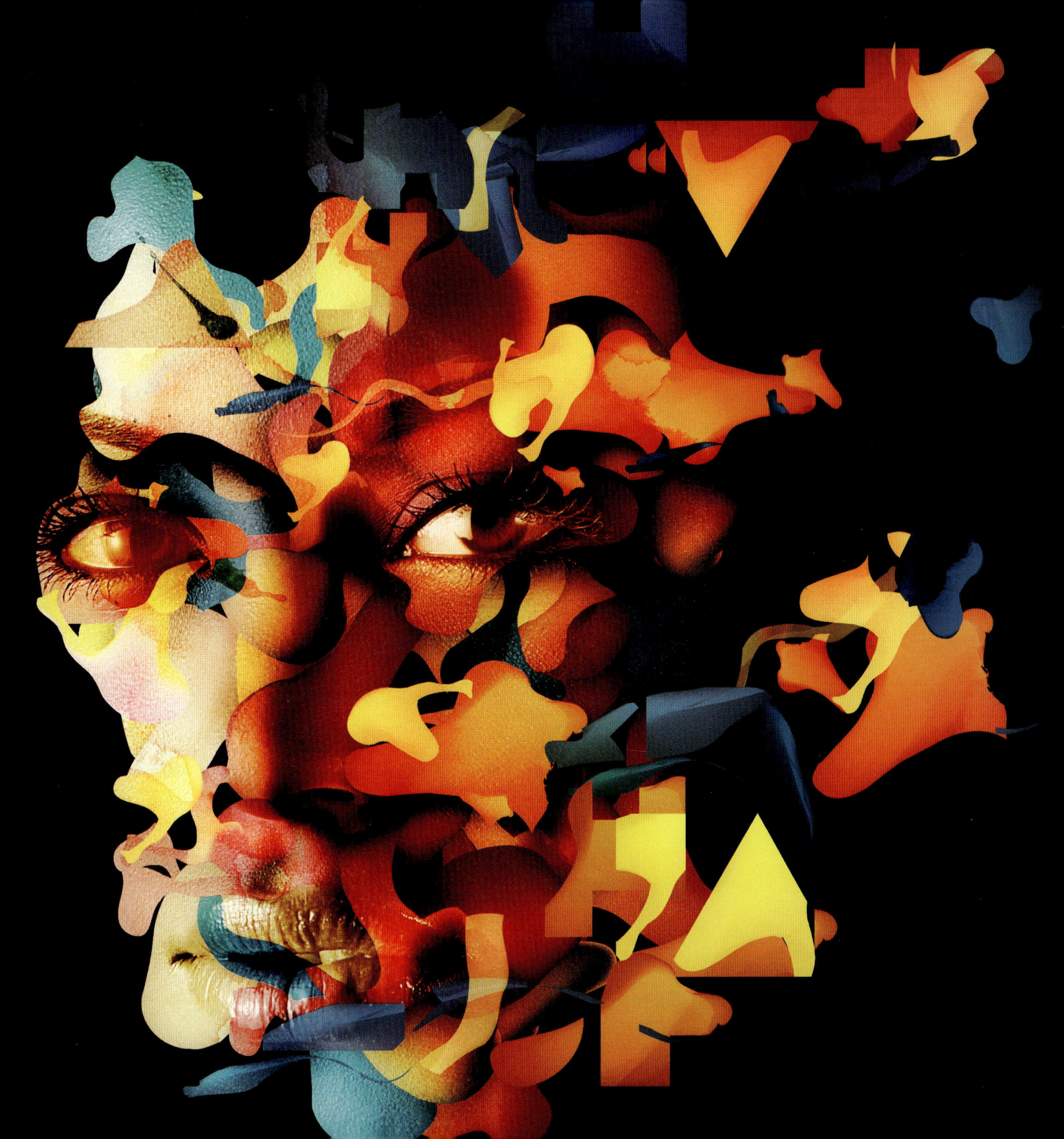

BERNARD DEMENGE

boitegrimace.blogspot.com

Who, bored in the midst of a Sunday afternoon, hasn't contemplated strapping a cheese grater to their chin for amusement? Few see it through. But for Bernard Demenge, strapping, squashing and generally manipulating his own face into a series of absurd grimaces has spawned an entire series of photographs.

'I love grimaces, pulling faces,' explains the French photographer. 'In a bid to win people over by making them laugh, I pursued this natural trait, punctuating my speech with furtive ape-like gestures. Now I can't help myself.' For *Parade*, a series of grimacing self-portraits, Bernard established a mini-studio – a kind of collapsible photo booth – in his apartment. He began without major accessories, contorting his face for the camera by means of a well-placed rubber band or some sticky tape. Then he graduated to household objects, from cotton buds propped in the mouth to a scrubbing brush lodged, moustache-style, under the nose. And then there was the aforementioned cheese grater. Bernard's work is an ode to absurdity, but *Parade* also has a deeper resonance, camouflaging an act of dissidence behind the childlike posturing. As he comments: 'I thumbed a grubby nose, made grotty faces in a nasty grotty world to trigger dry laughter, slightly shocking, not nice and polite; a way of rebelling.'

SELF-PORTRAIT WITH GRIMACE SECURED BY STICKY TAPE

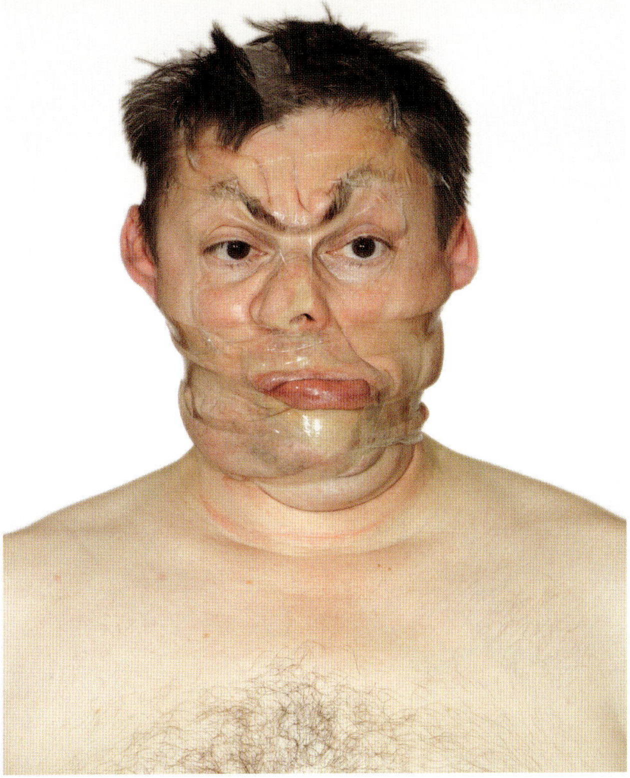

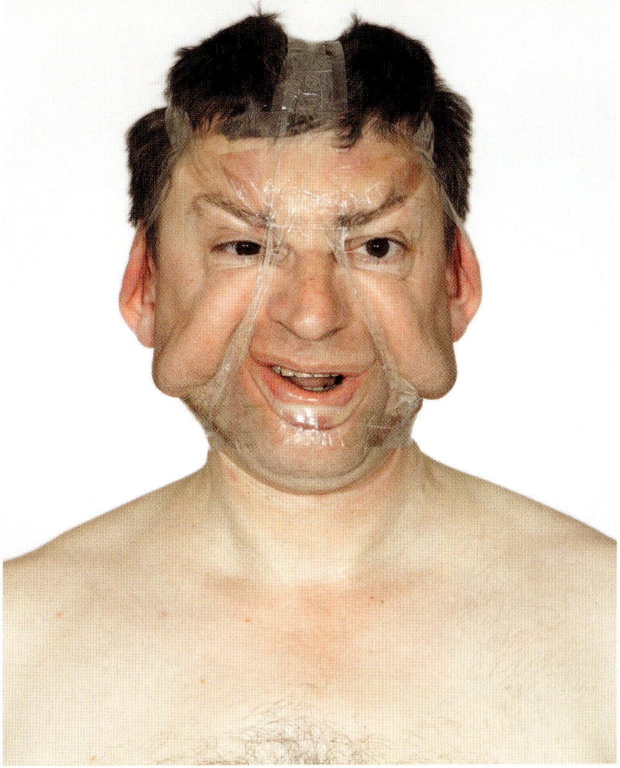

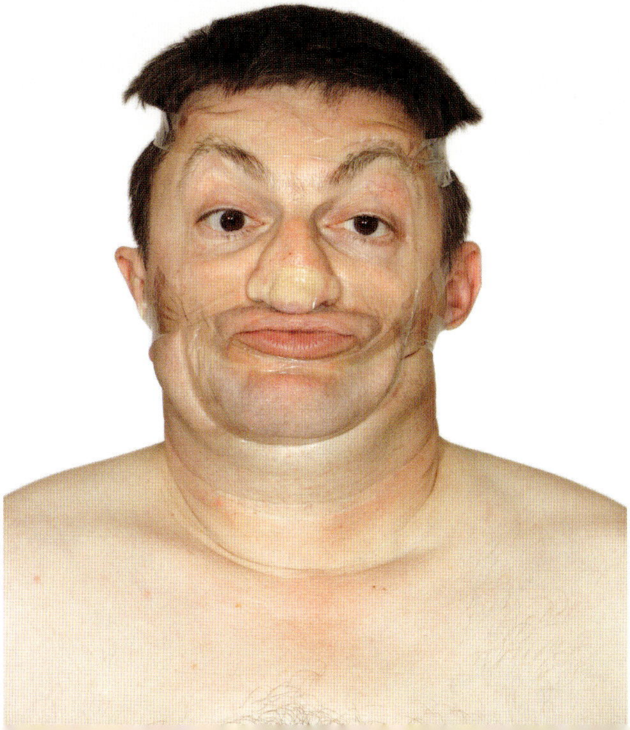

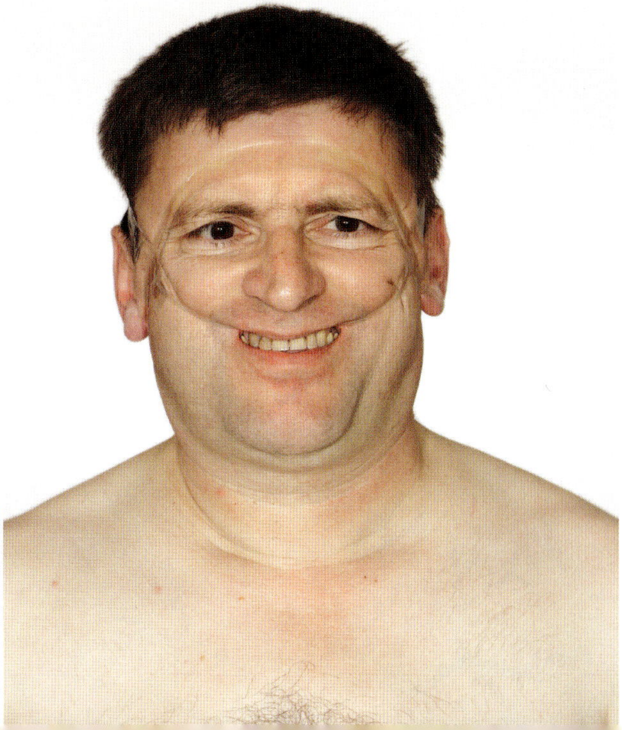

MR TOLEDANO

www.mrtoledano.com

All of the costumes in the *Hope & Fear* series of photographs are real. The outfits aren't digitally generated – the models are actually wearing suits made of guns or multiple naked toy dolls or fake breasts. It's all part of the socio-political oeuvre of Phillip Toledano, an English artist at work in New York.

'*Hope & Fear* is the external manifestation of internal desires and paranoia that are adrift in contemporary American society,' explains Mr Toledano (he drops the 'Phillip' in work mode). 'What are we afraid of? What do we love? How does our society function, and what does it worship?' He only became a full-time photographer and installation artist recently; prior to that, Mr Toledano held artistic directorships at various advertising agencies. His work consistently challenges our perceptions of contemporary society. In another series of images, *A New Kind of Beauty*, he raises questions about the use of plastic surgery to enhance looks; in *Stretch* he draws our attention to the depiction of the human body using mannequins enveloped like chrysalises in tensile fabric. Always, he leaves us room for contemplation, saying, 'Photographs should be like unfinished sentences. There should always be space for questions.'

STRETCH
HOPE & FEAR (Overleaf, left and right)

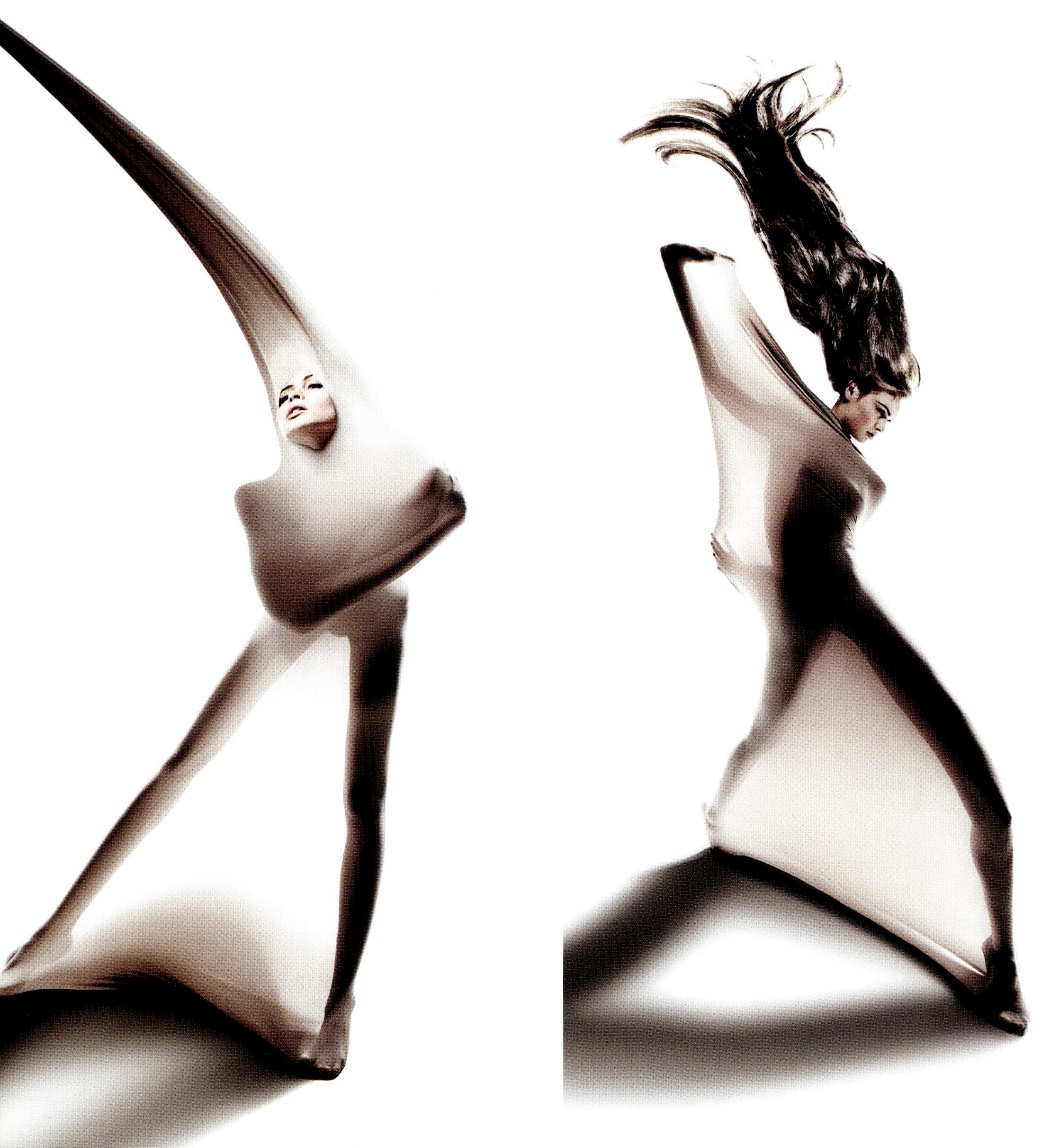

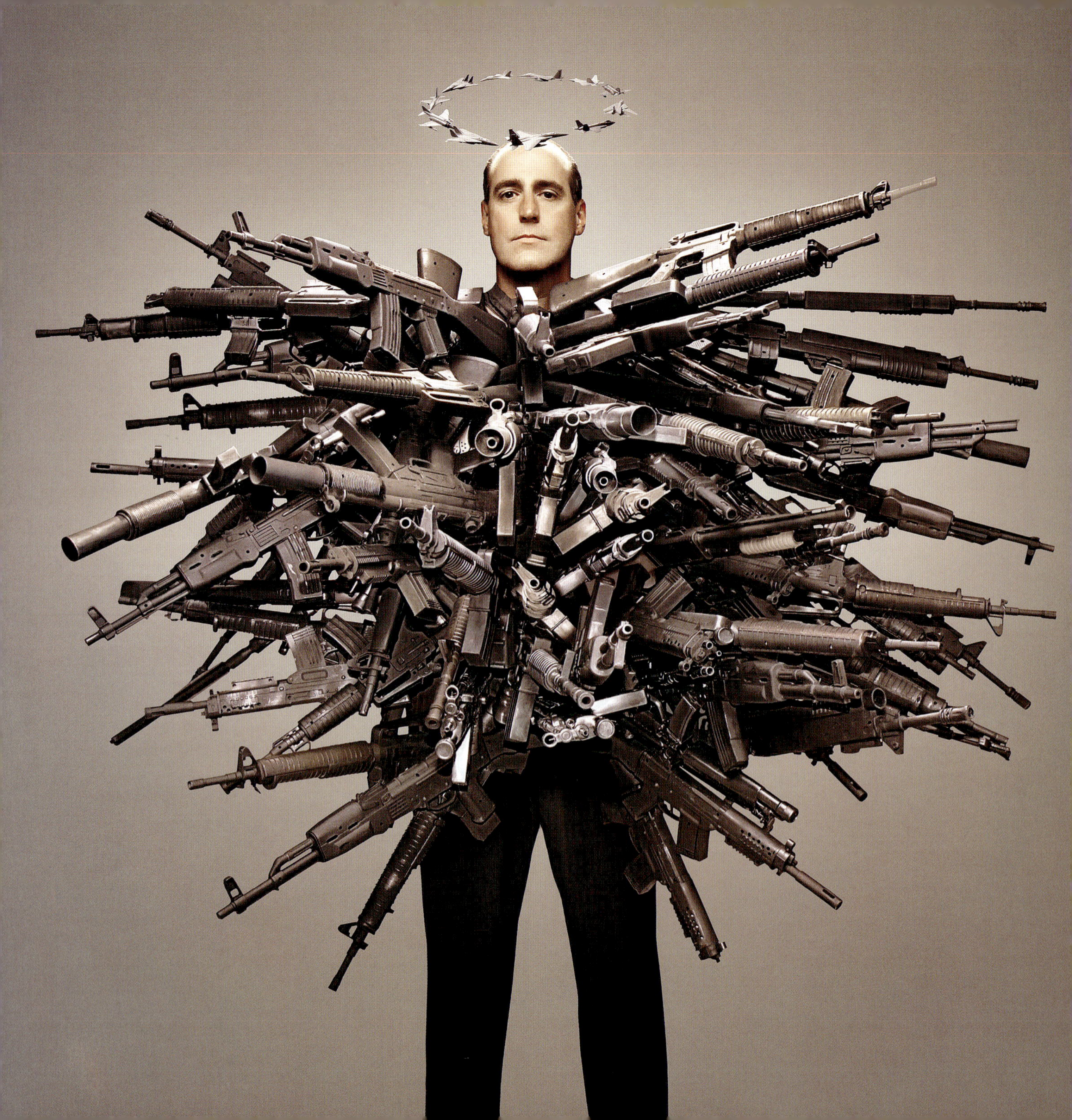

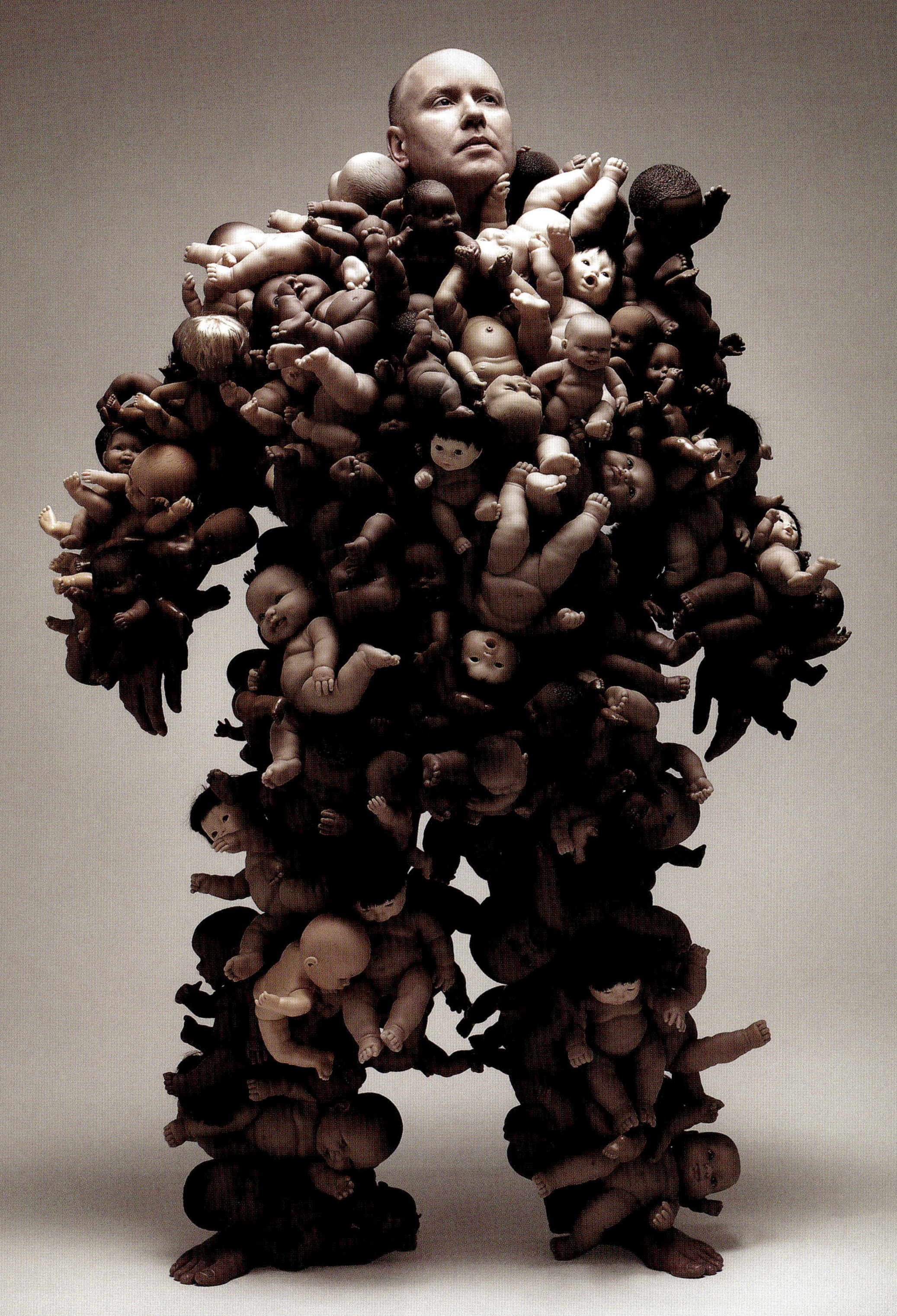

GIUSEPPE MASTROMATTEO

www.giuseppemastromatteo.com

Giuseppe Mastromatteo reinvigorates the figurative surrealism of René Magritte and Man Ray, using absurdity and beauty in equal measure to question established perceptions of the human body.

Indepensense, the US-based Italian artist's series of portrait photographs, presents a collection of transfigured bodies and reworked faces. With eyes peering out from the backs of heads, and ears seemingly transplanted from head to hand, the photographs depict a humanity of impossible, unrealistic dimensions. The digital collages displace the features of the face – the eyes, lips and ears – apparently ravaged, and yet the images carry no sense of violence. Indeed, each gives off an aura of timeless, emotion-free serenity. The photographs both attract and repulse, perhaps plunging the viewer into a reflection on the uncertainty of our times. Giuseppe's prints challenge the canonical definition of beauty, in which the emphasis is on harmony – how can we be so taken with these faces that are so clearly flawed?

INDEPENSENSE
(Right and overleaf, left and right)

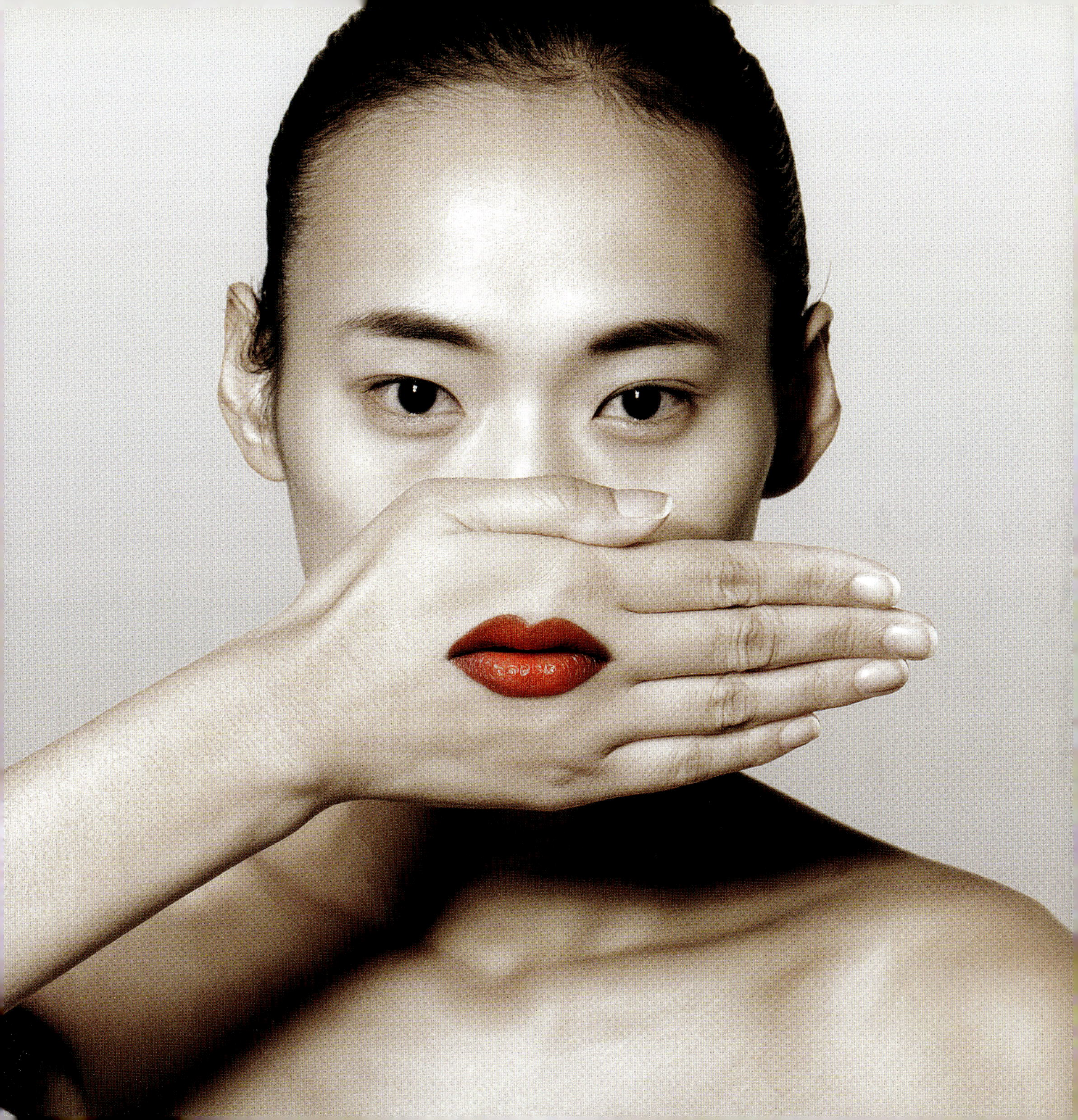

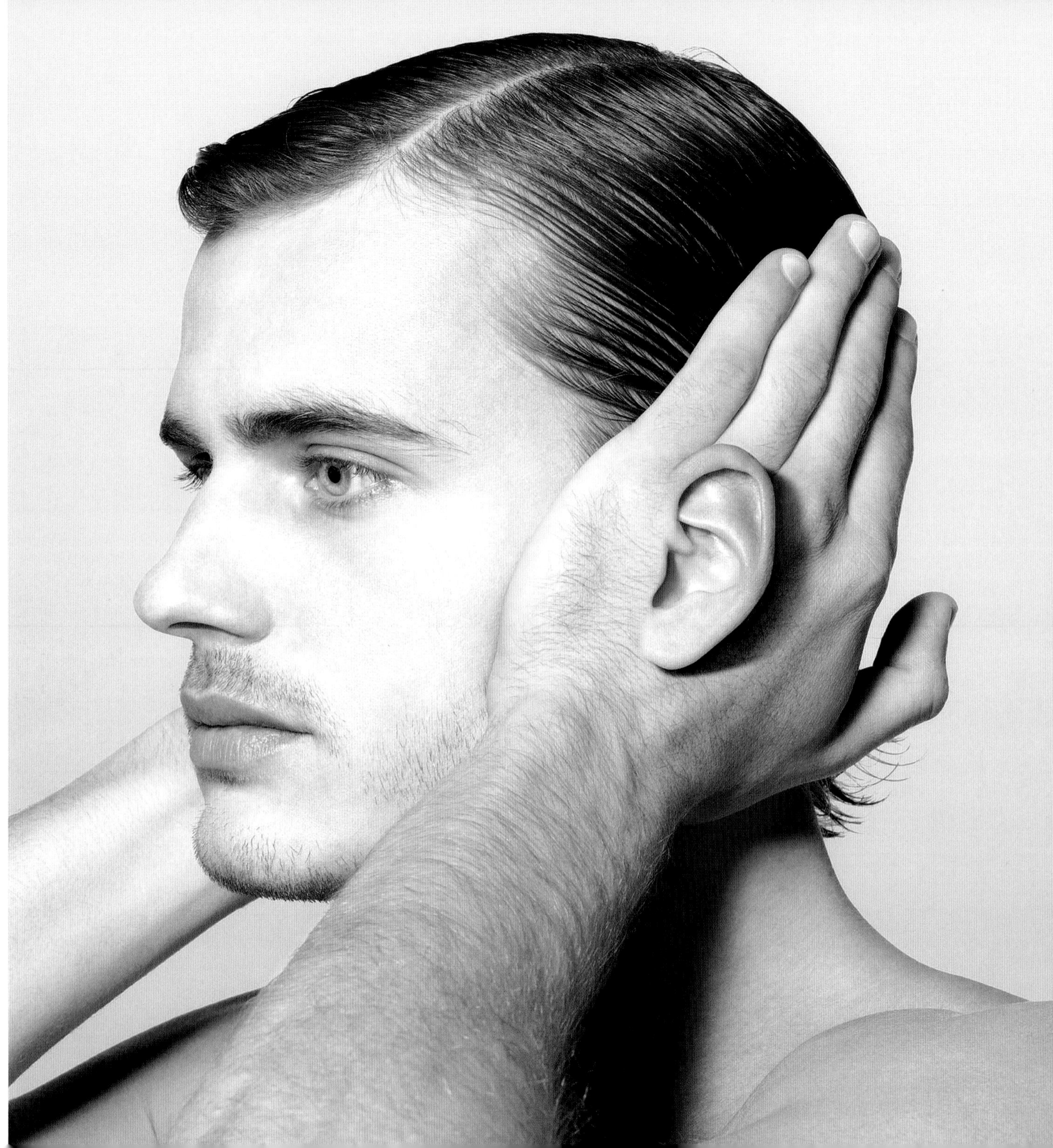

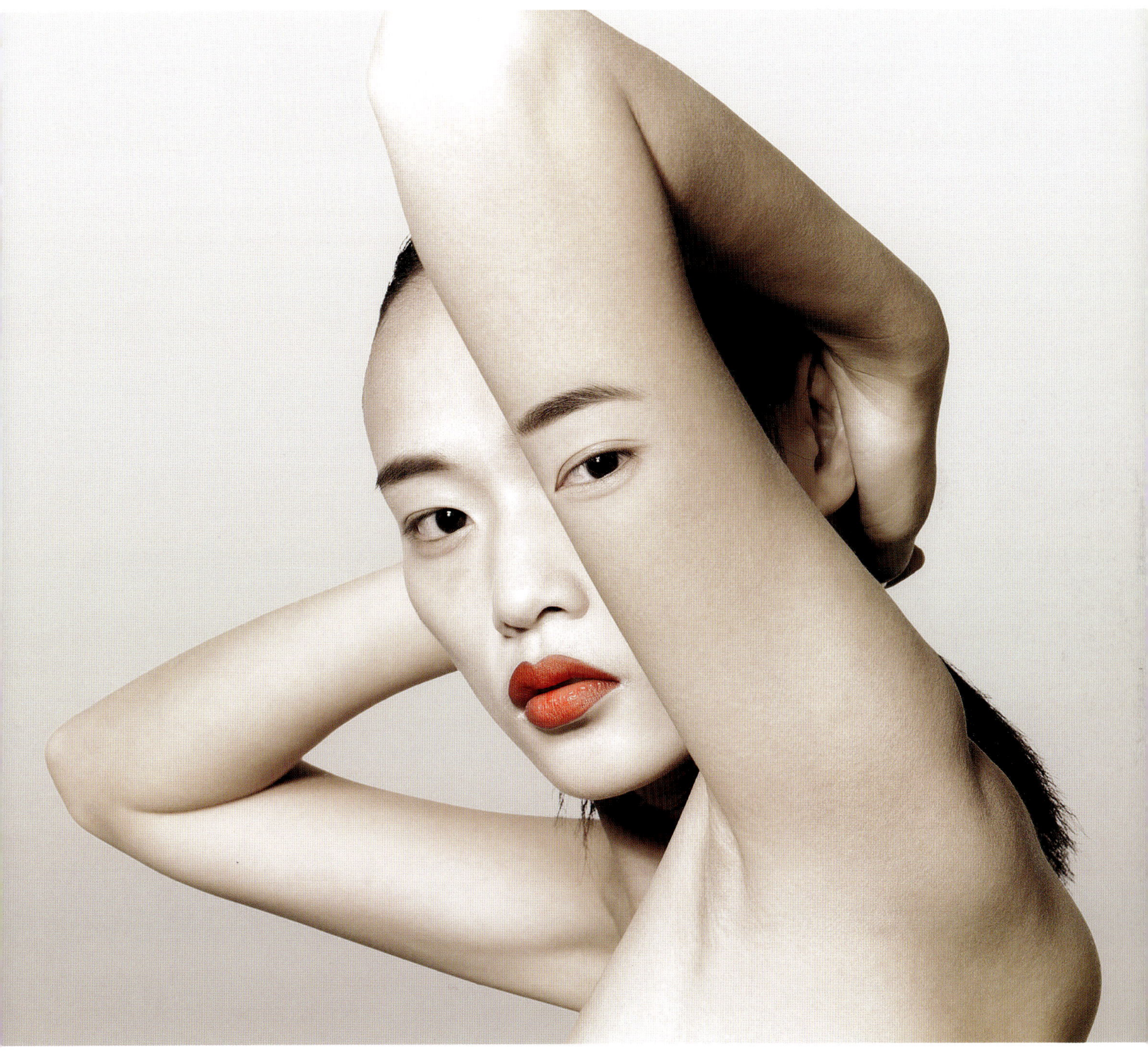

ROMAIN LAURENT

www.romain-laurent.com

Romain Laurent captures the dislocation of modern society with his camera. Walking at gravity-defying angles, standing alone amidst the chaos surrounding them or isolated inside a bubble, his subjects tap into the sense of isolation often manifest in 21st-century life.

The French artist created the *Tilt* series of photographs so that others might experience the disorientation that overcame him one day in the street. He discovered himself swaying, found his head spinning and realised that he could see the world from a different angle to everyone else. He felt like he was the only person standing upright. In *Tilt* the models lean at a sharp angle, albeit serenely, apparently anchored to the New York sidewalks. They bend impossibly at the ankles. The images blend digital manipulation with good old-fashioned theatre tricks. 'I had my assistant holding the actor leaning down on the side and I erased him in post-production,' explains Romain. Another series of images, *Something Real*, works to portray a particular sensation, specifically 'the moment in someone's life when that person disconnects from reality whilst (still) being a part of it, and suddenly wakes up.' Both series tap into the confusion of contemporary life – we're here but we're not entirely present. Instead, we're lost amongst the crowd.

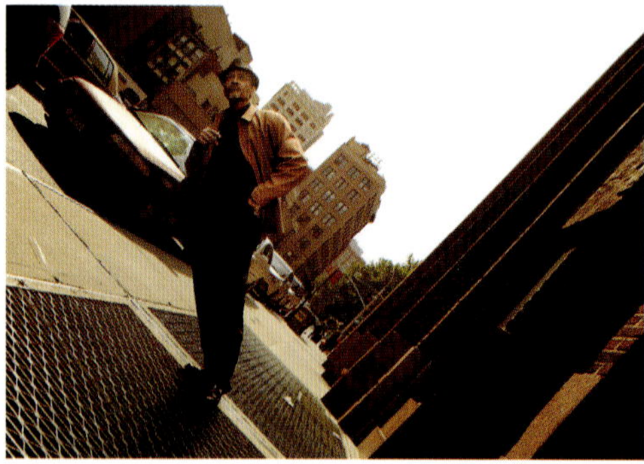

TILT (Left and right)
SOMETHING REAL (Overleaf)

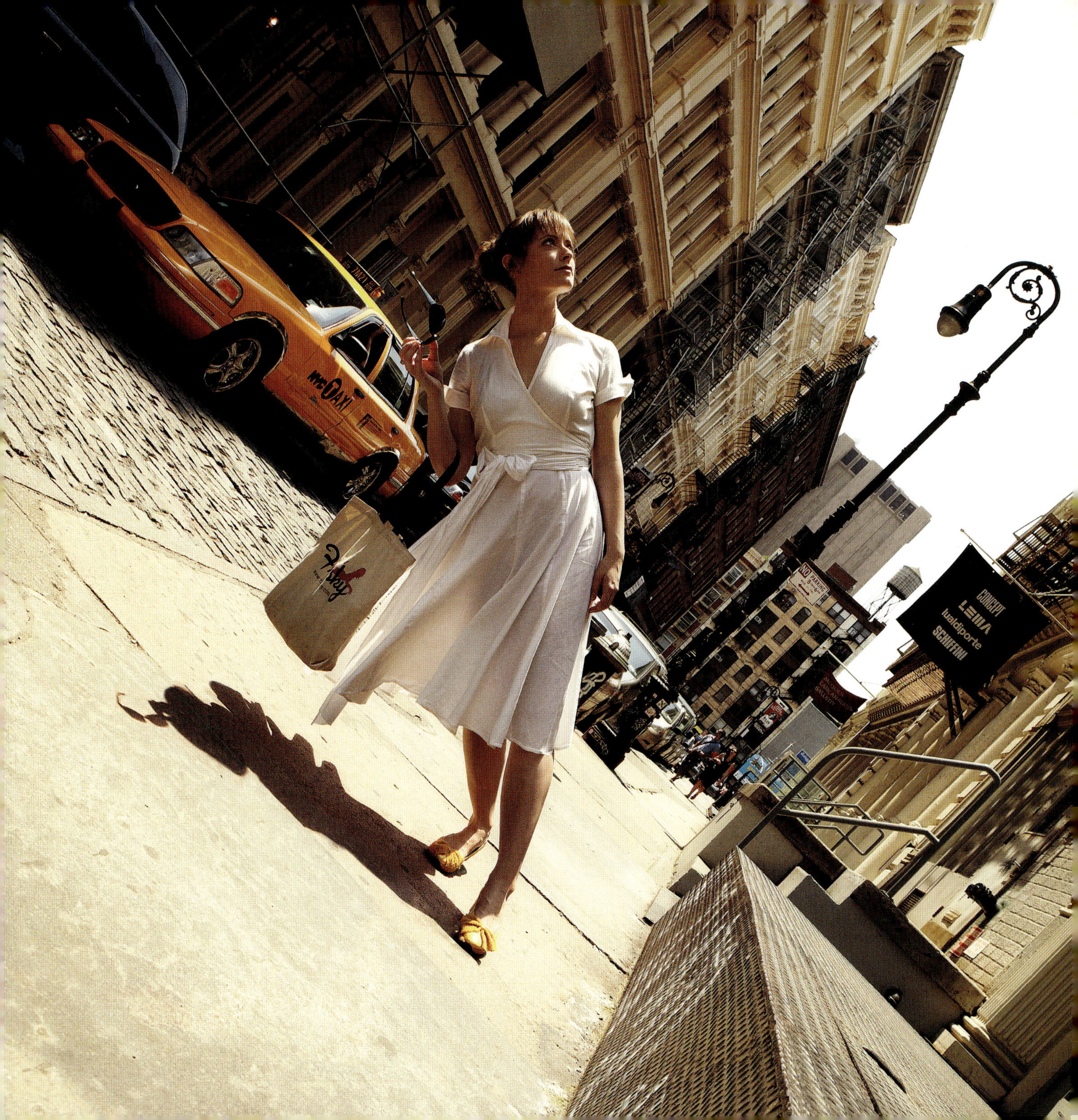
CONCEPT
LEMA
lualdiporte
SCHIFFINI

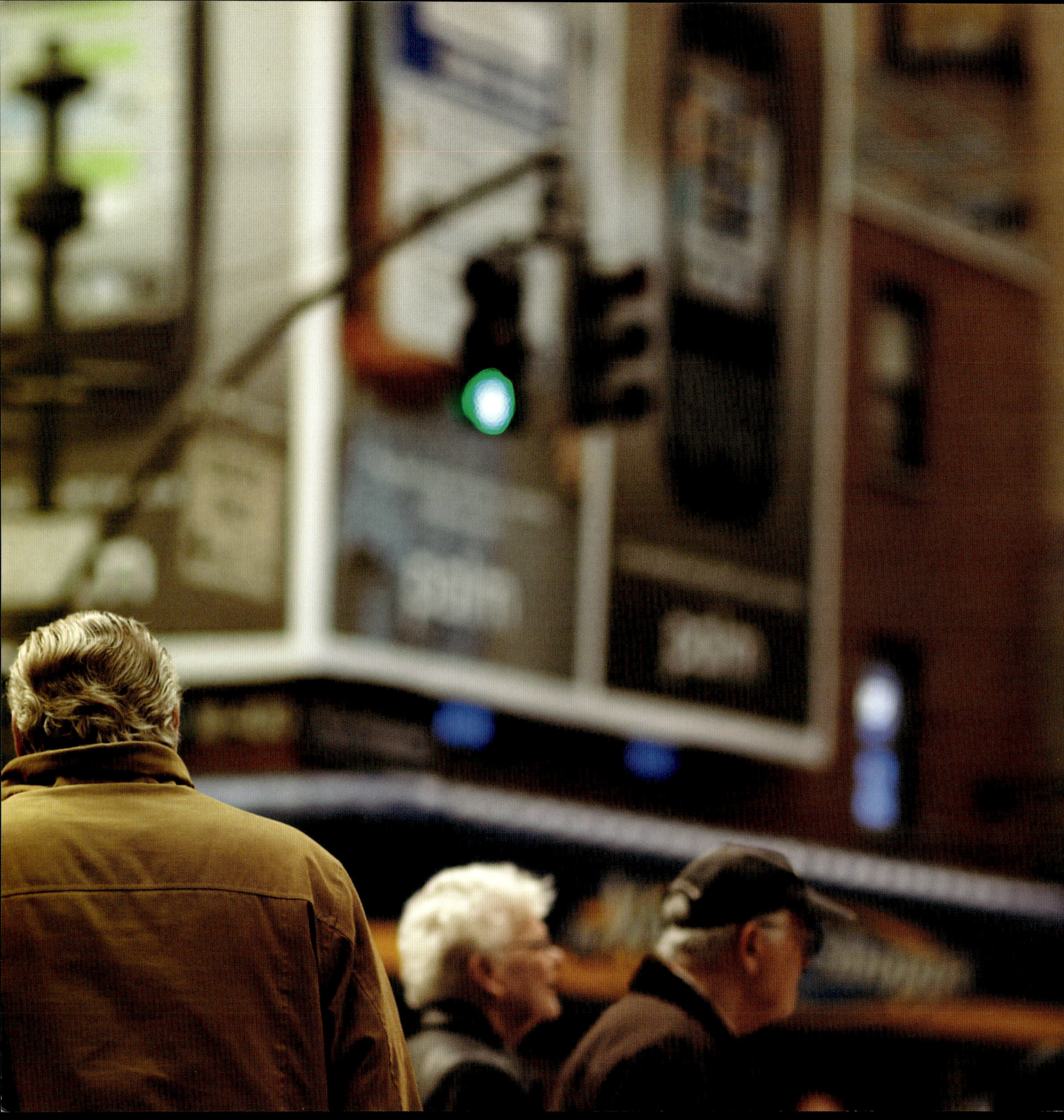

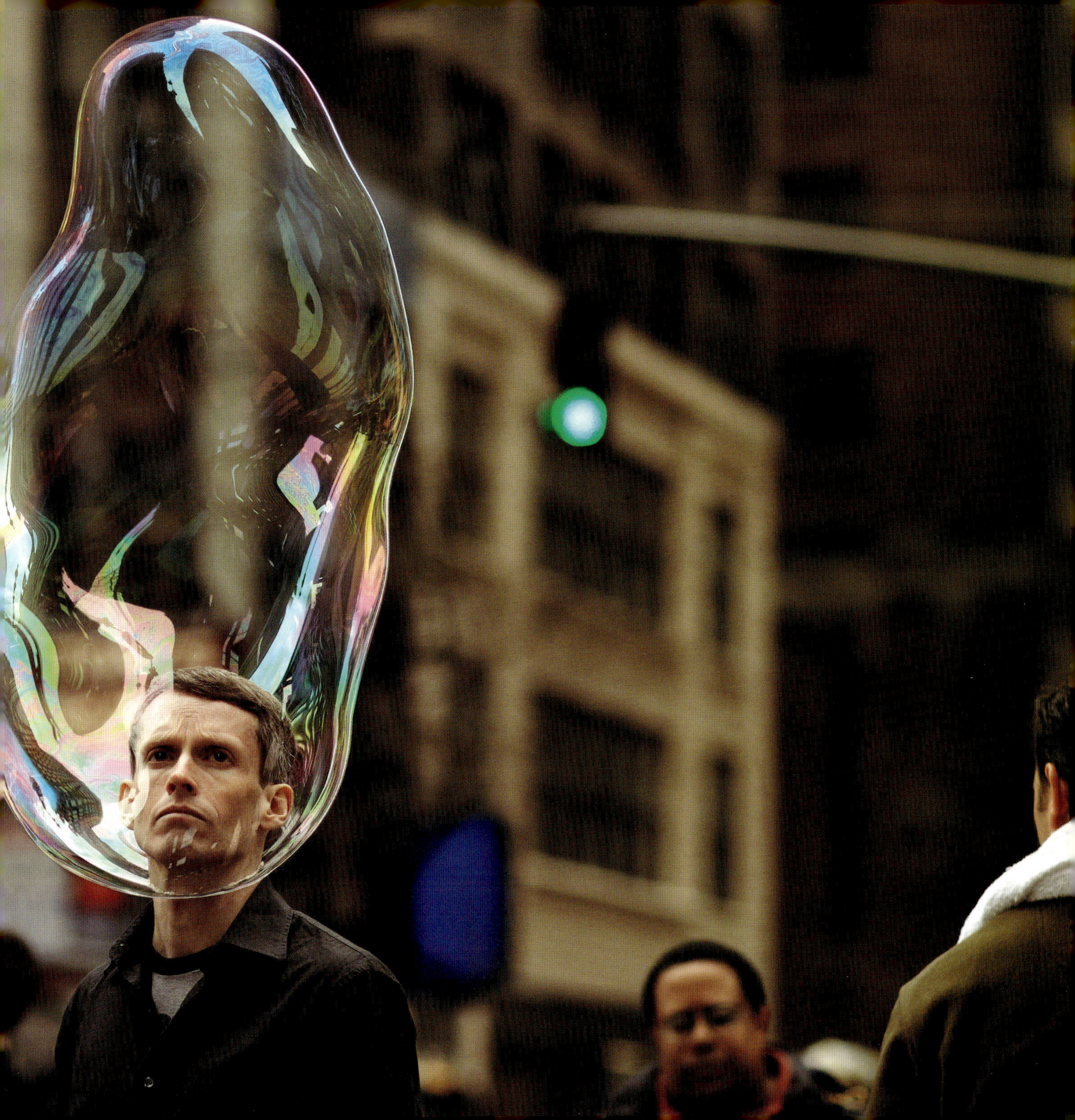

JENS SAGE

www.jenssage.com

Faces calm and serene, bodies relaxed – things couldn't be better for the models in Jens Sage's photographs. They seem to be sitting comfortably. And yet, clearly, something is missing.

Jens, a young Berliner inspired by artists as diverse as Erwin Wurm and Joel Sternfeld, describes himself as an 'amateur photographer' with an interest in design. His *Seats* series epitomises the qualities of the informal 'levitation photography' movement that has emerged around the world in recent years. As the name suggests, in Jens' work, the missing ingredient is the seat. And so subjects appear to levitate in the air. However, the use of familiar situations and natural light compels your imagination to fill in the gaps, to see the seat – whether bicycle saddle, public bench or car seat – where in fact there is none. The relaxed state of the models makes the images appear all the more natural, even whilst shadows confirm the absence of any physical support for the subject.

SEATS (Right and overleaf, left and right)

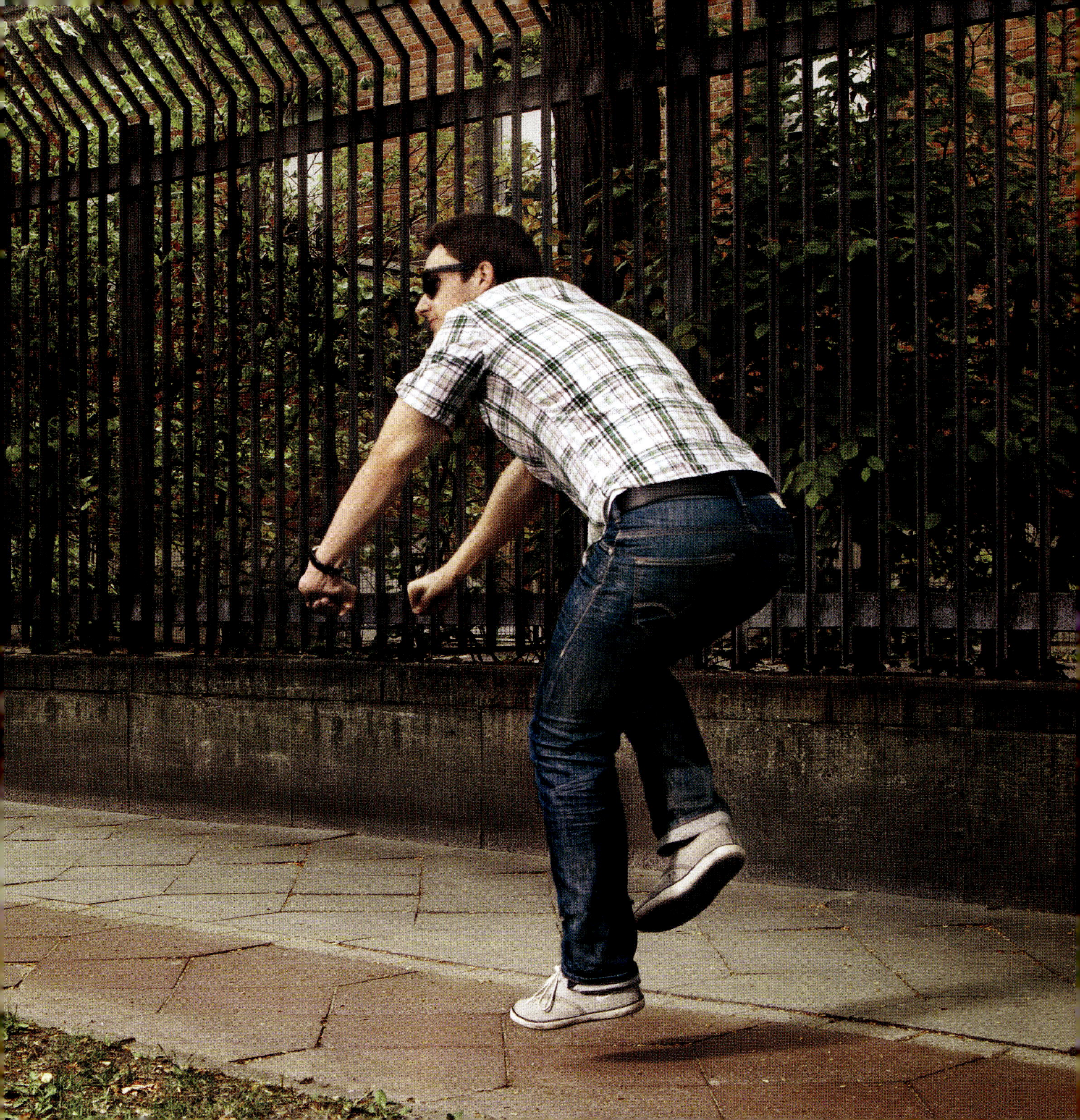

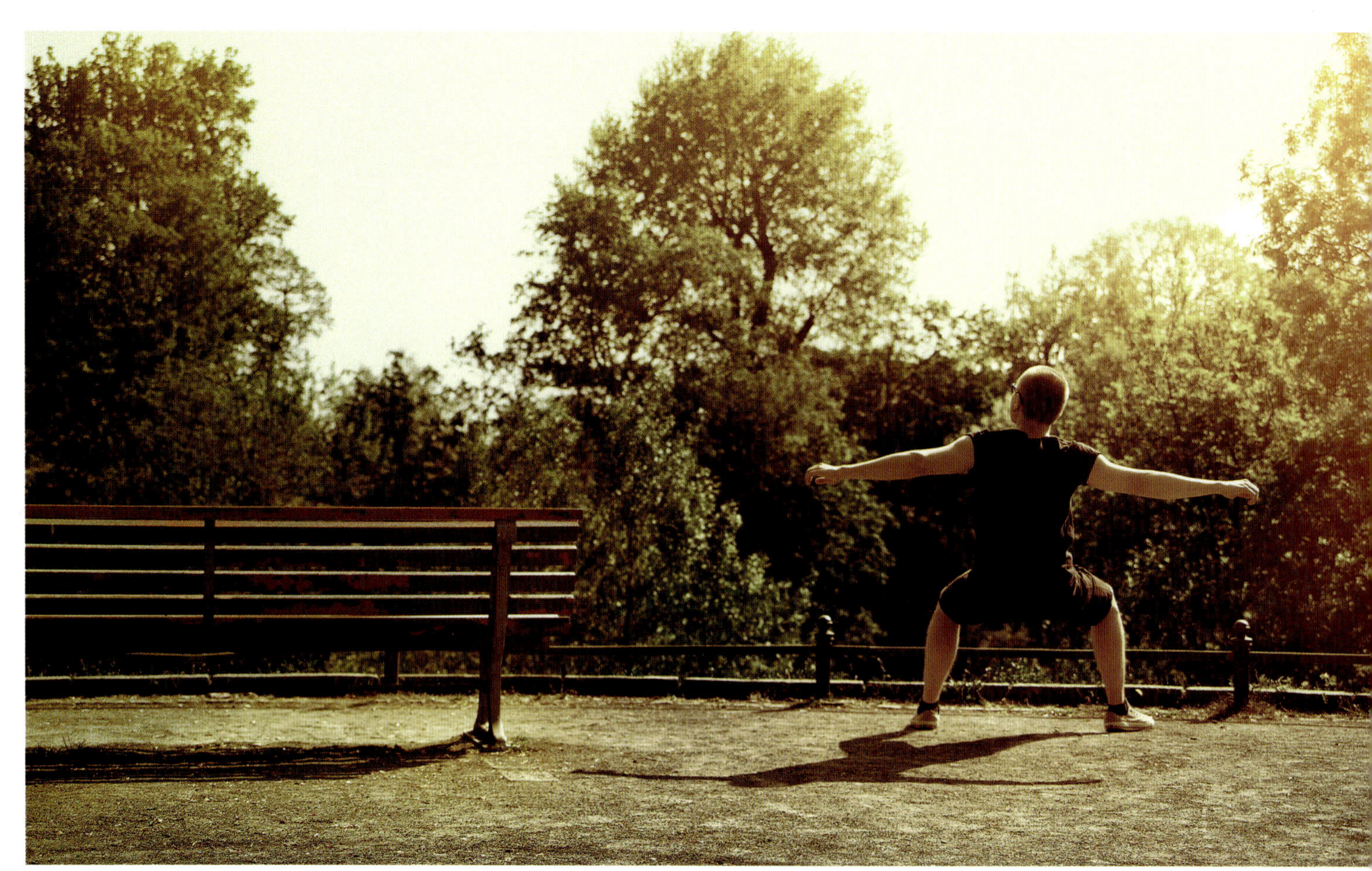

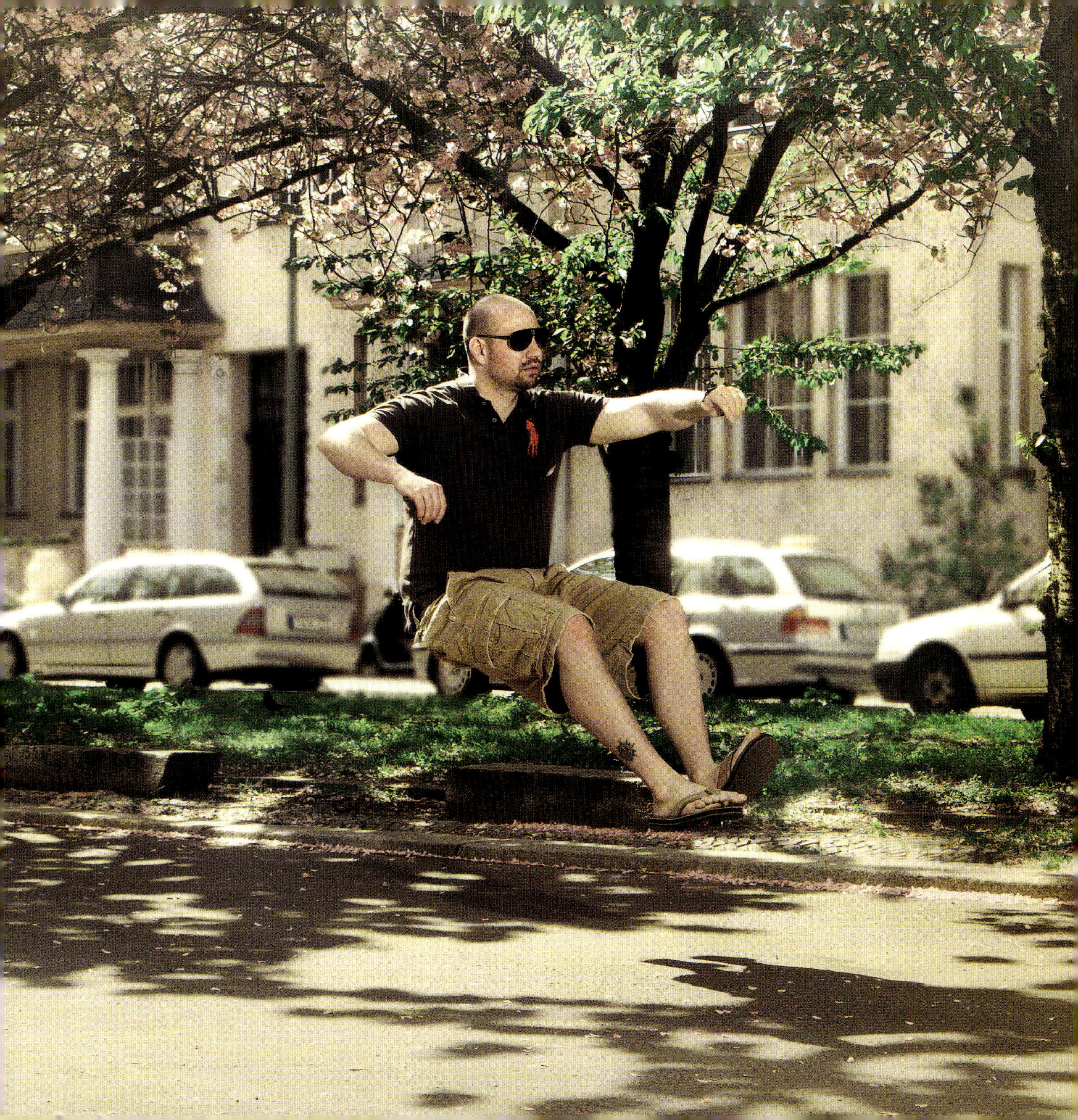

LIU BOLIN

www.ekfineart.com

Is Liu Bolin disguising himself amidst the landscape? Or are the surroundings actually swallowing him whole? By painting himself into the urban and rural milieu of his native China, the photographer raises some interesting questions about identity and control.

The artist's *Hiding in the City* series has deservedly met with growing acclaim in recent years. In camouflaging himself in the landscape, and yet doing enough to ensure that we're aware of his presence, Bolin achieves something remarkable. He articulates an esoteric question: how do you make your presence felt in an environment that consumes the individual? The work is inspired by the artist's own experiences of powerlessness, in particular the destruction of his studio by the Chinese authorities in 2005, which was razed along with everything else in Suojiacun, an artist's village on the edge of Beijing, on the grounds that it lacked the correct building permits. Bolin's photographs are made with the help of several assistants, and the shoots can take up to ten hours to complete. Having found success in his native China, the artist has subsequently expanded the series to include locations in New York and Venice.

TEATRO ALLA SCALA
LAGOON CITY OF VENICE (Overleaf, left)
HIDING IN THE CITY NO. 88 – SAWMILL (Overleaf, right)

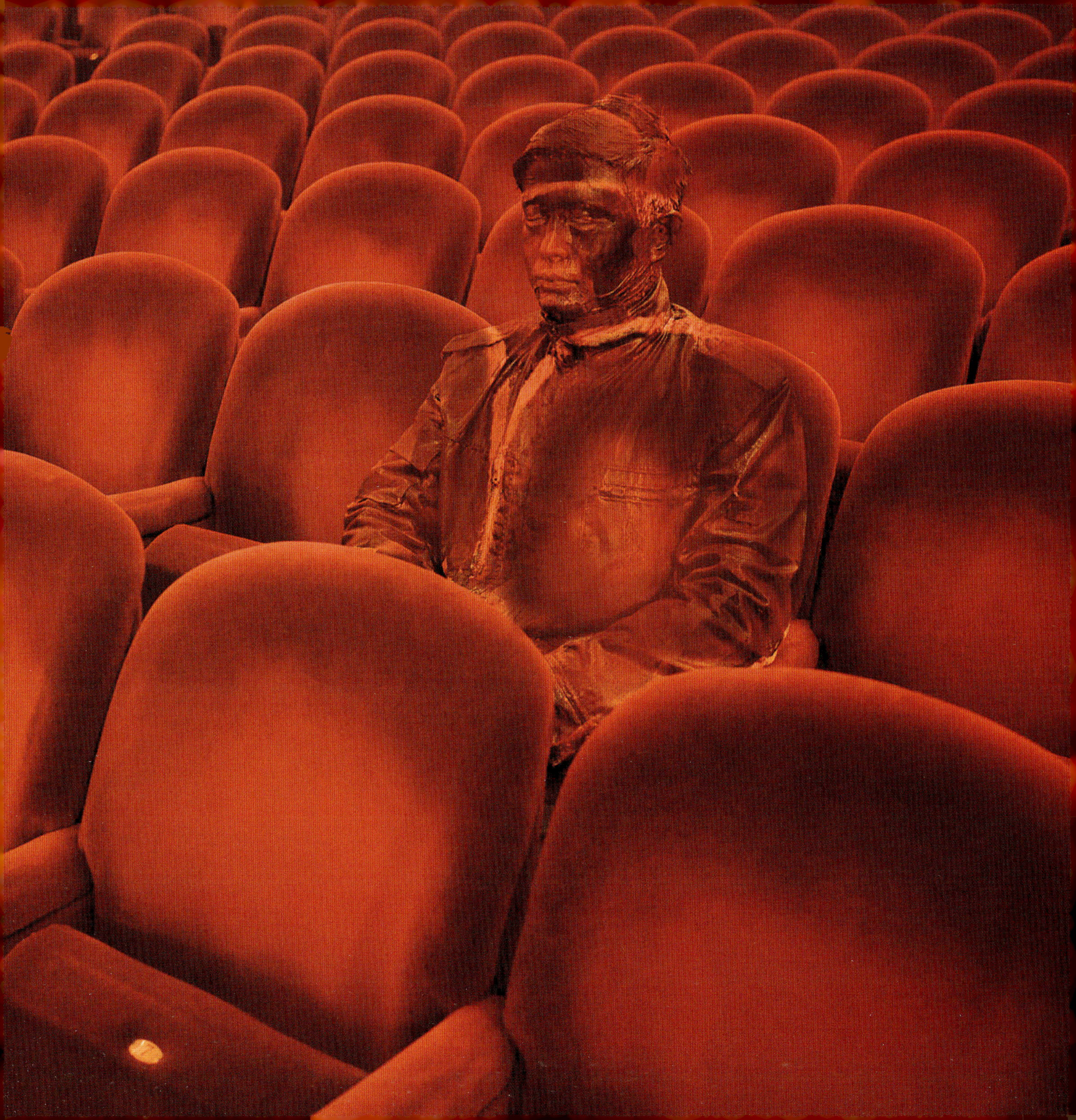

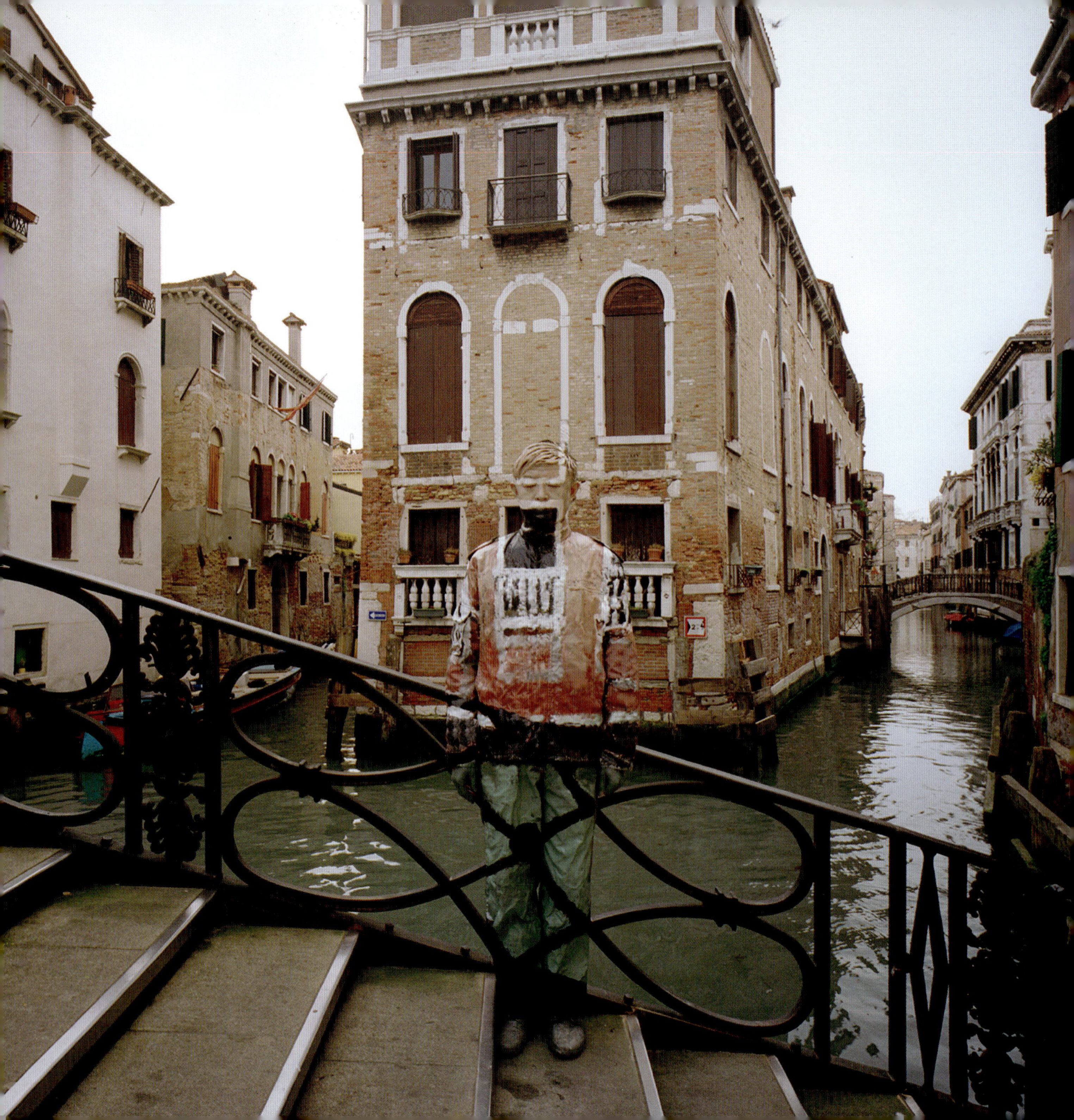

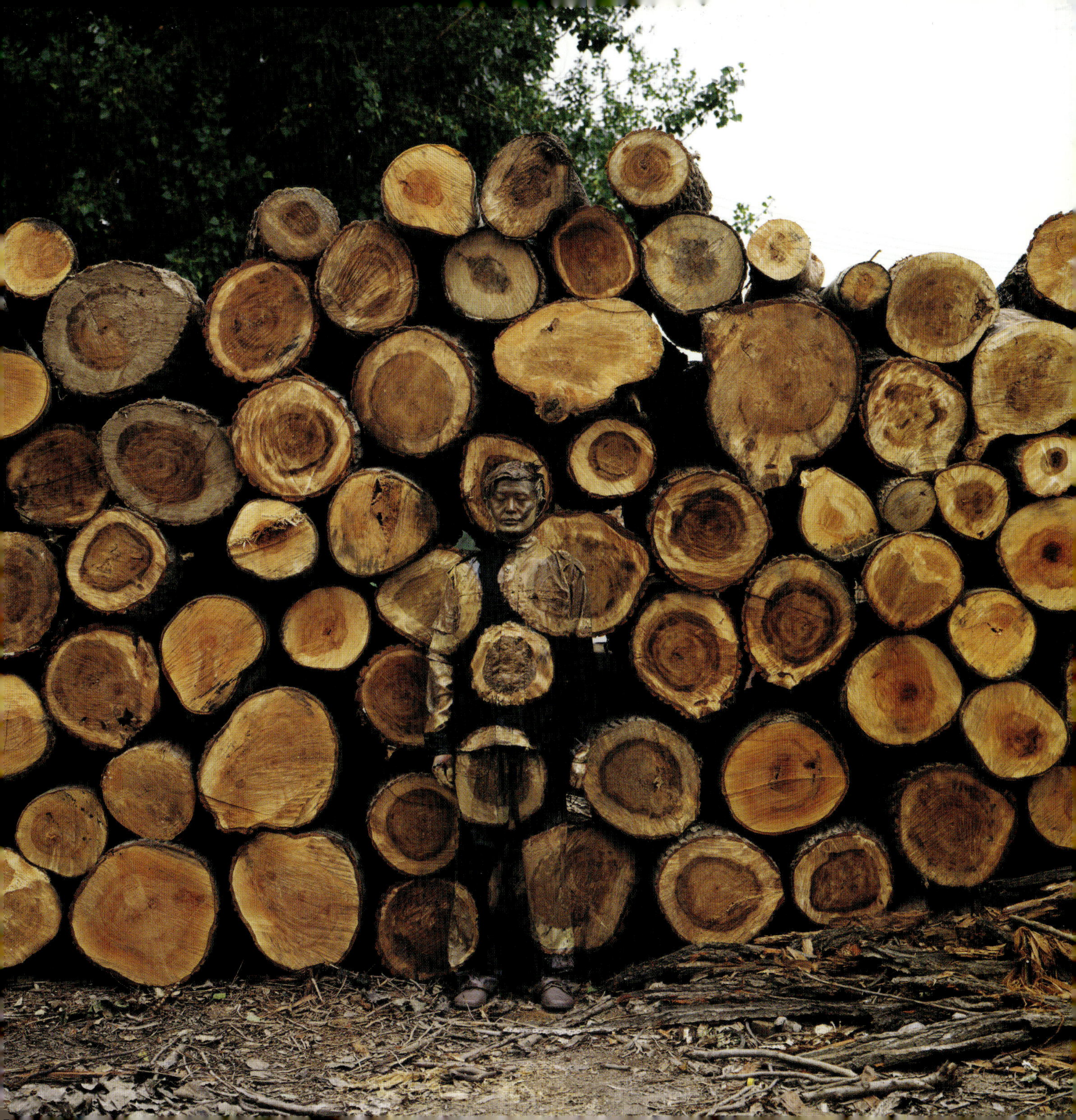

MOHAMMED AMINE NASSERI

www.aminenasseri.com

The intrigue in Mohammed Amine Nasseri's portfolio of *Dreamers* lies in discovering how the images were made. There was no post-production manipulation, no recourse to Photoshop. And yet somehow the subjects float, as if suspended in mid-air.

The Frankfurt-based designer created the series of photographs as a project for his course at Wiesbaden University. The brief, simply, was 'gravity'. His work captures the relaxation of deep sleep, the limp bodies within apparently consumed by fatigue. The use of such Spartan surroundings – with only a mattress, pillow, dishevelled sheet and blank wall for décor – works to focus our attention on the sleeping subject. Each figure in the series is positioned slightly differently, but in common they hover in the air, either rising up from the mattress or falling to earth from above. Unfortunately, Mohammed hasn't let us in on his production secrets, so we can only guess at how the images are produced.

DREAMER

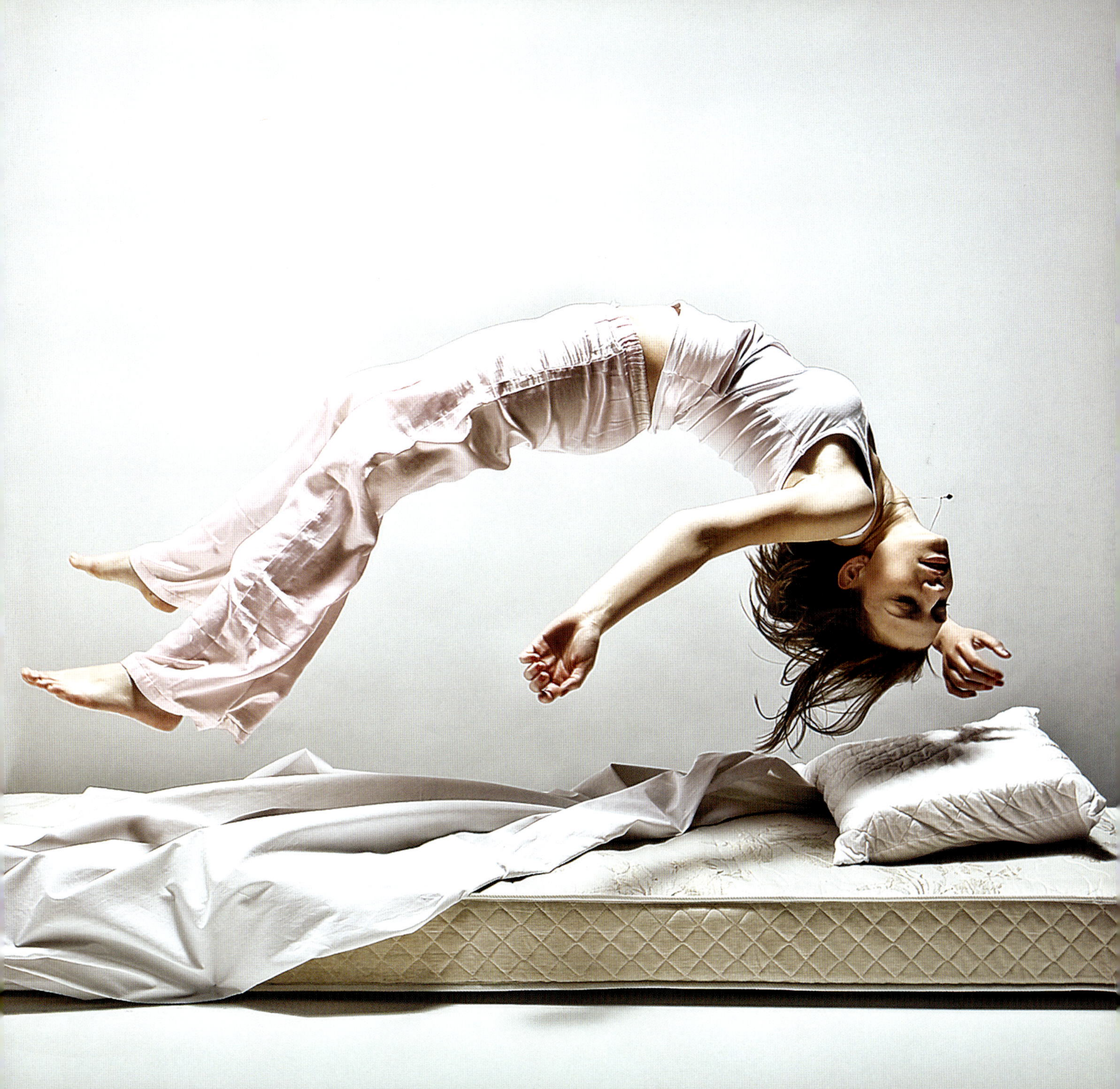

SCENERY

Photography can make us look at our surroundings in a different way. It removes us from the here and now and transports us to new worlds, new settings in which, far from being relegated to the background, the environment comes forward and envelops the onlooker. Traditional landscape photography has always placed distant scenery in front of our eyes, but today practitioners are pushing the boundaries further than ever before — carrying us off to miniature worlds made of food or to once familiar destinations now distorted or embellished almost beyond recognition.

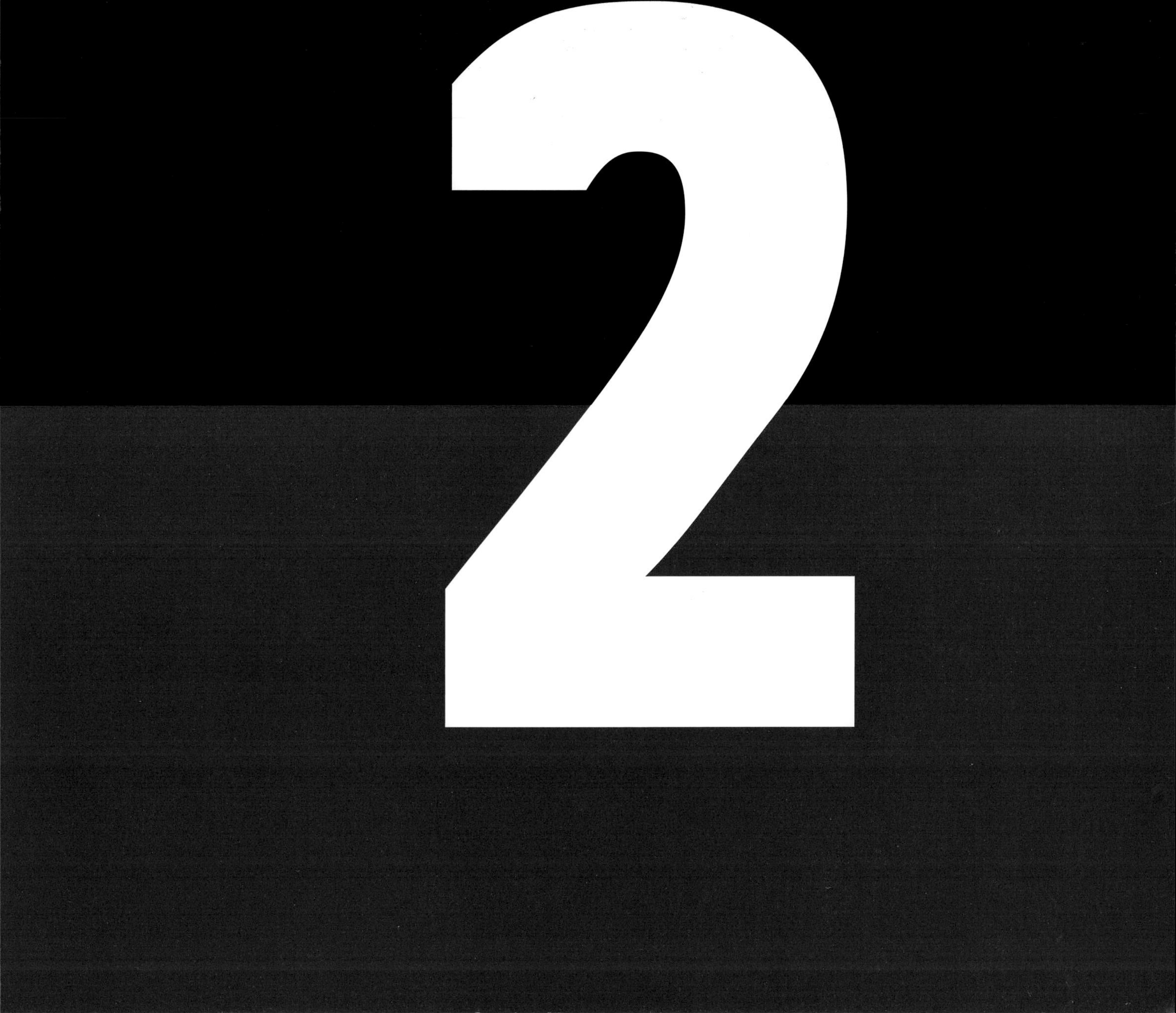
2

CARL WARNER

www.carlwarner.com

Carl Warner's landscape photographs look good enough to eat. The rocks have a hint of boiled potato about them, the waterfalls are bizarrely reminiscent of Parma ham and, yes, that giant cactus could well pass for an oversized gherkin. There's a very good reason why.

Carl was an only child and duly spent a significant amount of time alone in his bedroom with only his imagination for company. He would draw pictures, inspired in particular by the fantastical worlds of Salvador Dalí, Patrick Woodroffe and Roger Dean. These early influences are writ large in Carl's photography, for which he creates landscapes made entirely from food. That boyhood escape into other worlds and alternate realities is clearly visible, as is the influence of album cover art, which enjoyed its heyday – with graphic designers like Storm Thorgerson, forever associated with Pink Floyd – at around the same time that Carl was first getting into photography. Despite the food photographs' offbeat appeal, Carl considers himself something of a traditionalist. As he explains: 'I tend to draw a very conventional landscape using classic compositional techniques as I need to fool the viewer into thinking it is a real scene at first glance.' His work does indeed evoke that double take moment, the point at which you realise that rock is actually ciabatta bread or that what you first thought was the sea could well be slices of smoked salmon.

COWBOY VALLEY
CHINESE JUNK (Overleaf)

These images came from: Carl Warner's Food Landscapes (Abrams Image, 2010) and FoodLand (Abrams Books For Young Readers, 2010)

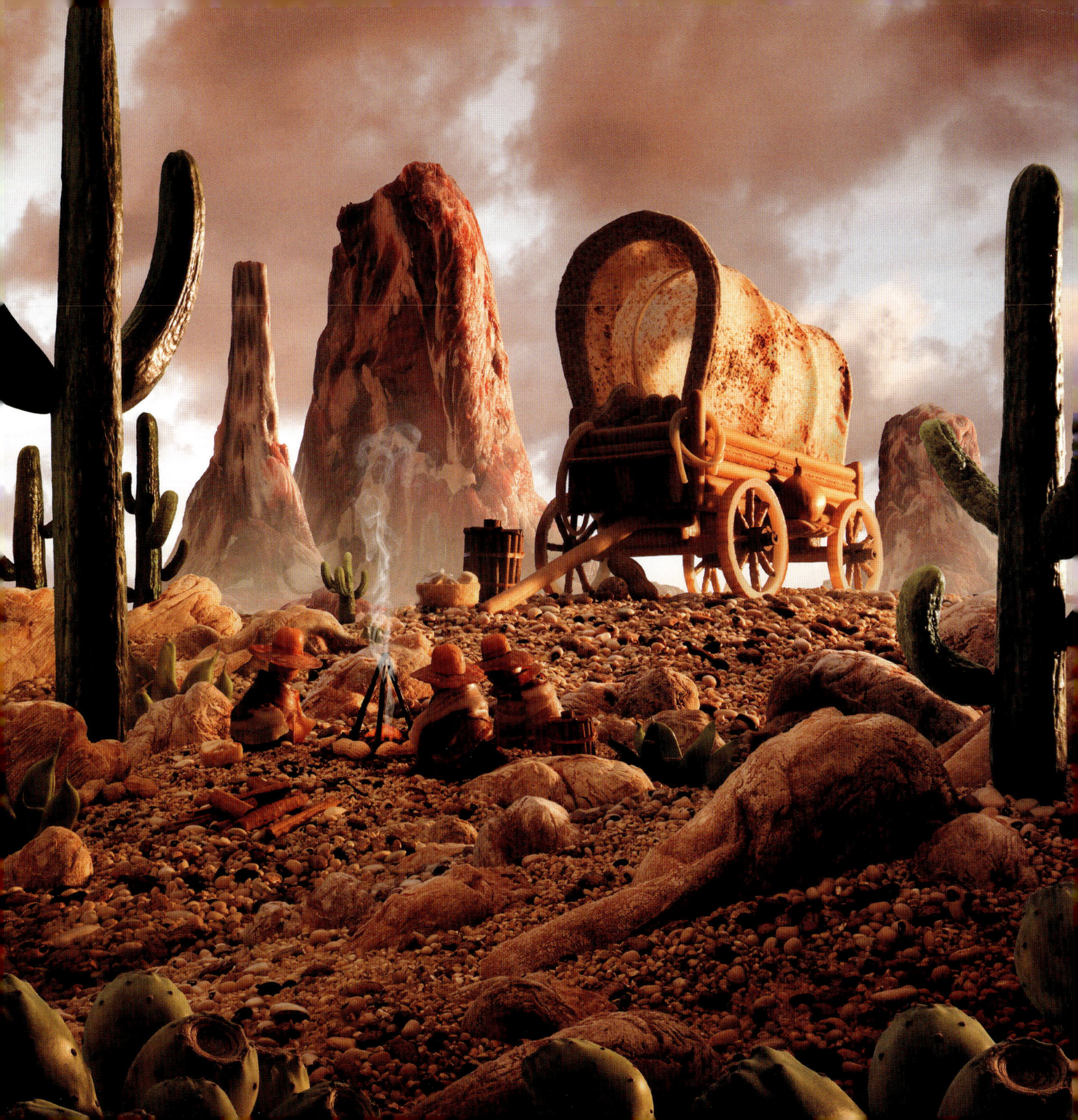

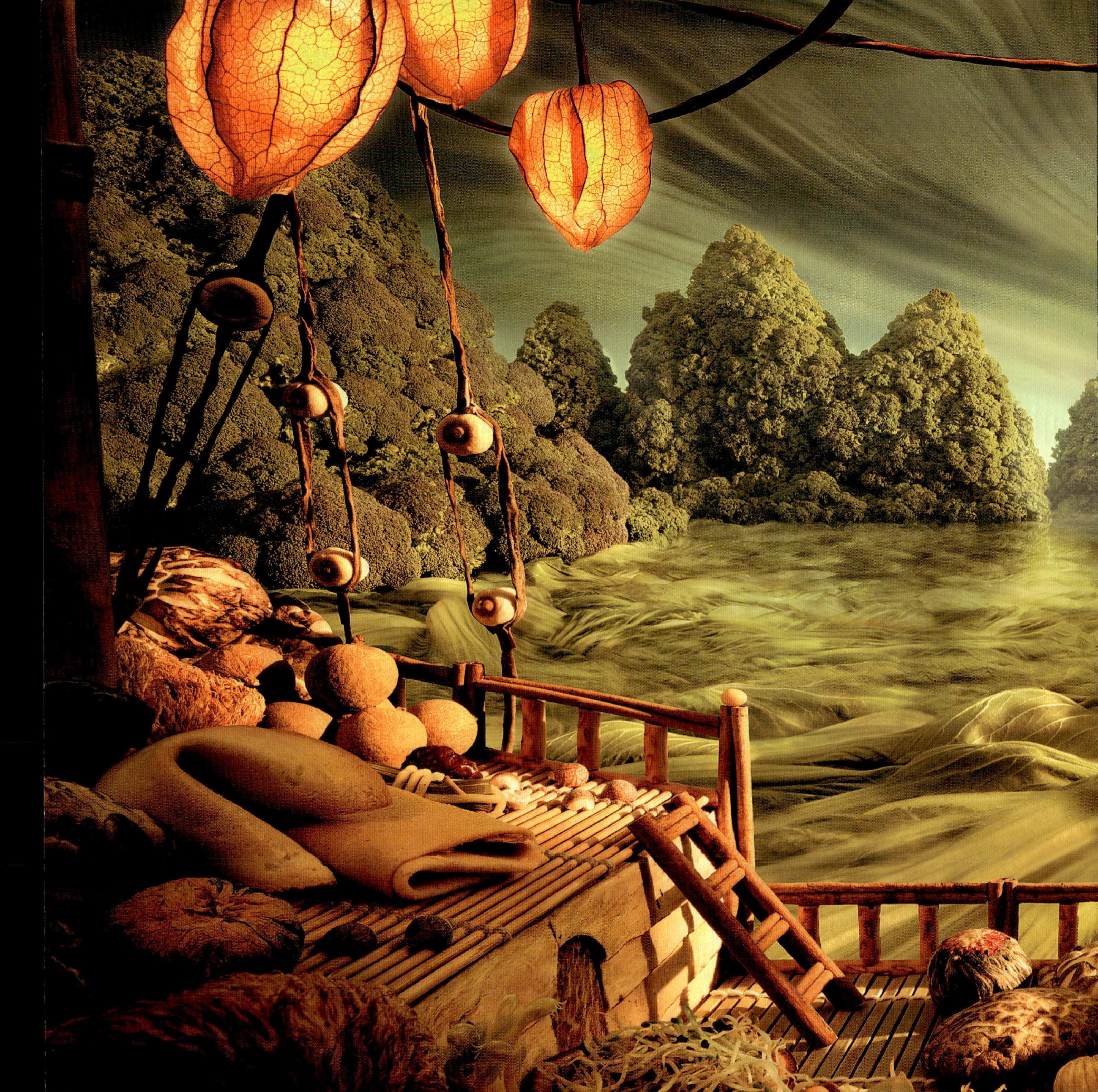

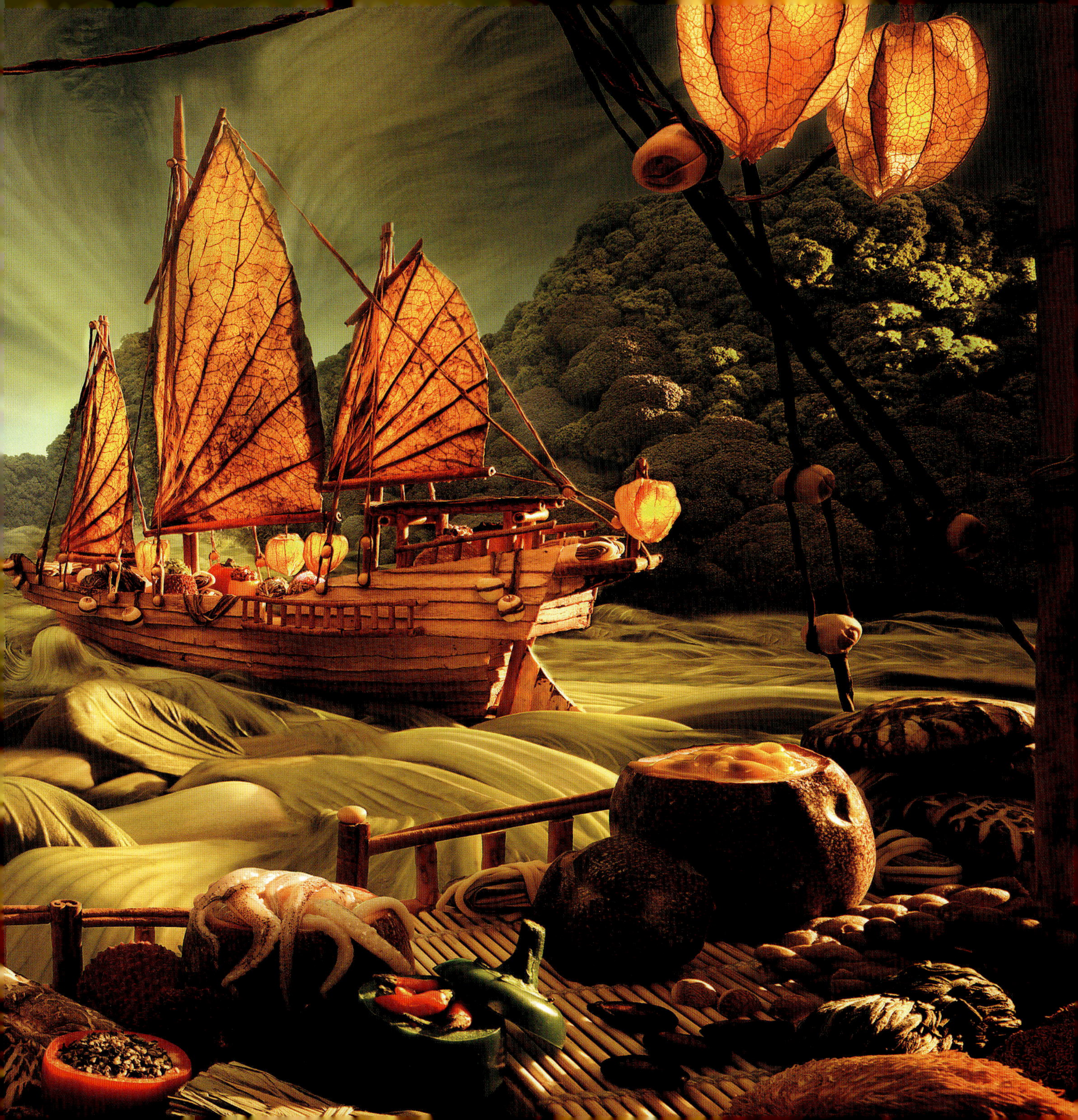

56

SCENERY

MICHAEL HUGHES

www.hughes-photography.eu

How many people photograph the Eiffel Tower every day? Or the humble NYC taxicab? Or Big Ben? Thousands, no doubt. It seems likely, however, that only one – British photographer Michael Hughes – has chosen to immortalise the scene with the addition of a cheap tourist souvenir.

Souvenirs is a collection of 150 photographs, each with the famous monument, figure or scene in some way obscured or joined by a miniature version of itself, as bought by Michael at a nearby souvenir shop. Michael has variously employed fridge magnets, lollypops and pencil sharpeners in the pursuit of his art. Each is perfectly aligned to replace the original subject, be it Mickey Mouse or the leaning tower of Pisa. In the course of *Souvenirs*, Michael has subverted the Golden Gate Bridge, the Sphinx, the Beatles (walking across Abbey Road), Don Quixote and the Statue of Liberty, each time inserting his own, much cheaper variant of the original into the photograph. The presence of the photographer's hand in the image, clutching the souvenir, is integral. It all began in 1999 as part of a reportage piece for a Finnish newspaper, before developing into an Internet phenomenon a few years later. There was even an invitation to the *Jay Leno Show* in Los Angeles.

NEW YORK, TIME SQUARE, TAXI AND NAKED COWBOY
HOUSES OF PARLIAMENT, BIG BEN MODEL AND TWO TOURISTS, LONDON

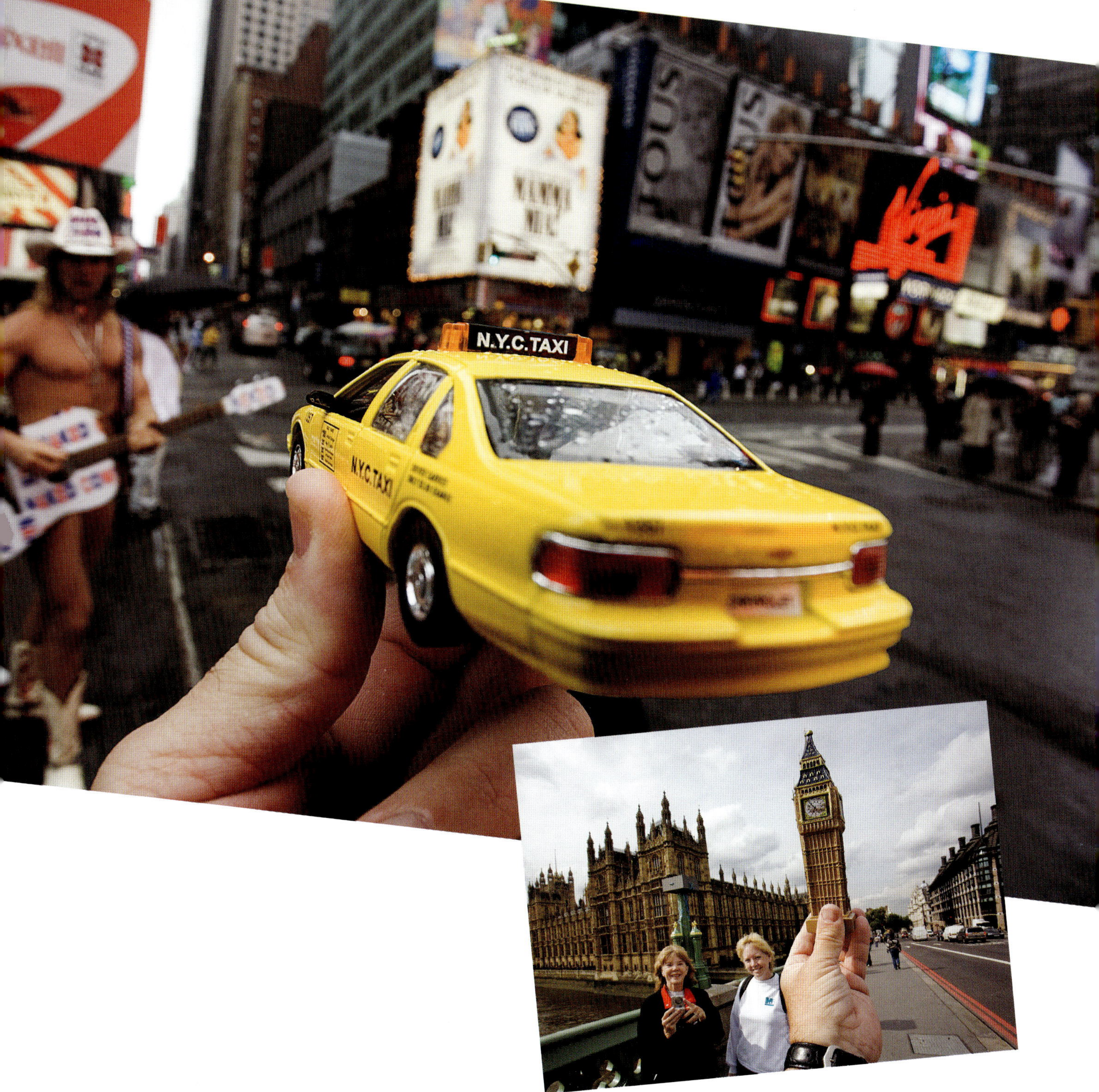
N.Y.C.TAXI
N.Y.C.TAXI

STUDIO PARRIS WAKEFIELD

www.parriswakefield.com

The famous skylines in the Studio Parris Wakefield's series of *Cityscape* photographs slide off the wall in a blur of light. The building shapes are instantly recognisable but presented as never before. They have no single, solid viewpoint, and despite their familiarity each is hard to grasp.

Howard Wakefield's and Sarah Parris' agency has an enviable reputation for design, having worked with rock bands such as Suede and on fashion campaigns for the likes of Dior. In the *Cityscapes* series of images, they hope to portray the great urban scenes of the modern age as churning, constantly changing environments in which the viewpoint alters with every pair of eyes, whether resident or visitor. 'These enigmatic cityscapes represent the profusion of perceptions from a constantly evolving city,' they confirm. 'There will always be something new to discover – from the distinct, to the obscure, these cityscapes portray their unique infinite quality.' The cities, from Copenhagen and Toronto to Milan, Perth, Chicago and London, are well known and yet the images of them here are illusive, the solidity of the scene hard to pin down. In presenting the cities in this way, Howard and Sarah flag up how differently each of us sees the urban landscape.

LOS ANGELES

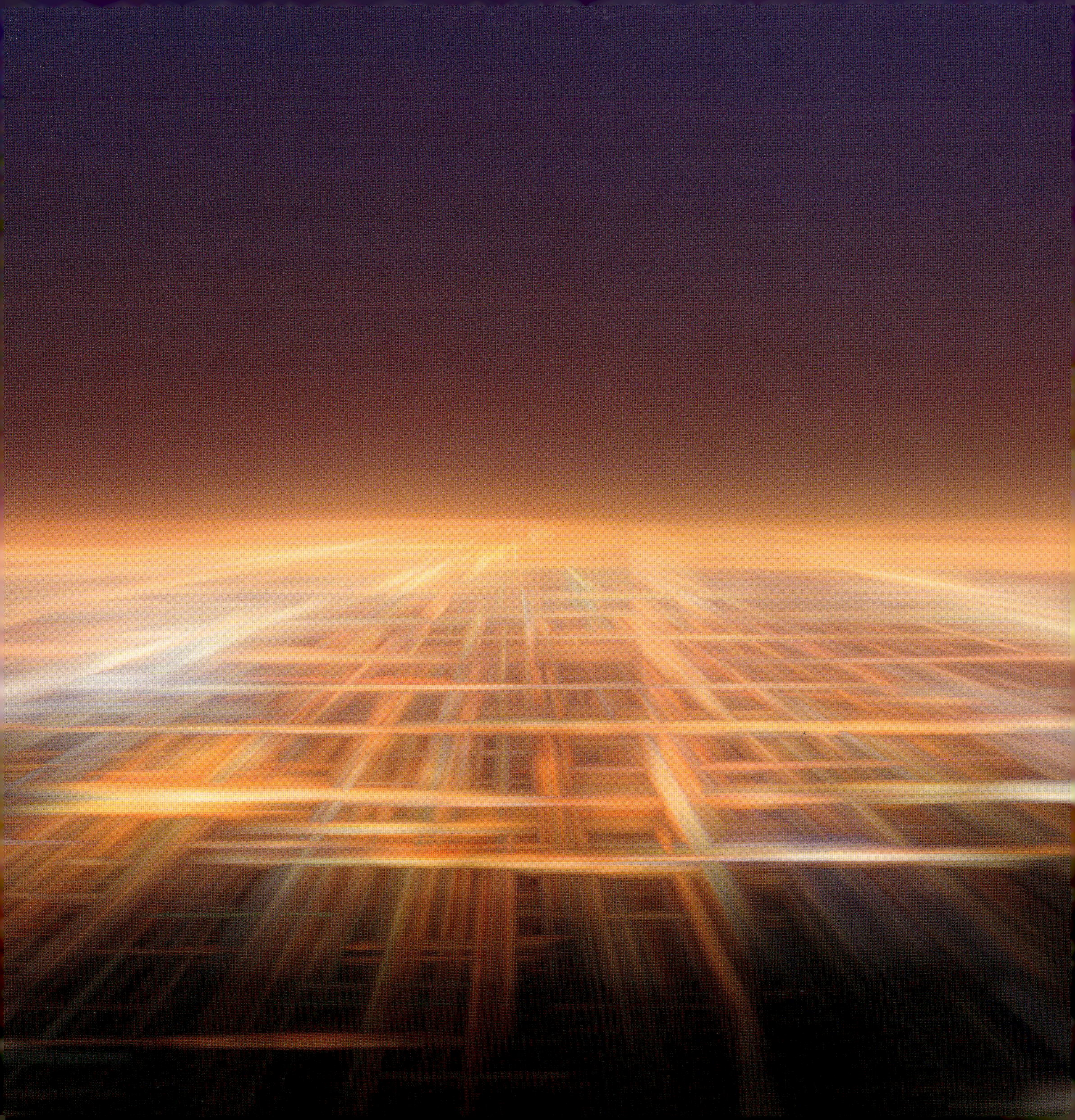

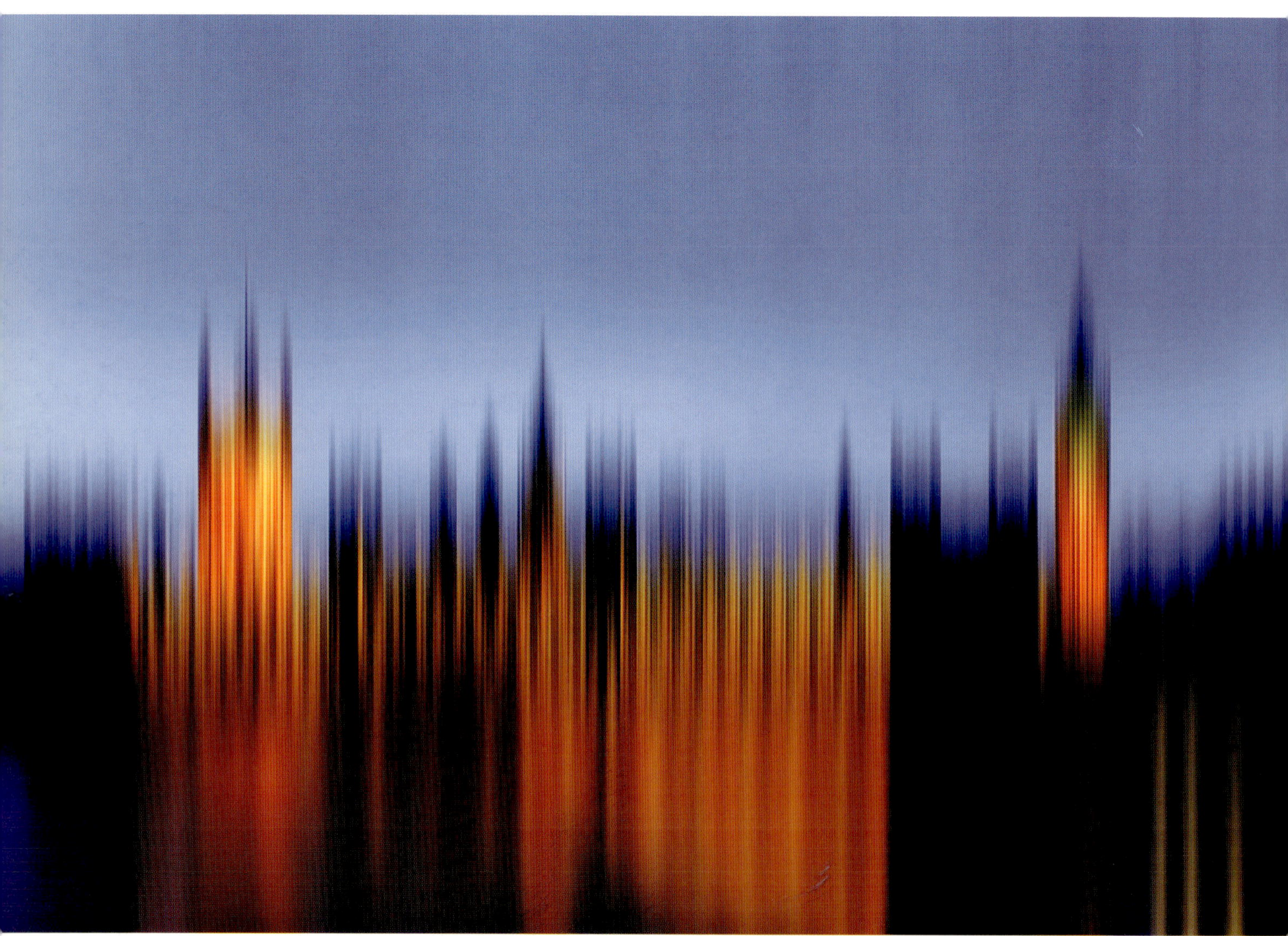

LONDON

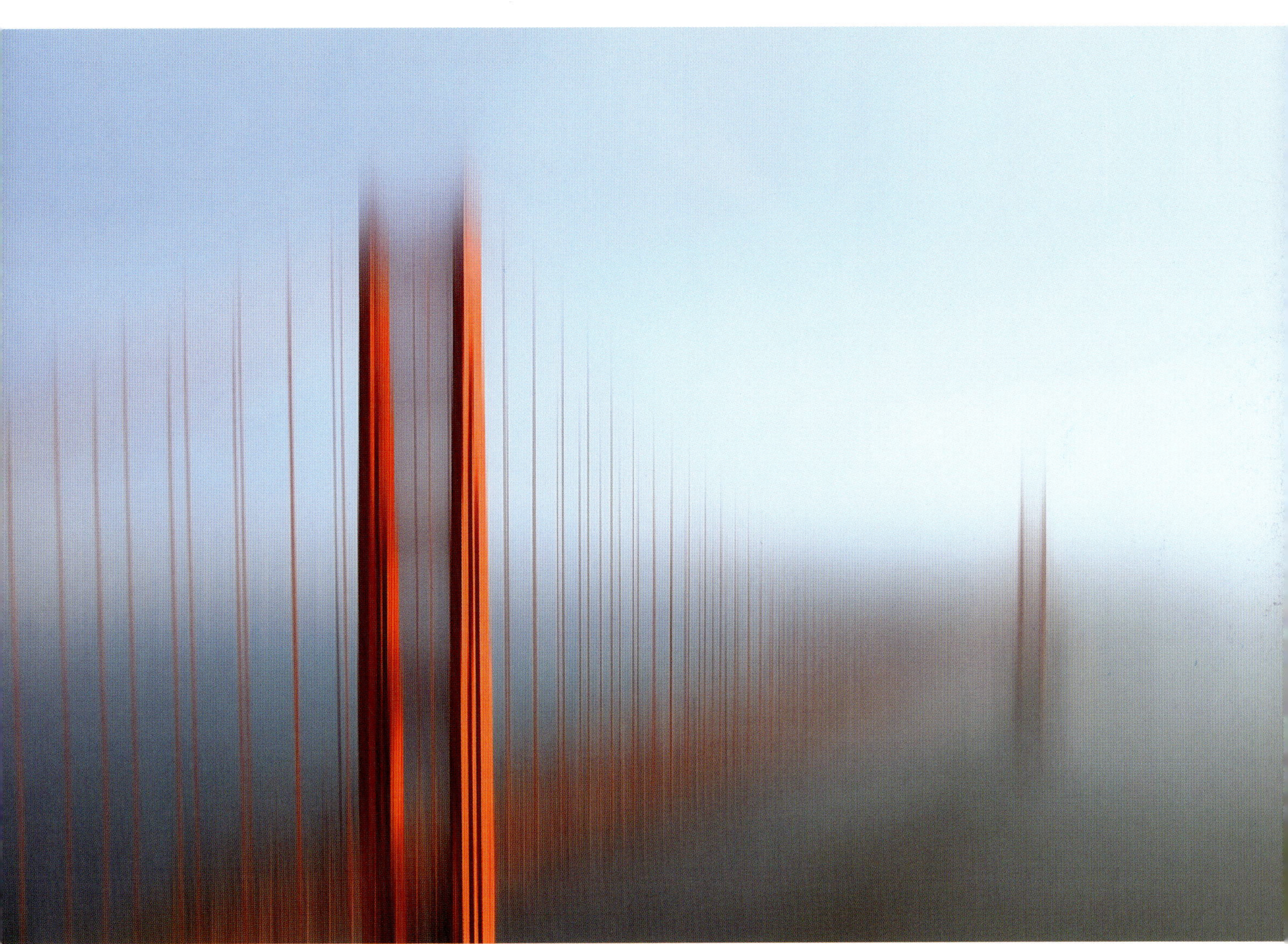

SAN FRANCISCO

TODD MCLELLAN

www.toddmclellan.com

Do you know what the inside of your old radio-alarm clock looks like? Or any of the other mechanical objects that we all use on a daily basis? Each conceals hundreds, if not thousands, of tiny components, without any of which the whole would not function. Canadian Todd McLellan draws attention to this familiar, but ignored world, by dismantling and meticulously photographing lawn mowers, telephones and typewriters.

Todd, from Saskatchewan, says it all began in a kindergarten finger painting class. It was there that he first enjoyed working with his hands. Today, he's moved beyond splashing paint around, to the highly detailed *Disassembly*, a series of photographs depicting objects such as radios or typewriters that have been painstakingly dissected and rearranged according to a strict rationale. Each subject is photographed twice. In the first shot, the dissected parts are laid out on a flat surface and tweezered obsessively into place according to size, type or function. In the second image, all hell breaks loose – the dismembered object is captured in the throws of destruction, apparently exploding in mid air. Using this approach Todd asserts order over confusion or, alternatively, injects chaos where once there was harmony. Either way, by photographing the extensive entrails of everyday mechanical and electronic objects, the artist breathes new life into things that tend to be wiped from the memory with alarming alacrity.

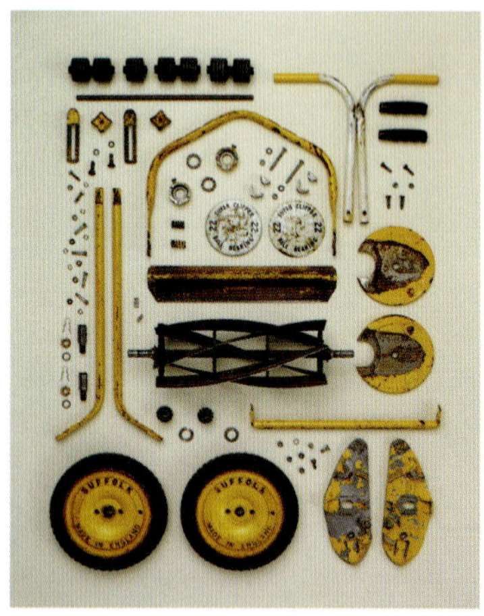

APART PUSH LAWN MOWER
OLD PUSH LAWN MOWER (Left)

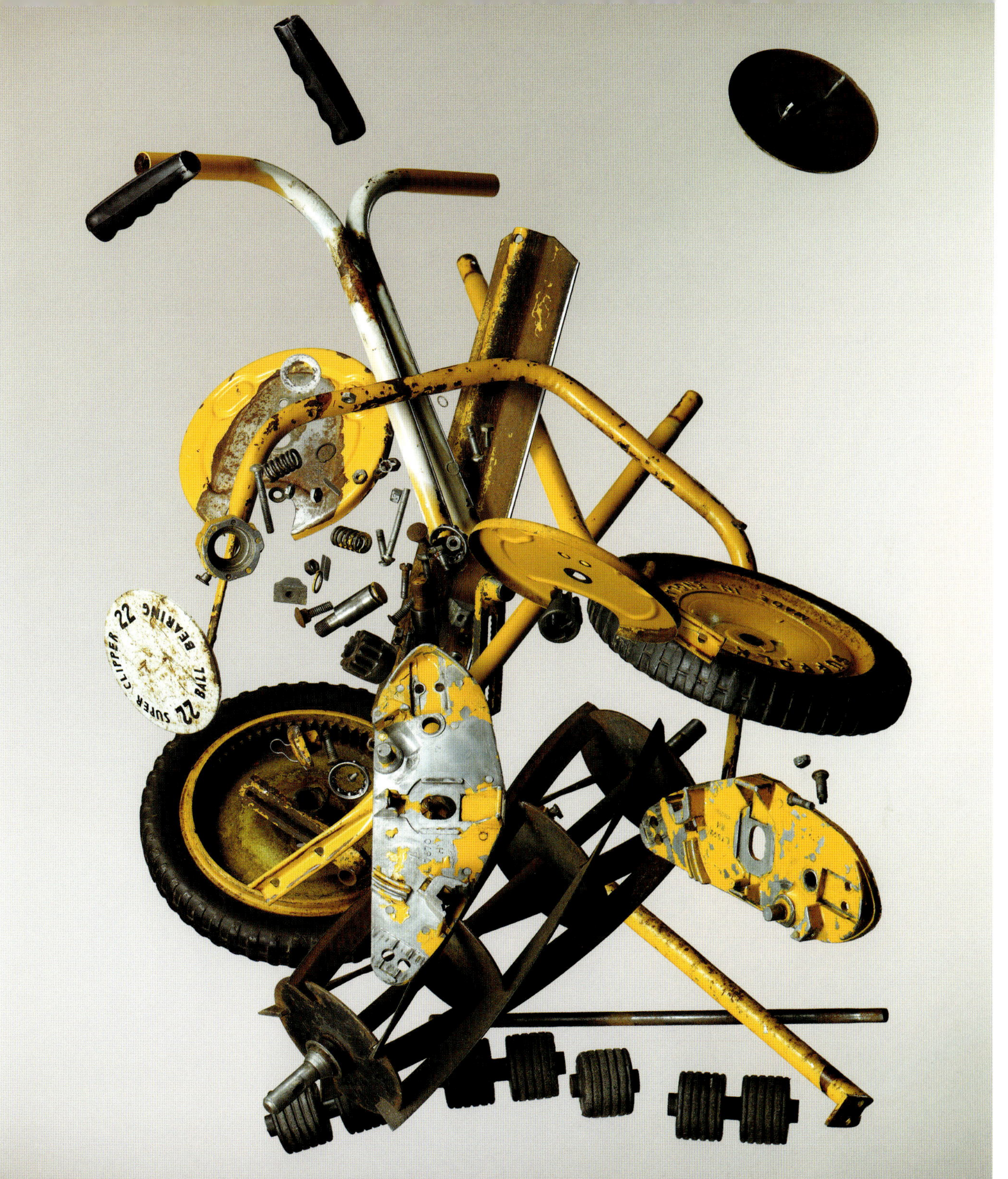
SUPER CLIPPER 22 BALL BEARING 22

JACK AMBRIDGE

www.jackambridge.com

Artists have long spent their time convincing us that their work renders the real world as they see it. So encountering a photographer who makes the actual world look like something he (or we) might conjure from the imagination can confuse the senses.

Jack Ambridge, a photographer based in southeast England, photographs actual cityscapes, landscapes and seascapes but, by dint of some very clever technology, presents them as fictitious, scaled-down models of the real thing. In his *Little Land* series Jack shows us photographs of Hastings in which the south coast town looks like a model. The grass, snow, houses, cars and people are given a hyperrealism that makes them look somehow false. He achieves the effect using 'tilt-shift', a process that entails working with a special lens or post-processing software for that 'toytown' look. The plane of focus is manipulated to give the impression that the camera is only centimetres away from the scene, when in truth the image is shot from a significant distance. The results take some studying. Indeed, even protracted staring may not convince you that these are actual places rather than simply models.

BOAT – WINTER

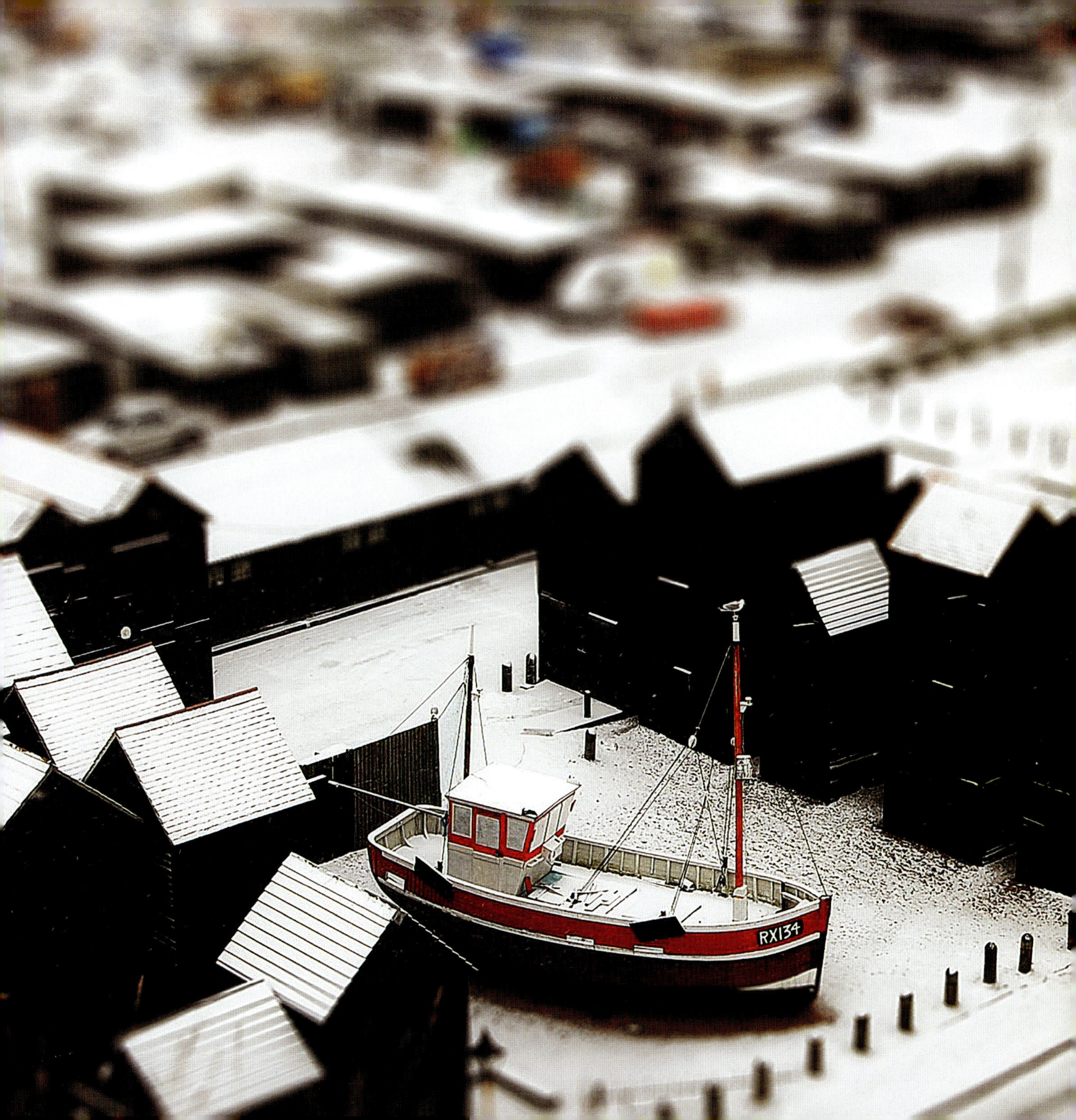
RX134

66

YANG YI

SCENERY

www.galerieparisbeijing.com

For many years the colossal Three Gorges Dam in the Chinese province of Hubei was the largest construction site in the world. The building project displaced over 1.2 million people and destroyed eleven cities. For one Chinese artist, the destruction created by the dams' advance became a very personal matter.

Yang Yi saw his old city dismantled amid the dam's construction. He was born and raised in Kaixian, but like its other inhabitants was compelled to move out in 2007, ahead of relocation to a new, purpose-built town. He captured the city on camera at the point of abandonment, creating the *Uprooted* series of images that depict a ghost town submerged beneath the water, where the few remaining inhabitants adapt as best they can with masks and snorkels. The photos reflect three phases of life in the city: the present is portrayed by everyday scenes; the past by sepia tones; and the future by the omnipresence of water. The real city was eventually flooded in 2009. For Yang Yi, the images preserve something very personal. 'I don't intend to dwell on the meaning to be found in my photography,' he comments. 'What is important for me is that I came from that town. It is about all that we have in common there: our accent, our spicy coriander, the nod we give each other, a friendly signal to say hello when we pass one another on the street.'

UPROOTED – 13, EAST RIVER BRIDGE

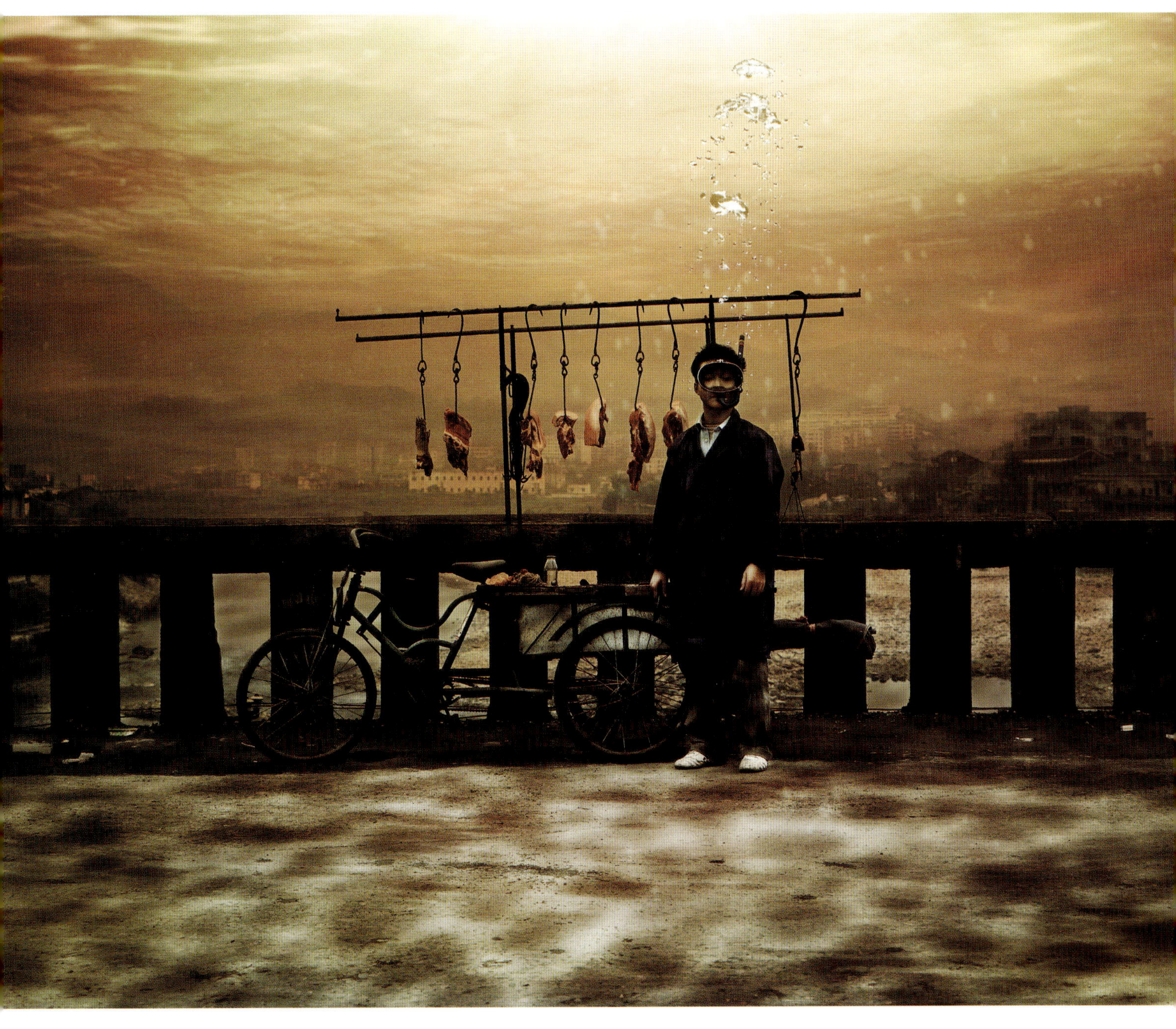

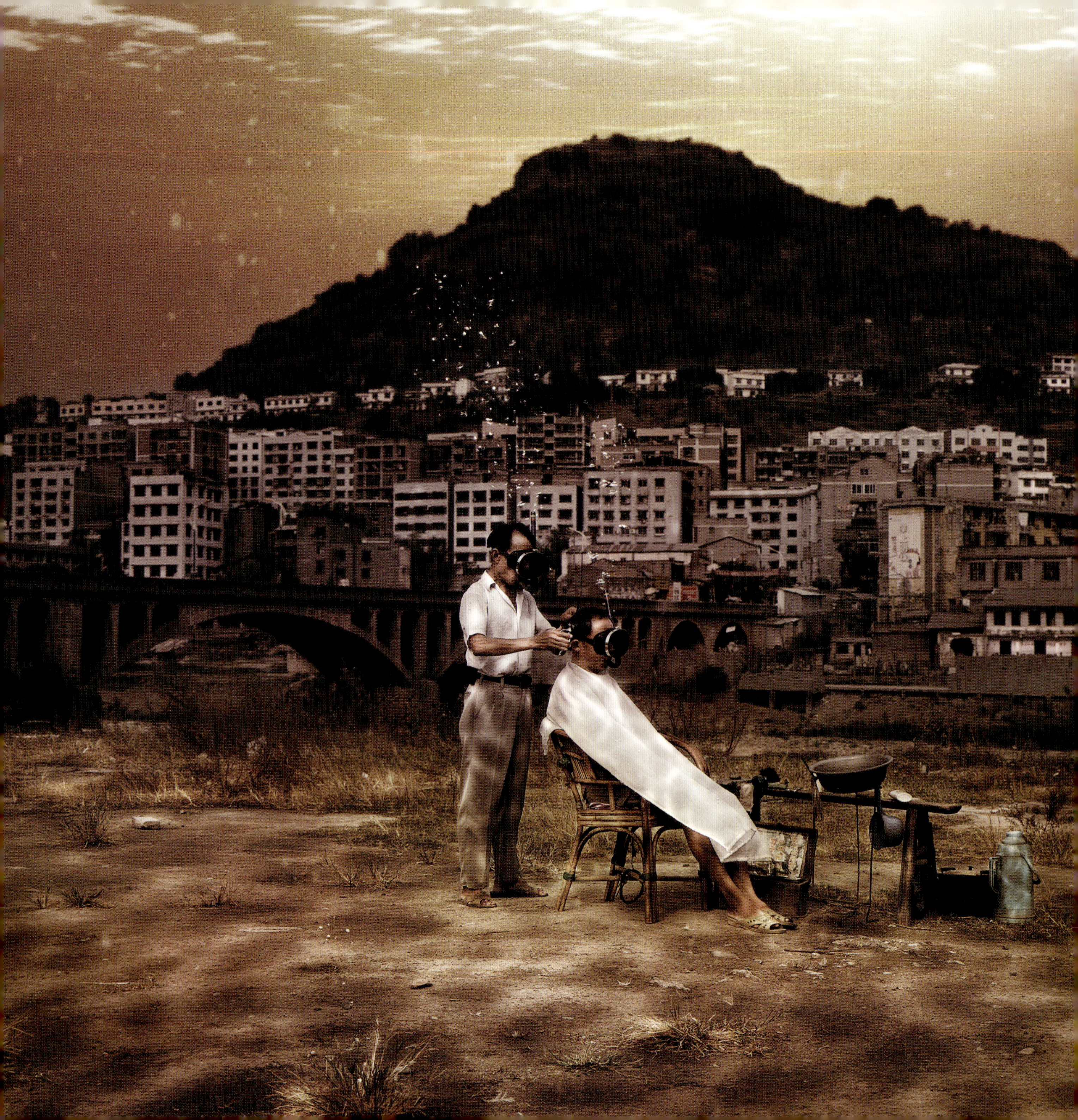

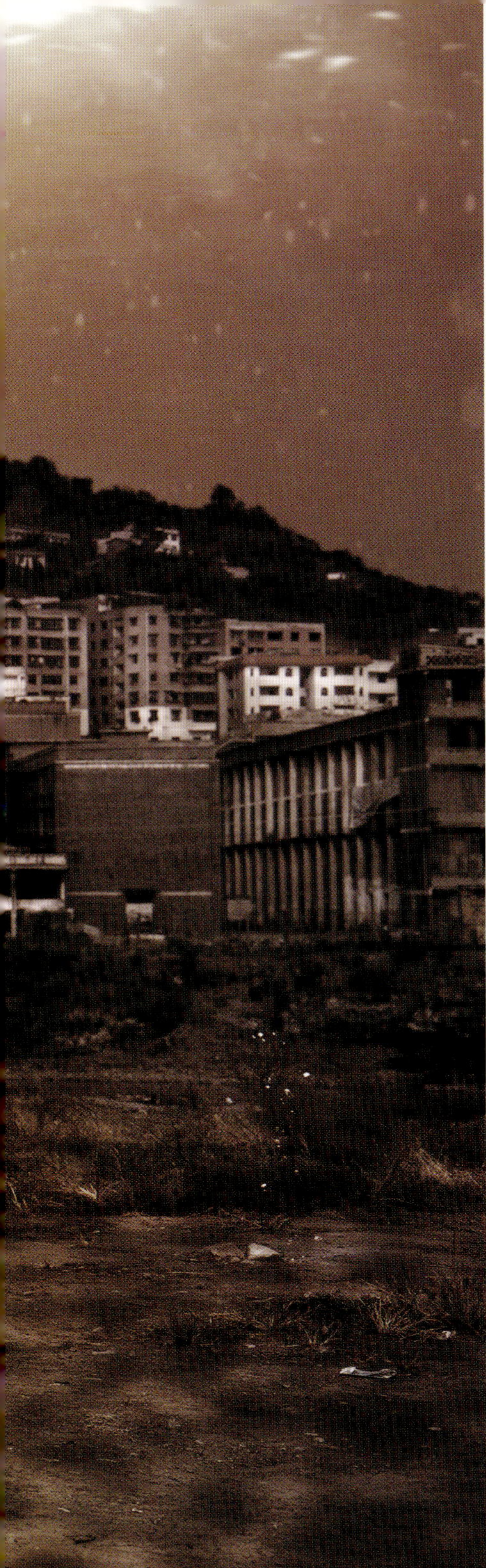

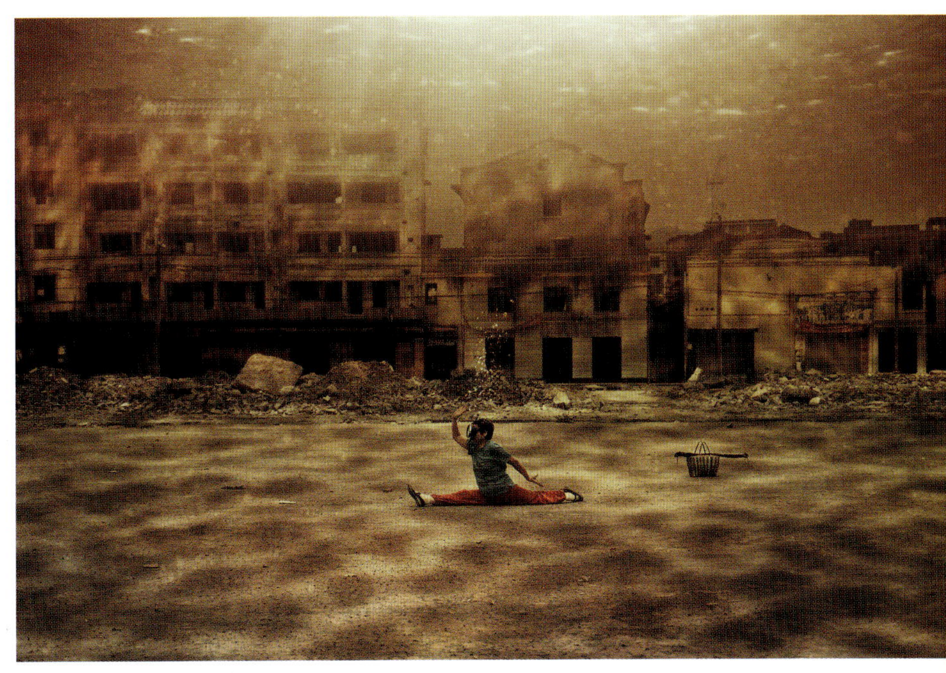

UPROOTED – 17, PLAYGROUND
UPROOTED – 11, EAST RIVER BANK (Left)

70

ALEXANDRE ORION

SCENERY

www.alexandreorion.com

Metabiosis occurs when a new organism is formed from the substrata left behind by another organism after its death. Think, for example, of a hermit crab in a predecessor's shell or, if you can bear it, maggots feeding on a corpse. This metabiotic process has proved inspirational to one young graffiti artist and photographer from Brazil.

Alexandre Orion began his artistic career aged fourteen, painting T-shirts which he then sold in the markets of his native São Paulo. Soon, he graduated to graffiti art, and started to consider how passers-by perceived his murals, and whether it was possible to strike up a dialogue between the art and the pedestrian. And so the *Metabiotics* series was born. For Alexandre, the metabiosis operates between painting and photography. The artist has the two disciplines sharing the same environment, like two inseparable yet incompatible organisms. It begins with his murals on the walls of São Paulo, which take on a life of their own as they interact with the locals. This new dynamic is then transposed into photography as Alexandre captures the changed scene with his camera.

METABIOTICS 14, 2004

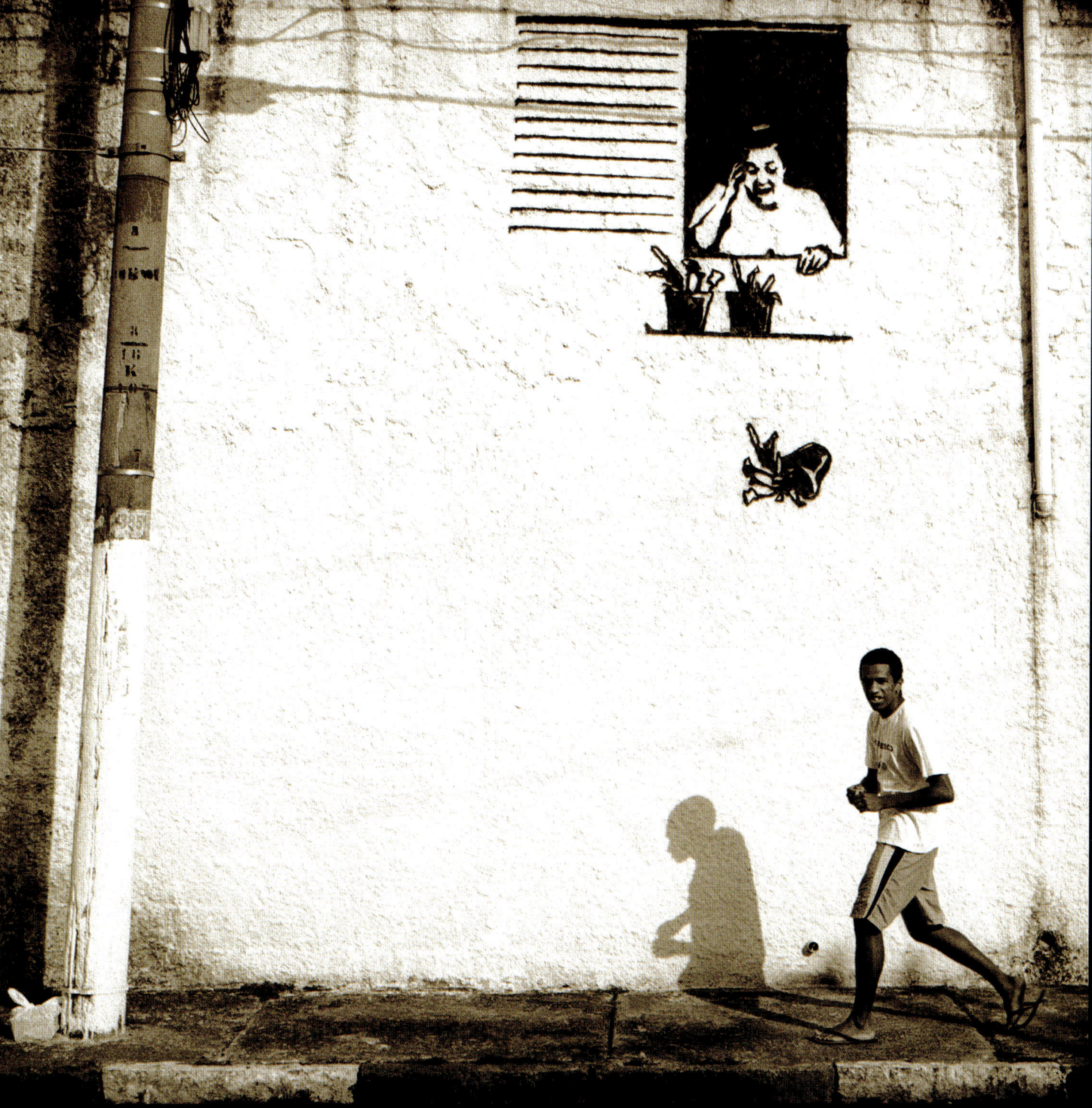

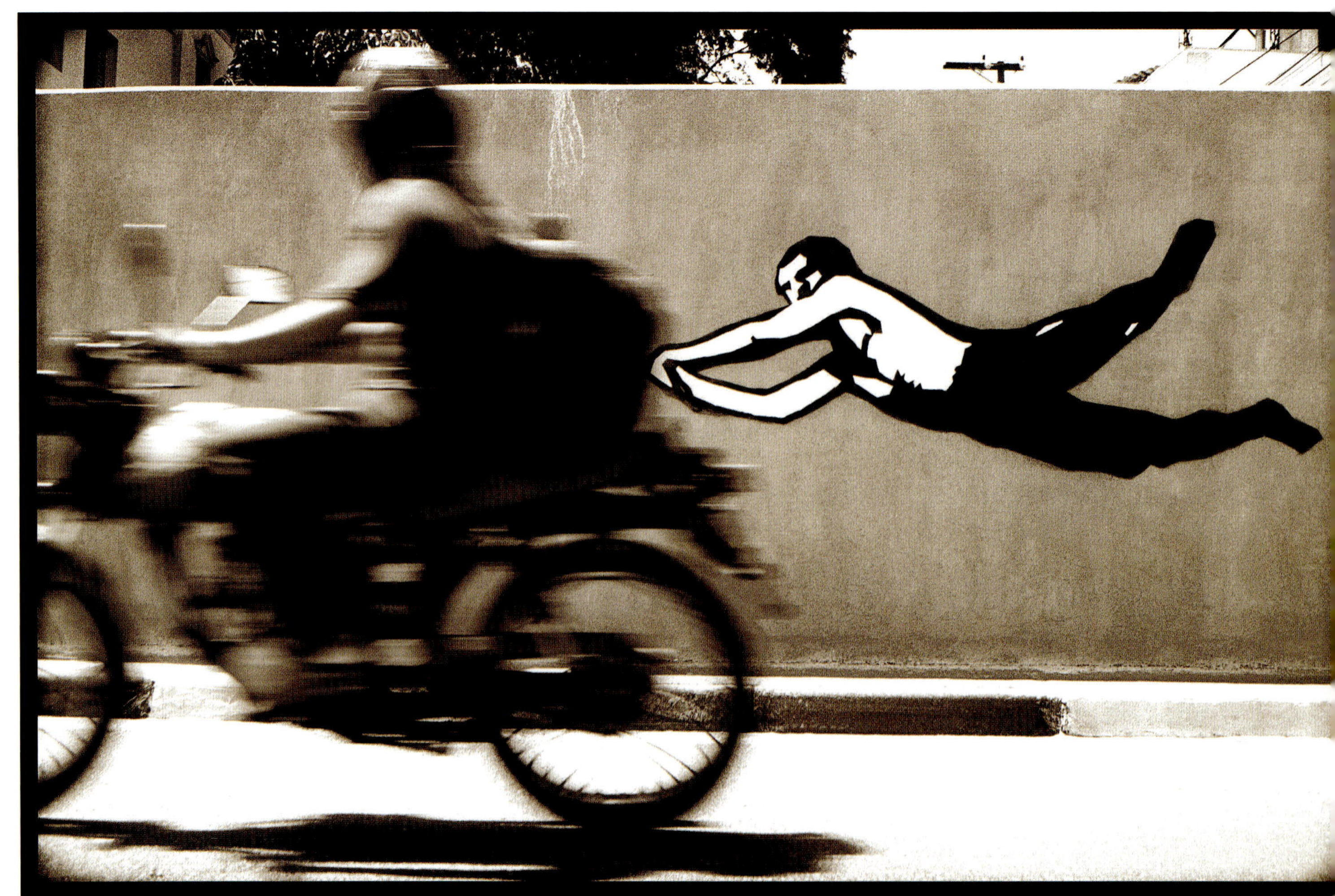

METABIOTICS 8, 2003

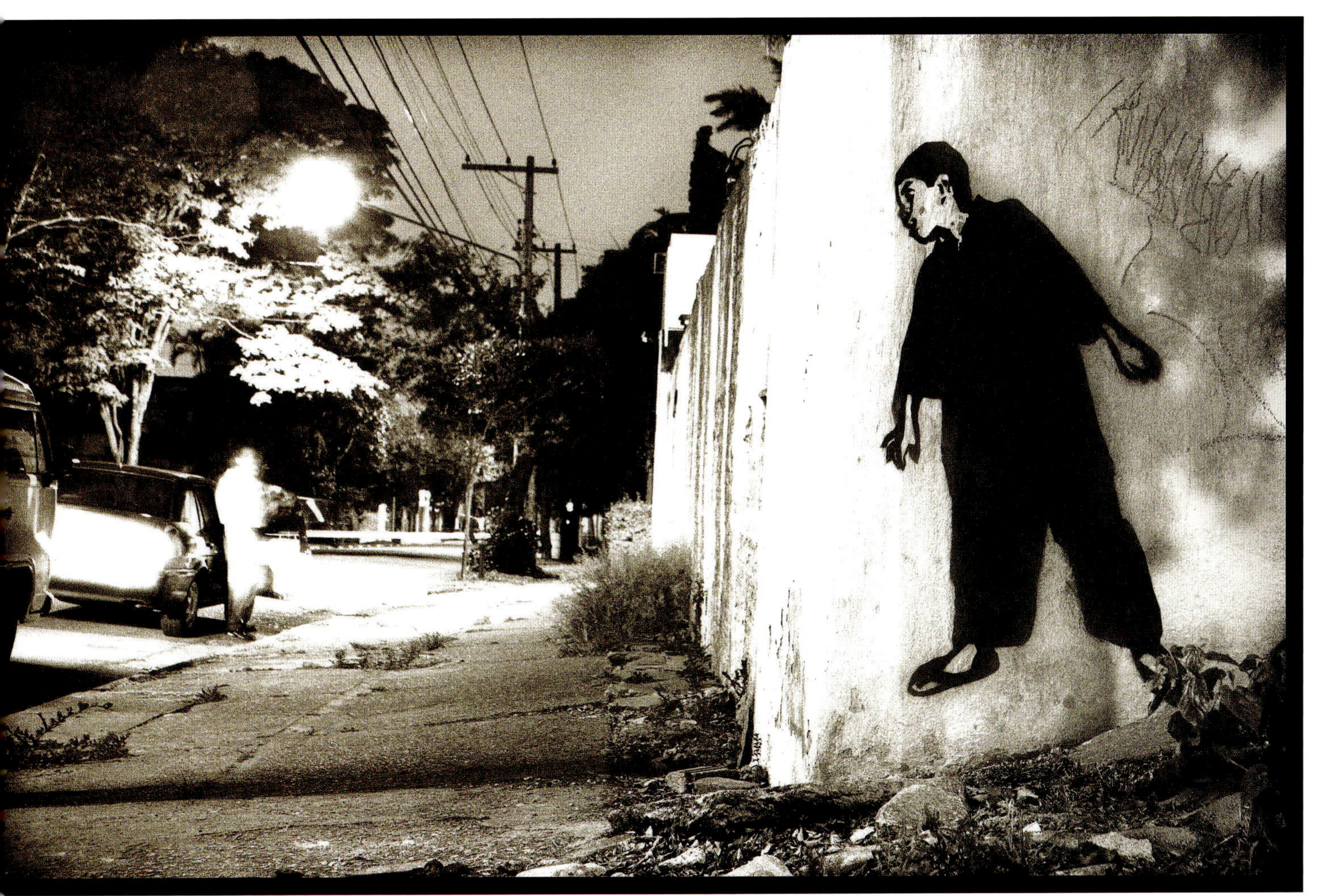

METABIOTICS 7, 2003

PEP VENTOSA

www.pepventosa.com

Pep Ventosa describes his photography as an exploration of the medium itself. By deconstructing and then rebuilding myriad photographic images of iconic architectural sites he creates new visual experiences.

In the *Collective Snapshot* series, the California-based Catalan photographer gathers together several dozen photographs all depicting the same view but at different times of the day. The chosen scene is usually an iconic tourist spot, a site such as the Sydney Harbour Bridge or the Brandenburg Gate in Berlin. He layers the photographs of the site together, recomposing the panorama rather like a sandwich. By splicing so many different photos on top of one another, Pep generates an overall image that celebrates collective memory, creating an abstract vision which, he hopes, will make even the stranger feel at home in a foreign land. 'What grows is a unique new narrative space that never actually happened, where the whole has travelled mysteriously further than what the camera documented,' he explains. 'Part memory, part imagination. Not unlike the way we see.' The resultant image shimmers, as reminiscent of a J.M.W. Turner painting as anything photographic.

THE TAJ MAHAL

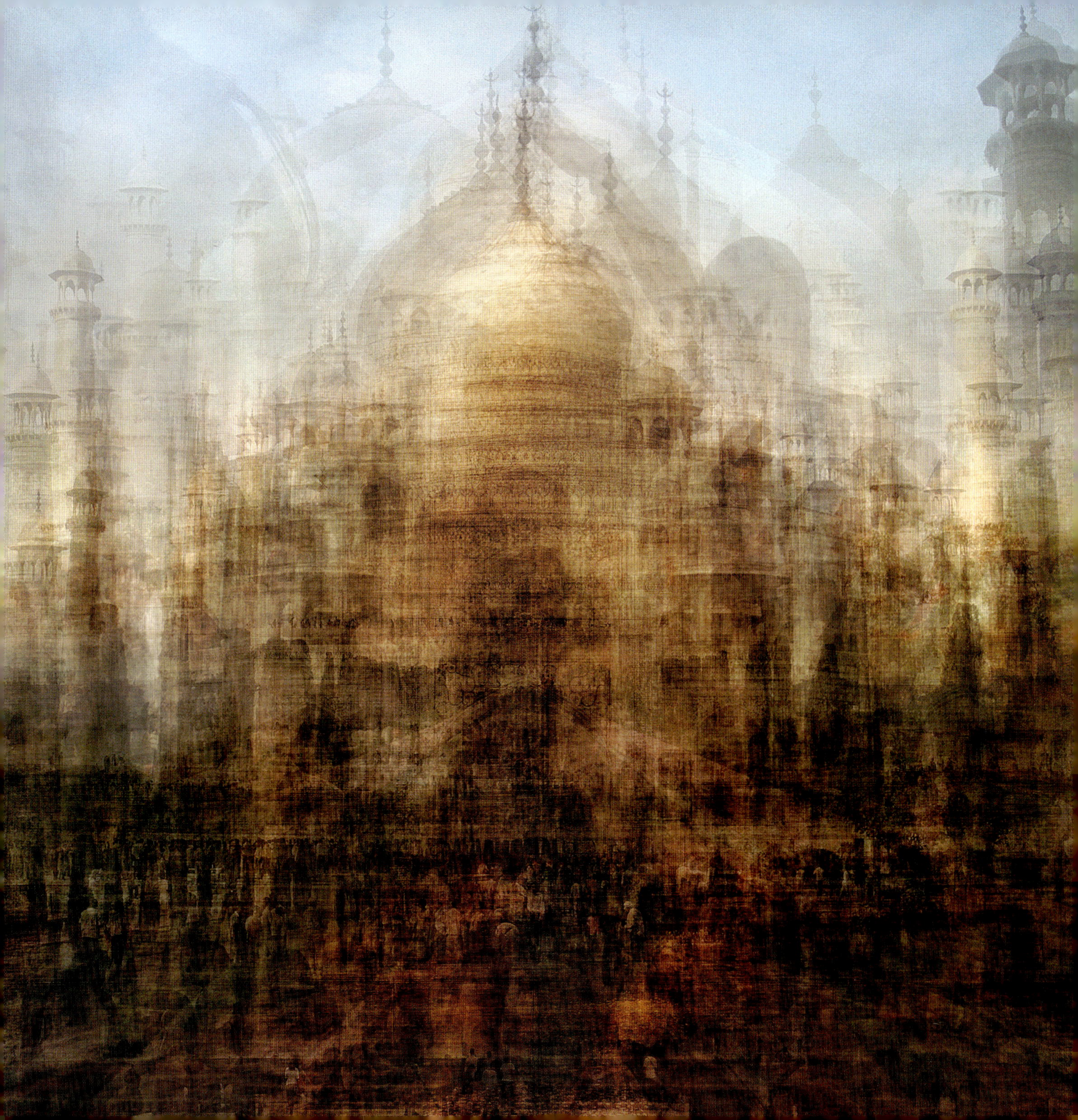

BARRY UNDERWOOD

www.barryunderwood.com

American artist Barry Underwood projects us into a twilight world illuminated by surreal lights and shapes. His photographs lie somewhere between performance and static art, their spectral lights drawing the viewer into a fantasyland.

The images are taken from the artist's *Scenes* series, a collection of dioramas – or illuminated landscapes – created on-site in the far reaches of the natural world. They're the product of a marriage; a combination of traditional photography and stage setting. 'I approach my photographic work with a theatrical sensibility that permits me to intermingle issues that arise from contemporary painting, cinema and land art,' explains Barry. 'The resulting images are surreal images, given that they result from this cross-pollination between traditional photography and theatre.' Lights installed in the landscape by the artist appear as intrusions and interventions since they contrast with the inherent atmospheric properties of natural light and thereby render the forms of the landscape abstract. For Barry, the *Scenes* series explores the themes of illusion, imagination, narrative and the inventive potential of the ordinary.

AURORA GREEN
RODEO BEACH (Overleaf, left)
TRACE BLUE (Overleaf, right)

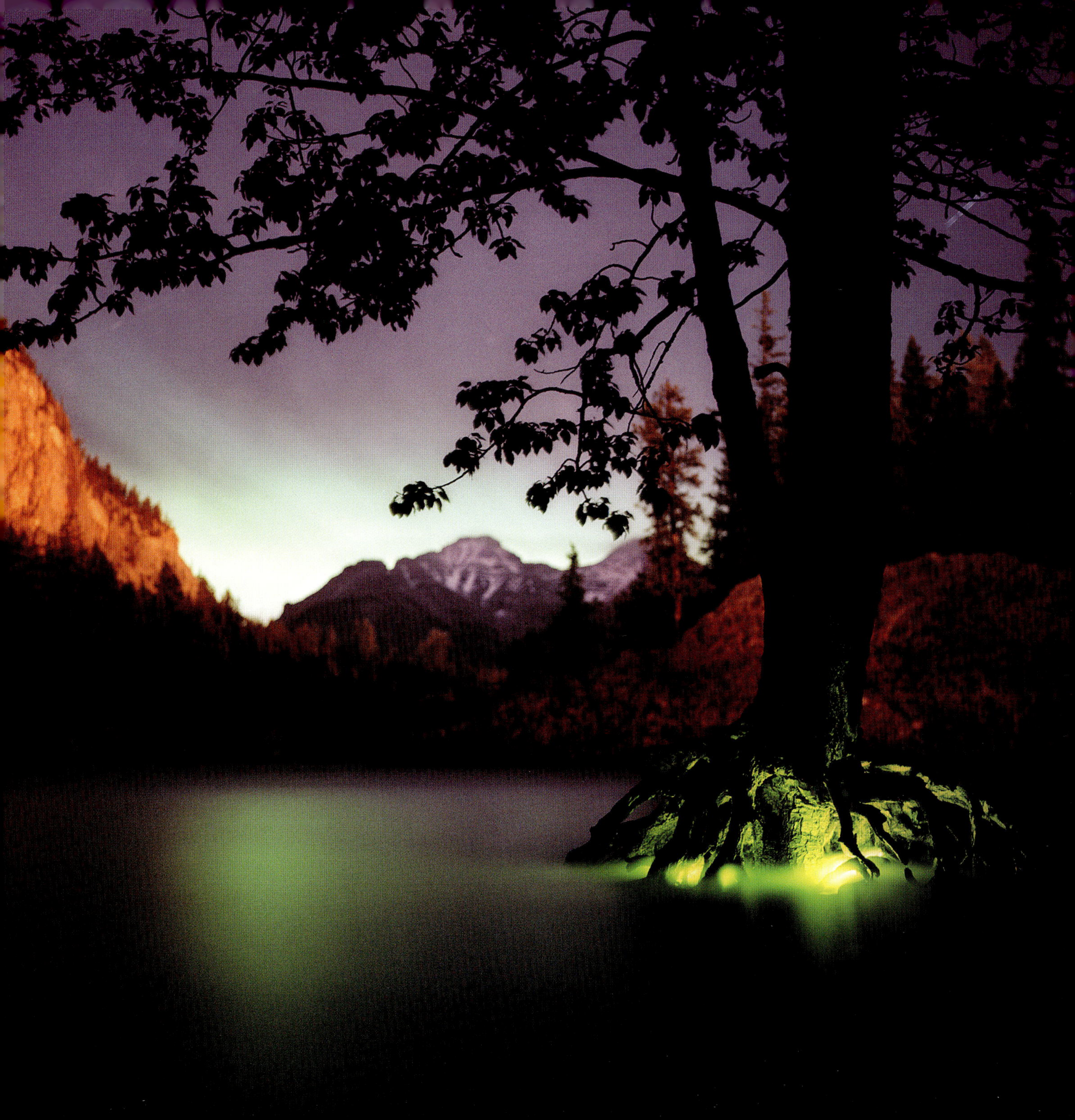

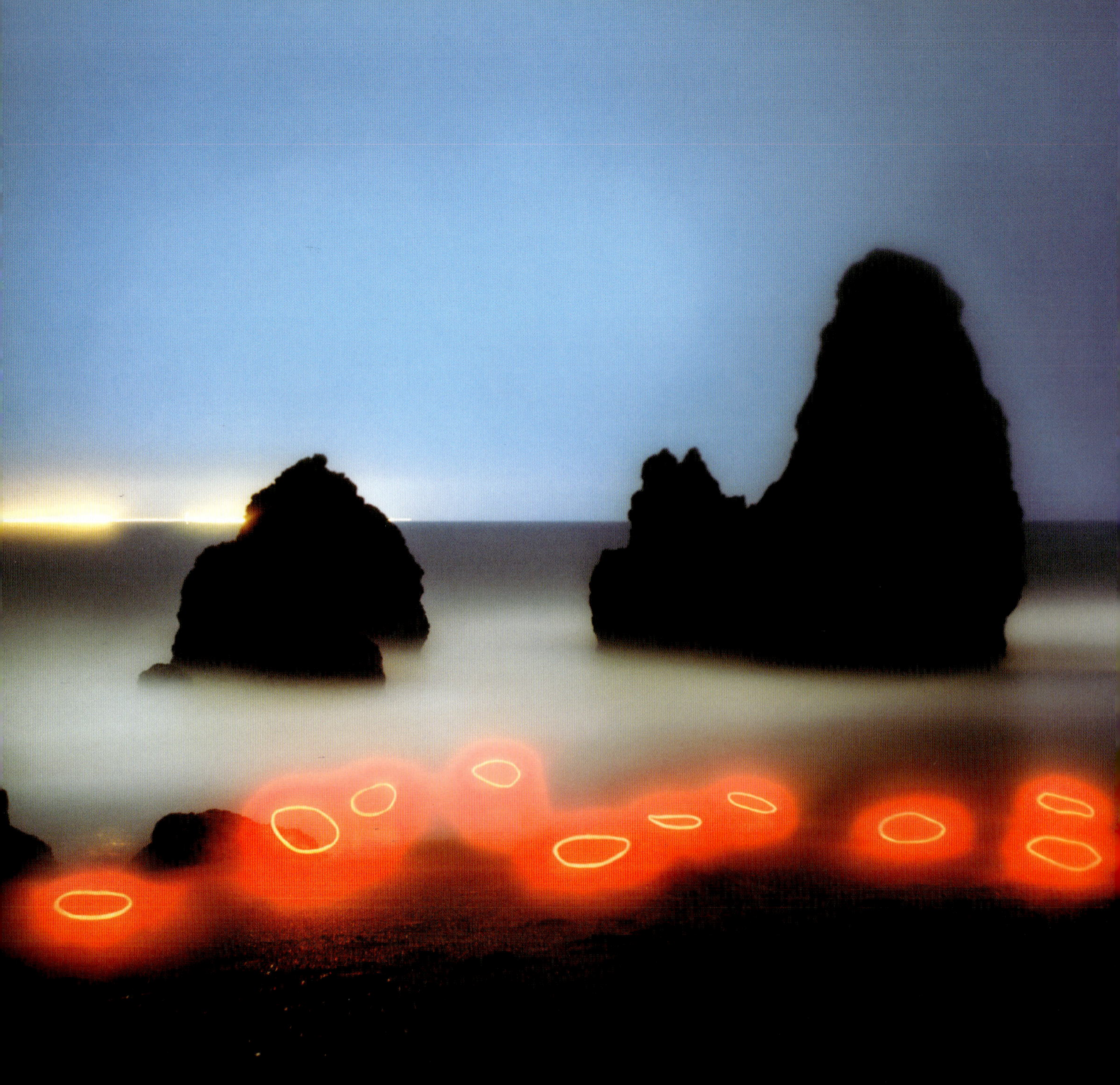

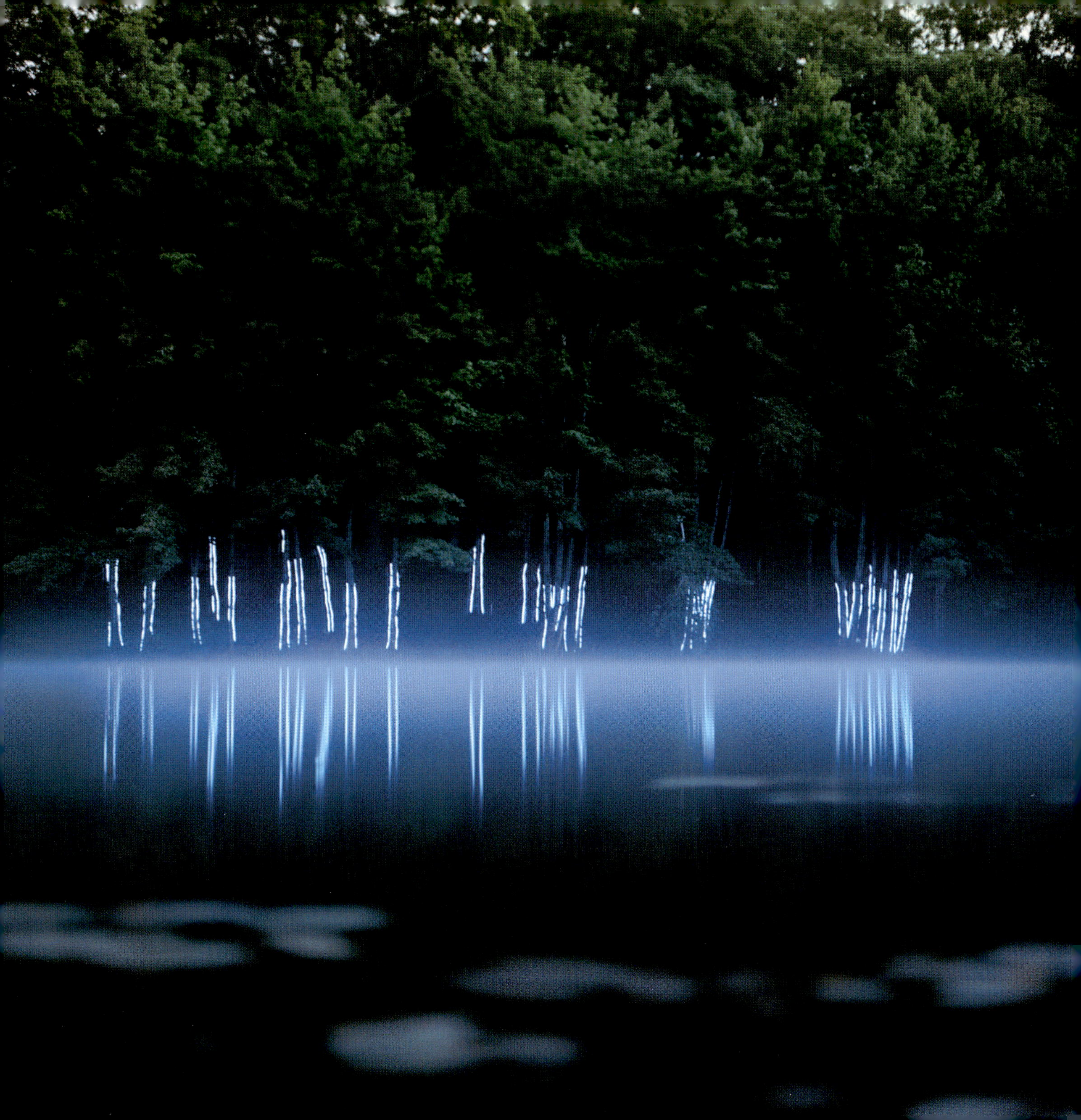

MICHAEL PAUL SMITH

SCENERY

http://www.flickr.com/photos/24796741@N05/

In Michael Smith's world it's still 1950 something. The cars are curvaceous monsters, like the Studebaker Champion, and the jukebox remains the most visited piece of furniture in the local diner. Welcome to Elgin Park, Michael's nostalgia trip in miniature, where everything exists on a scale of 1:24.

Some twenty-five years ago, the Pennsylvanian photographer decided to have some fun with his collection of miniature cars, and reconstructing the small American towns of his childhood seemed like a good place to start. Today, he's still making models of Elgin Park. Shot with a genuine scenic backdrop – in which the trees, electric wires and distant buildings are all real – the images are remarkably lifelike. Often, it's only the absence of people from the sets that betrays their diminutive scale. Michael doesn't use photo-editing software to enhance his photographs, although he does rely on filters that age the image in view. Other than that, his equipment consists of a six-megapixel Sony camera and a distinctly aged Mac computer. Although fictitious, Elgin Park has become something of a tourist attraction via Michael's *Flickr* page, which receives thousands of visits every day.

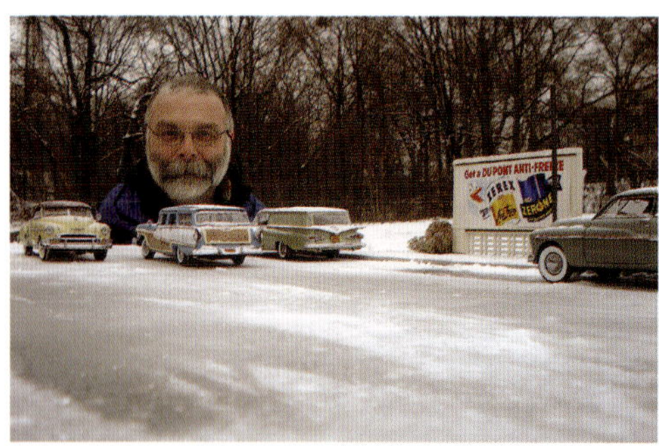

LAST WASH
JANUARY FIRST PHOTO SHOOT (Left)
JANUARY SNOWFALL 1959 (Overleaf)

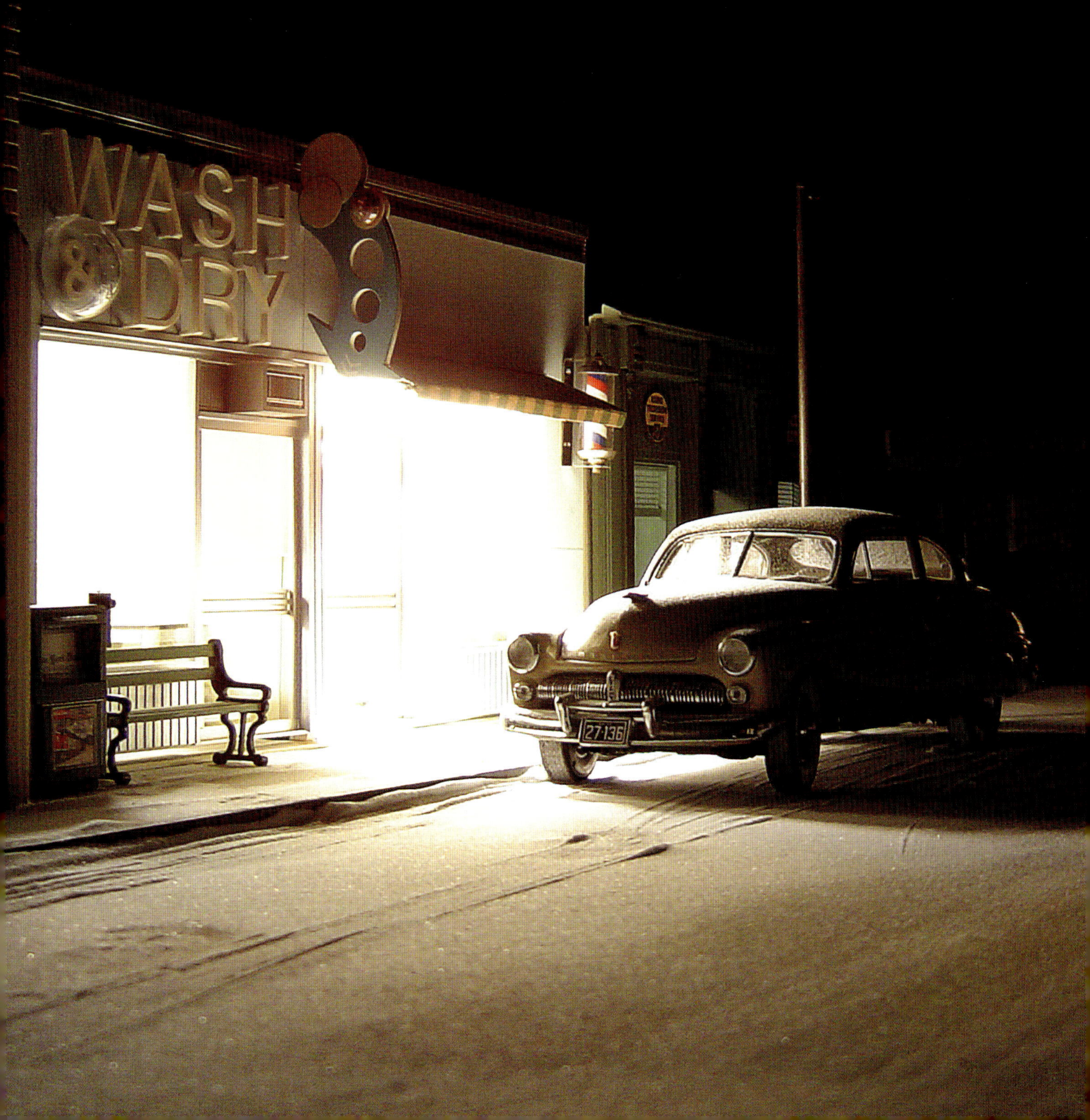
WASH
& DRY
27·136

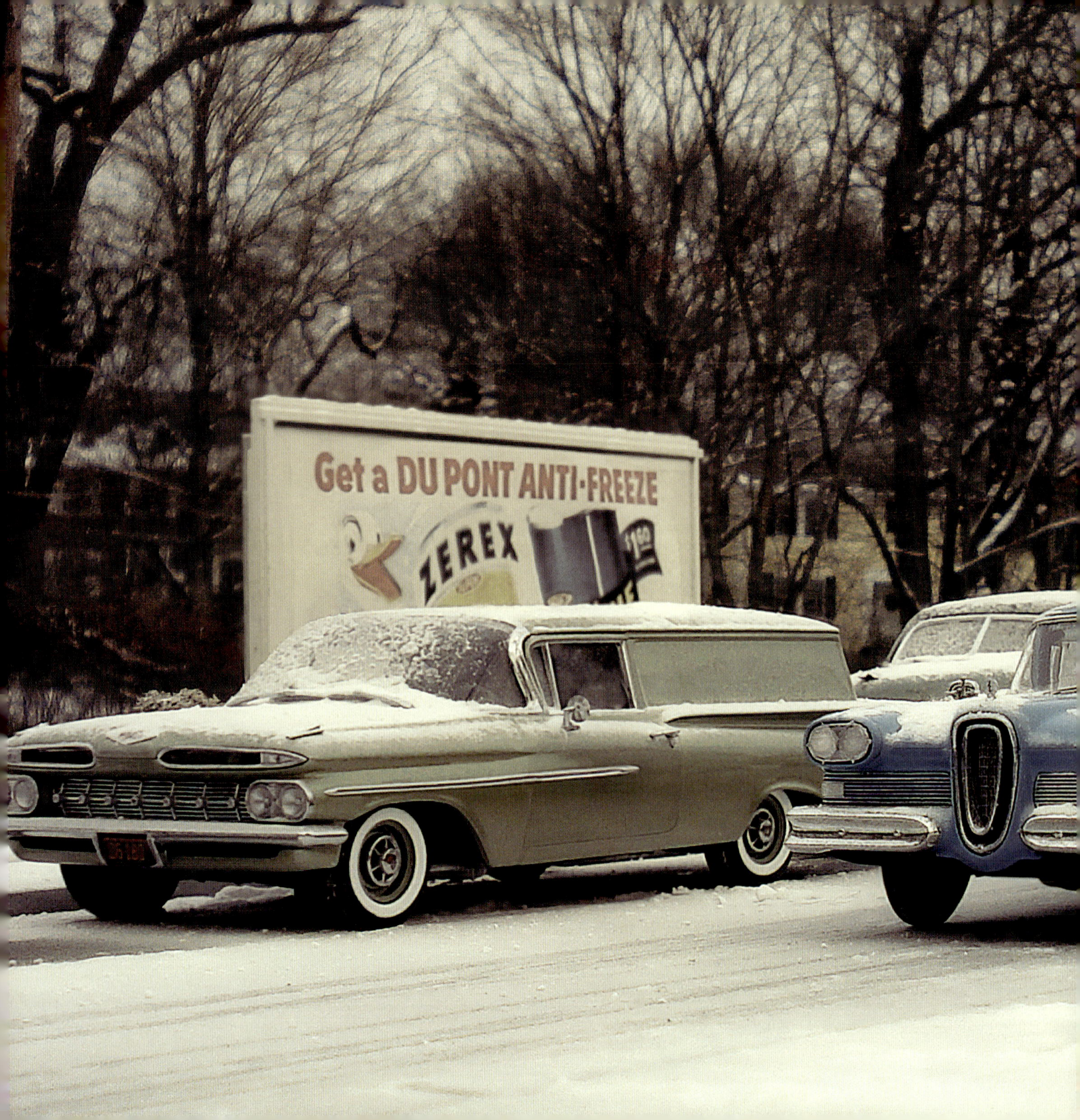
Get a DU PONT ANTI-FREEZE
ZEREX

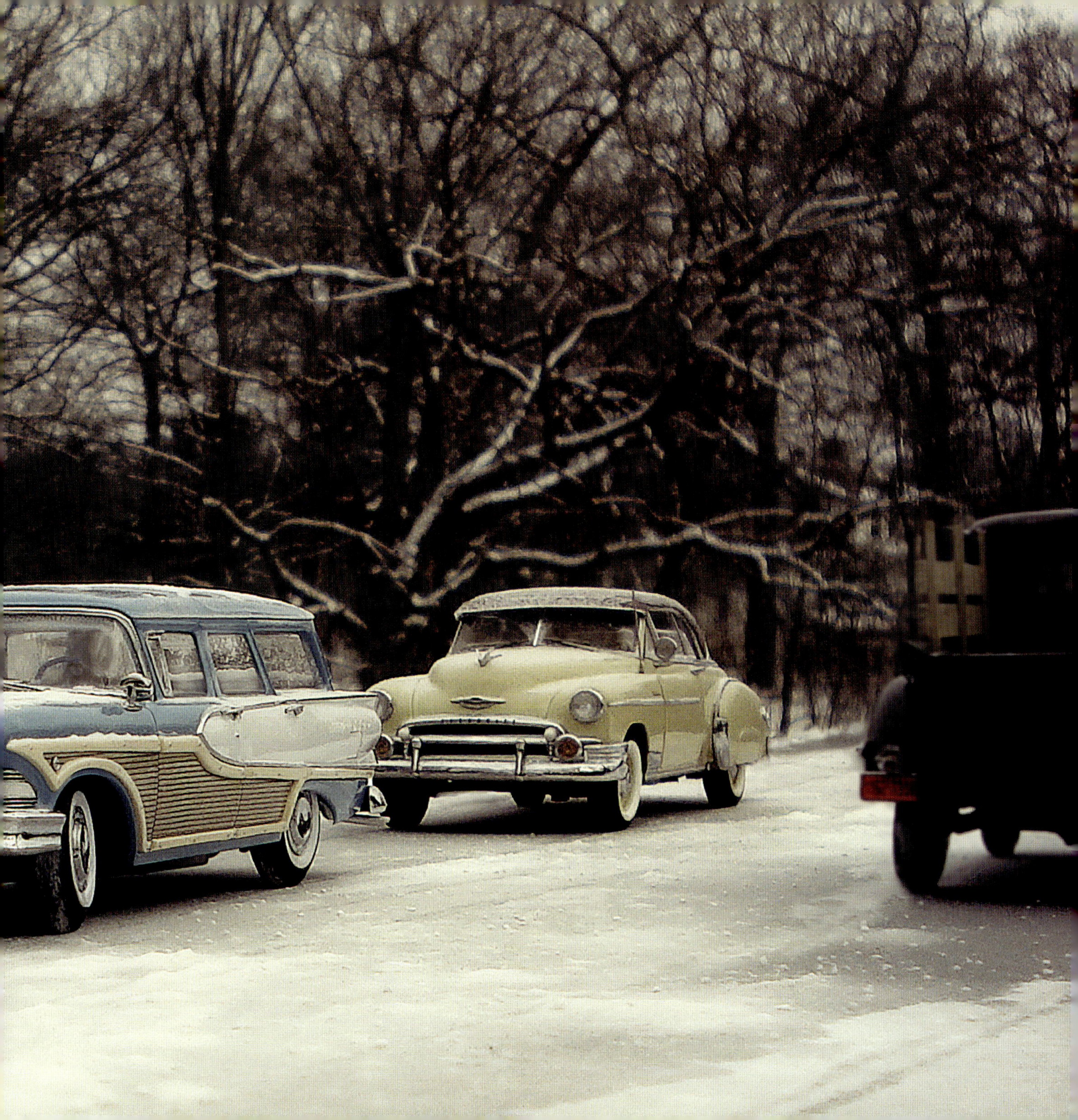

PIERRE JAVELLE & AKIKO IDA

www.minimiam.com

'Don't play with your food!' goes mother's famous mantra, aimed at children the world over for generations. But, as Pierre Javelle and Akiko Ida have artfully proved, playing with food can unlock a world of ingenuous creativity – a universe where skiers plummet down slopes of Chantilly cream, or where penguins dodge polar bears on icebergs made of marshmallow.

Pierre and Akiko met whilst studying photography at the school of Arts Décoratifs in Paris. He, Burgundian by birth, had grown up on a diet of Robert Doisneau and Henri Cartier-Bresson; she, from Japan, spent her childhood baking and photographing bread. Both graduated to a career in food photography. Together, they created the *Minimiam* project, in which foodstuffs become a microworld populated by tiny plastic figures only 1.5 centimetres tall. Some of the figures busy themselves with relatively mundane activities, pushing a tiny lawn mower over the furry surface of a kiwi fruit for example; others inhabit dangerous, fantastical worlds, in which they dress as ninjas and aim guns at trays of sushi. Clearly, Pierre and Akiko generate a sense of fun through their photography, but they also draw our attention to the fantastic details of food – the unconsidered colours or textures of the things that we consume every day.

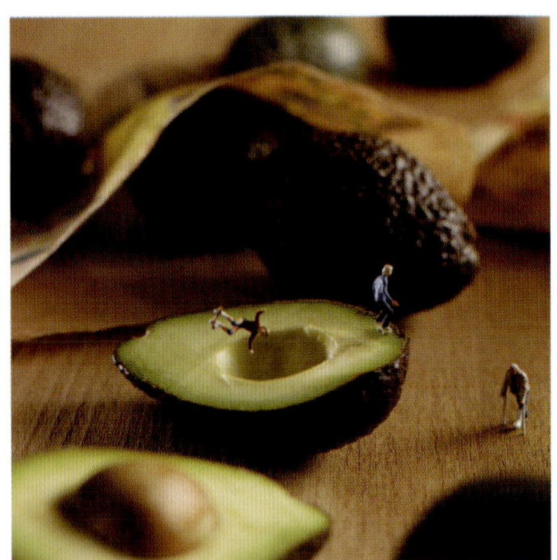

THE TUB (Left and right)
BENTO BREAK (Overleaf, left)
MARSHMALLOW FELLOWS (Overleaf, right)

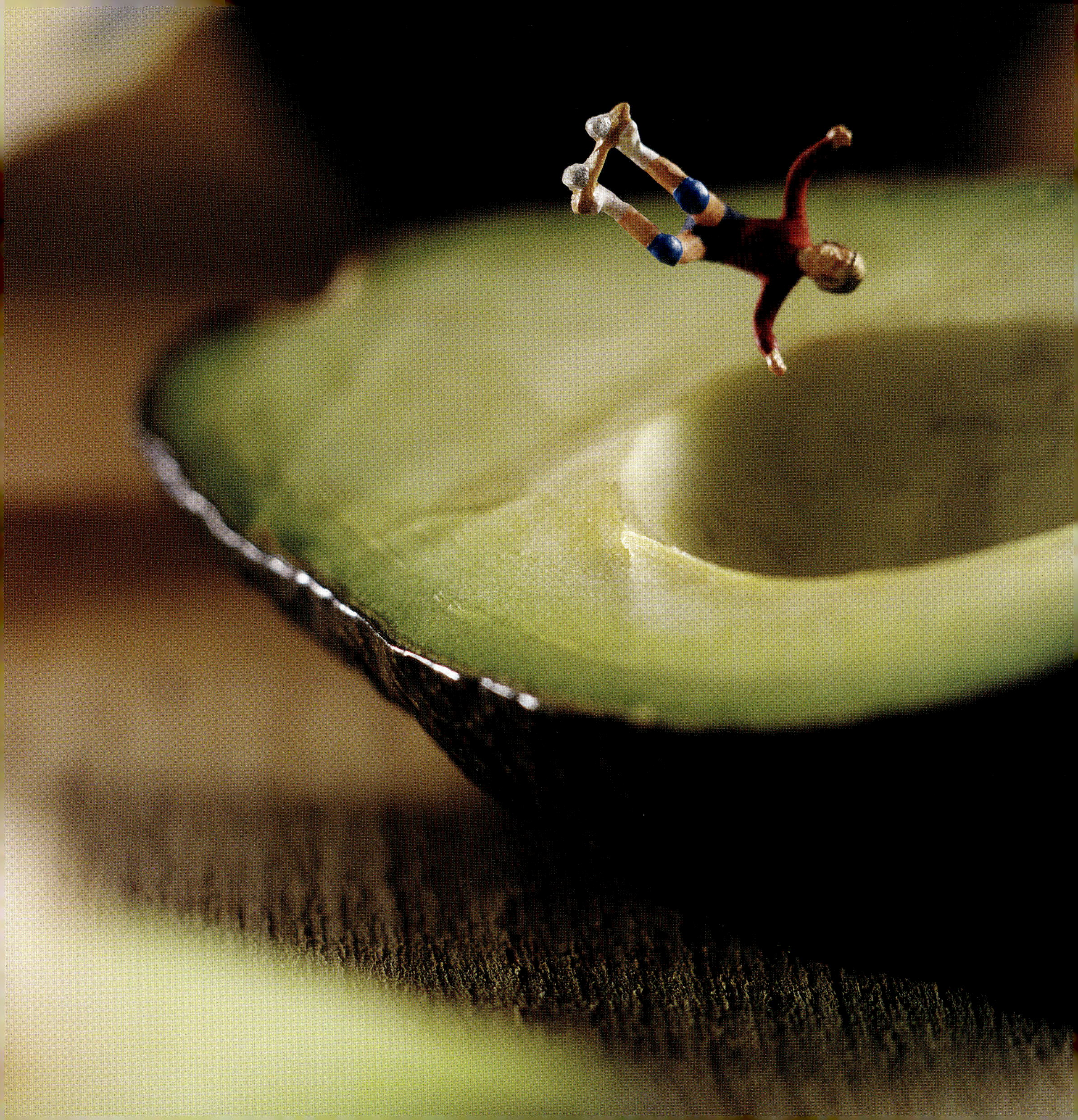

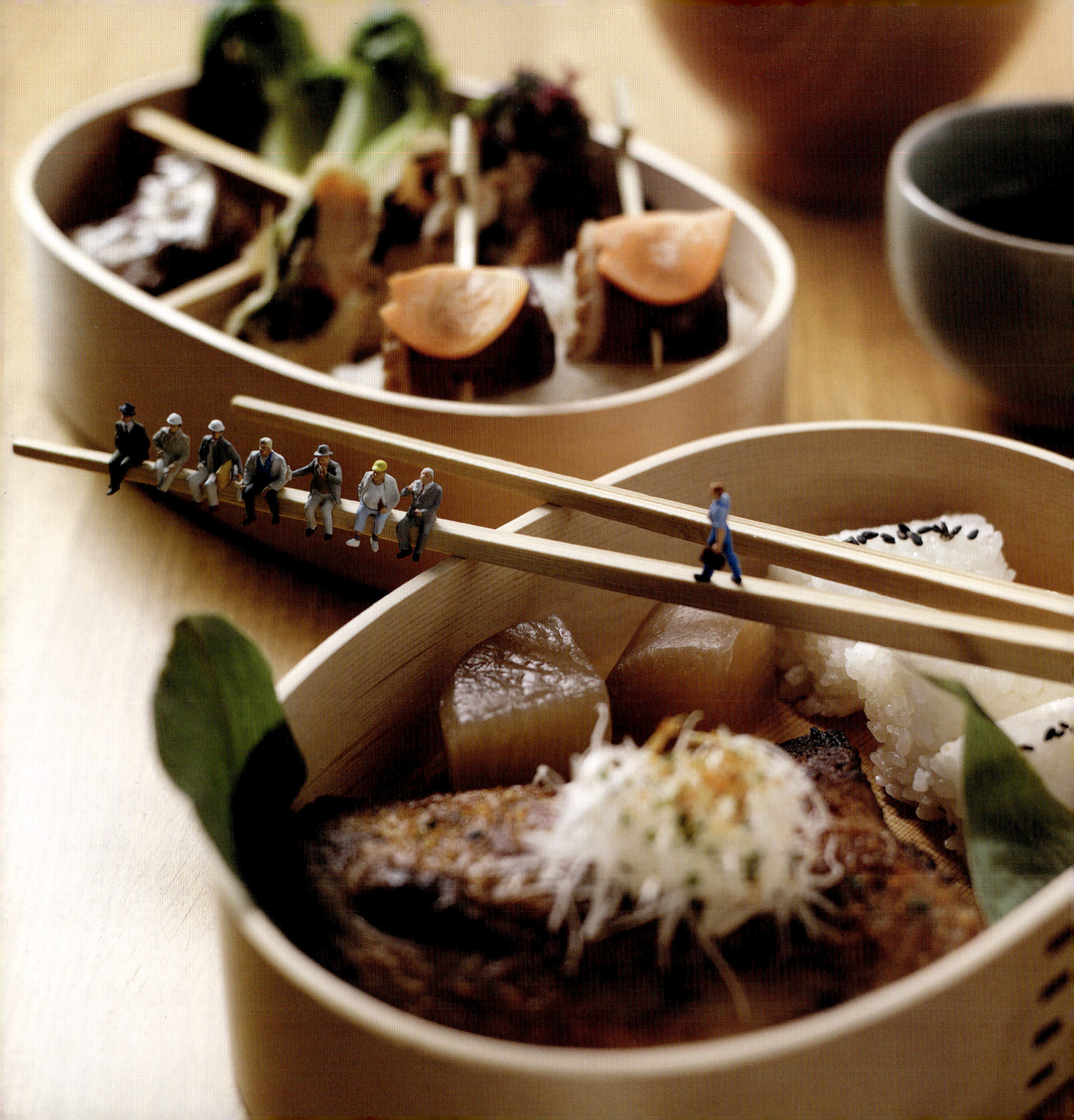

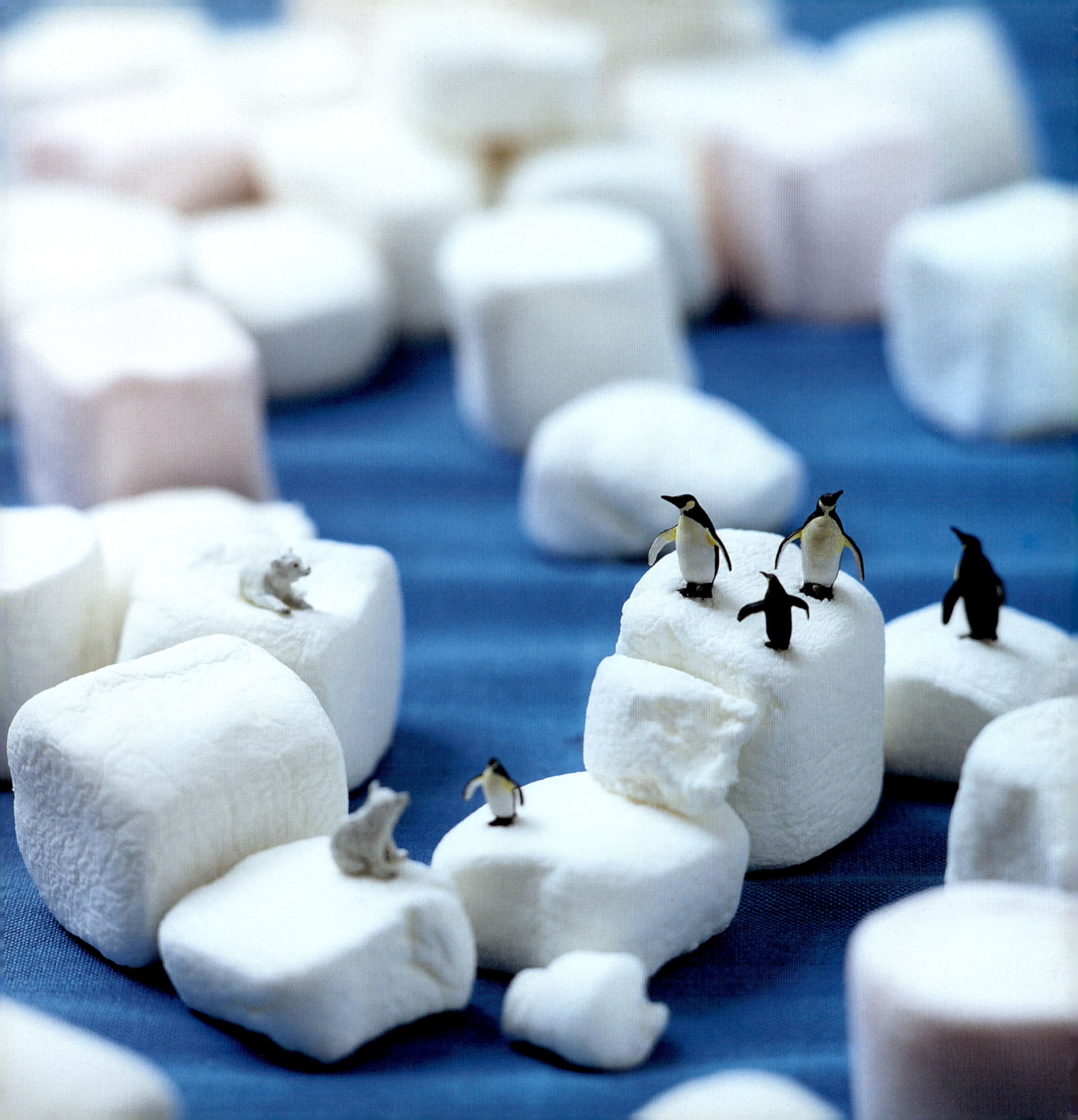

FEARS

Photography has always had the ability to shock, playing on the fears of its audience whether the source of that fear is real or imagined. Today, in the Photoshop age, the stuff of nightmares has become significantly easier to render in print. Digital manipulation can conjure monsters from the deep or rip flesh from the human body. And whilst some artists employ photography to draw out collective fears about repressive regimes or environmental catastrophe, others are more interested in schlock, unsettling with their use of sex and violence.

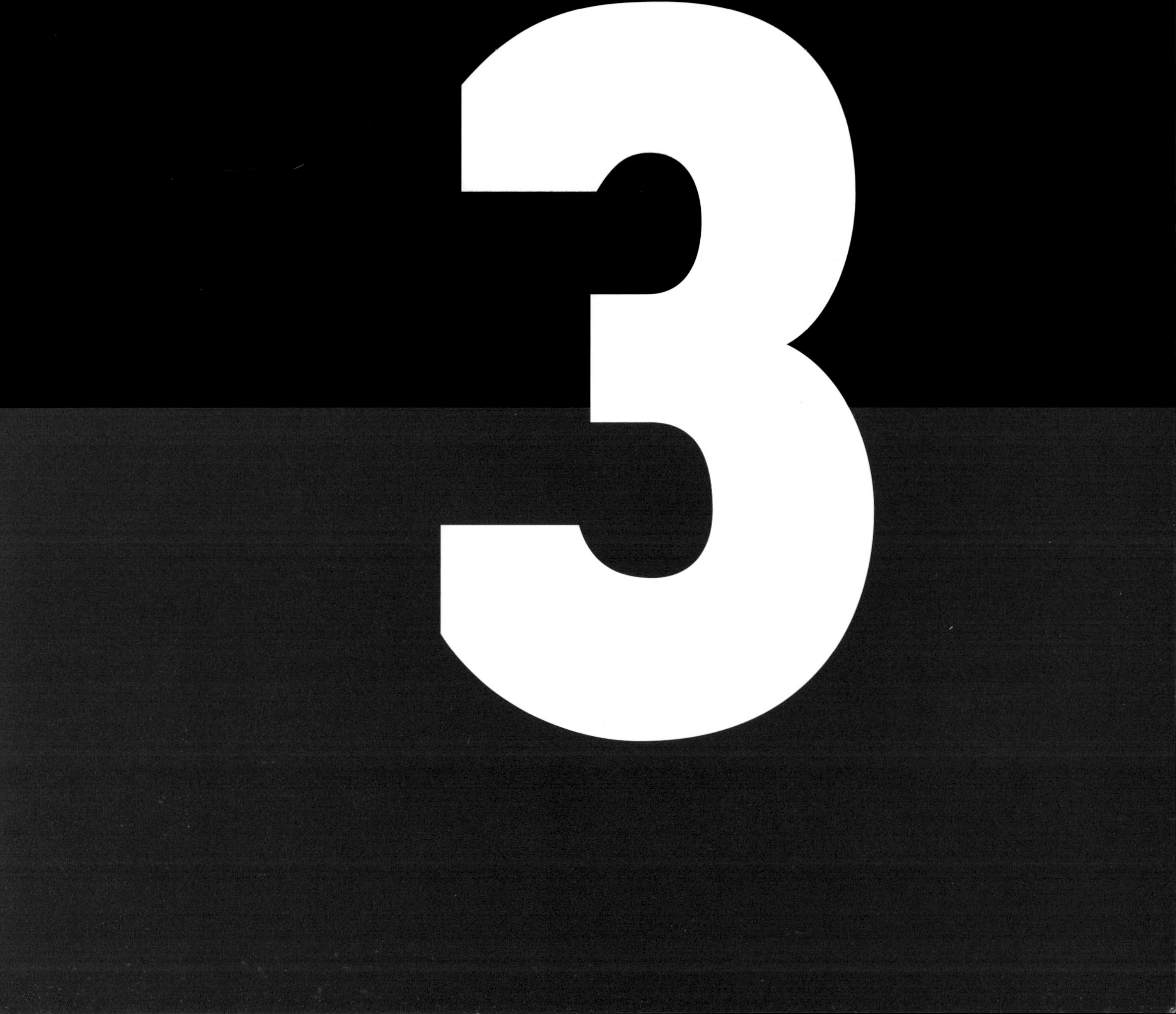
3

JAN OLIEHOEK

www.janoliehoek.com

Photo manipulation has given artists the scope to create new worlds and to shape illusory, fantastical objects and figures. For Jan Oliehoek it has brought the opportunity to sire a menagerie of mutant animals.

Jan draws inspiration at random from whatever images he unearths on the Internet. He finds a suitable photo, one that appeals either technically or aesthetically, and appropriates it for his art – chopping, melding and grafting to create surreal, humorous new worlds and figures. The physiognomy of animals, in particular, appears well suited to the effects of digital hybridisation. But Jan is more than just a master of manipulation; he works in the tradition of the great trompe-l'oeil painters, deceiving the eye and inducing the double take. It's not statement art – Jan isn't passing comment on genetic engineering or cloning. Instead, he hopes simply to create beautiful images.

HIPPO FROG
CROGGY (Overleaf, left)
ZEBRA FROG (Overleaf, right)

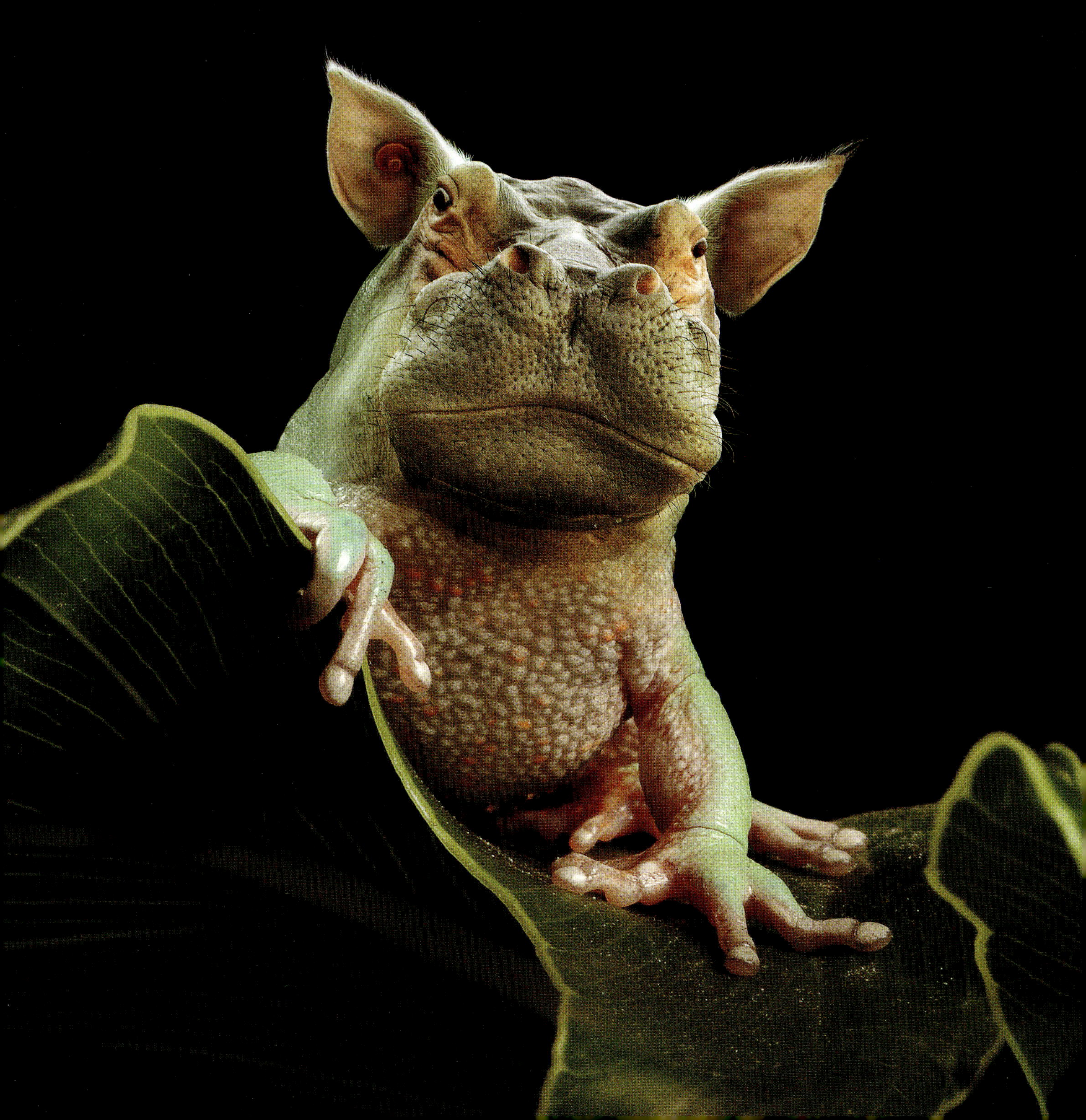

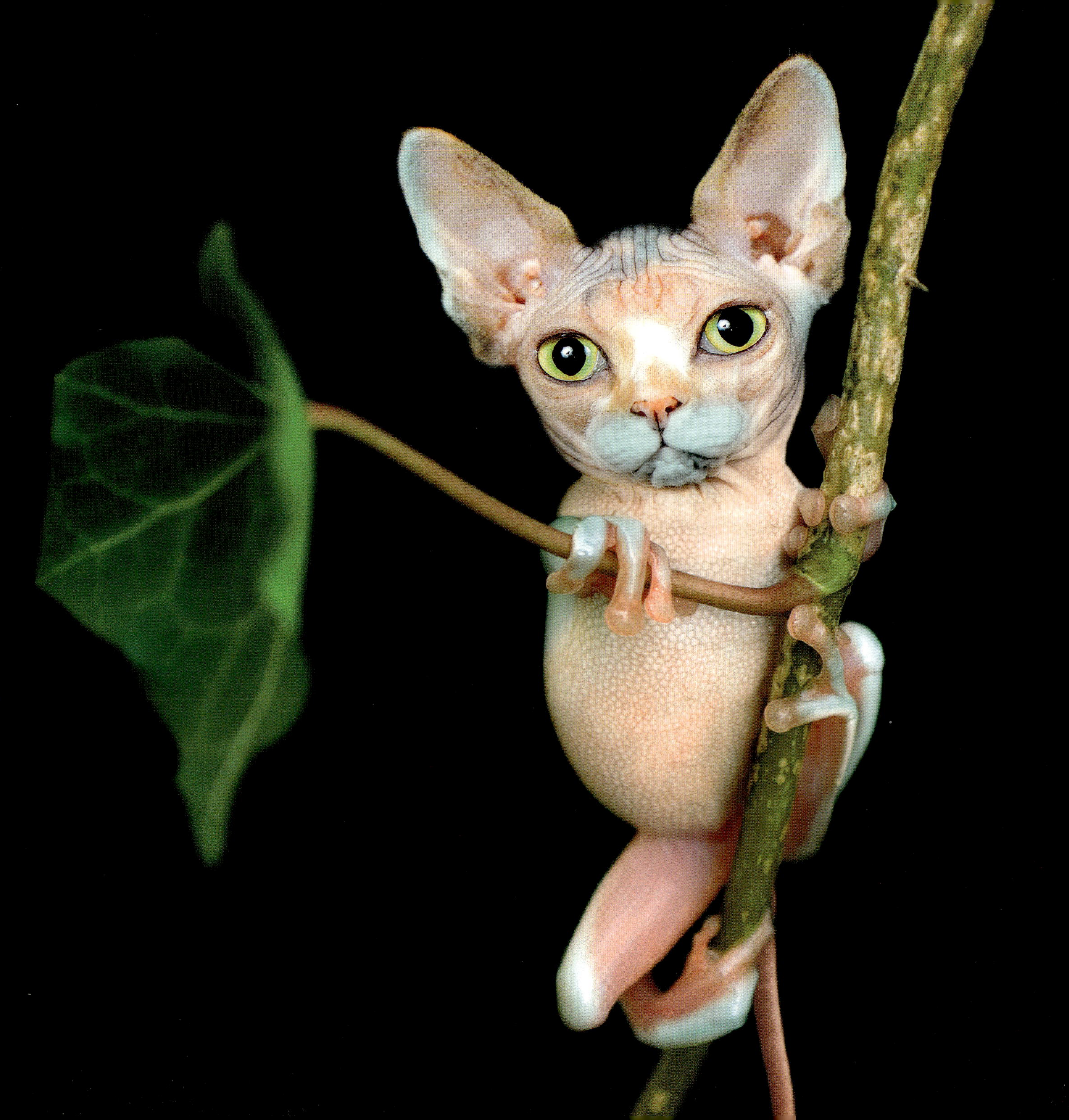

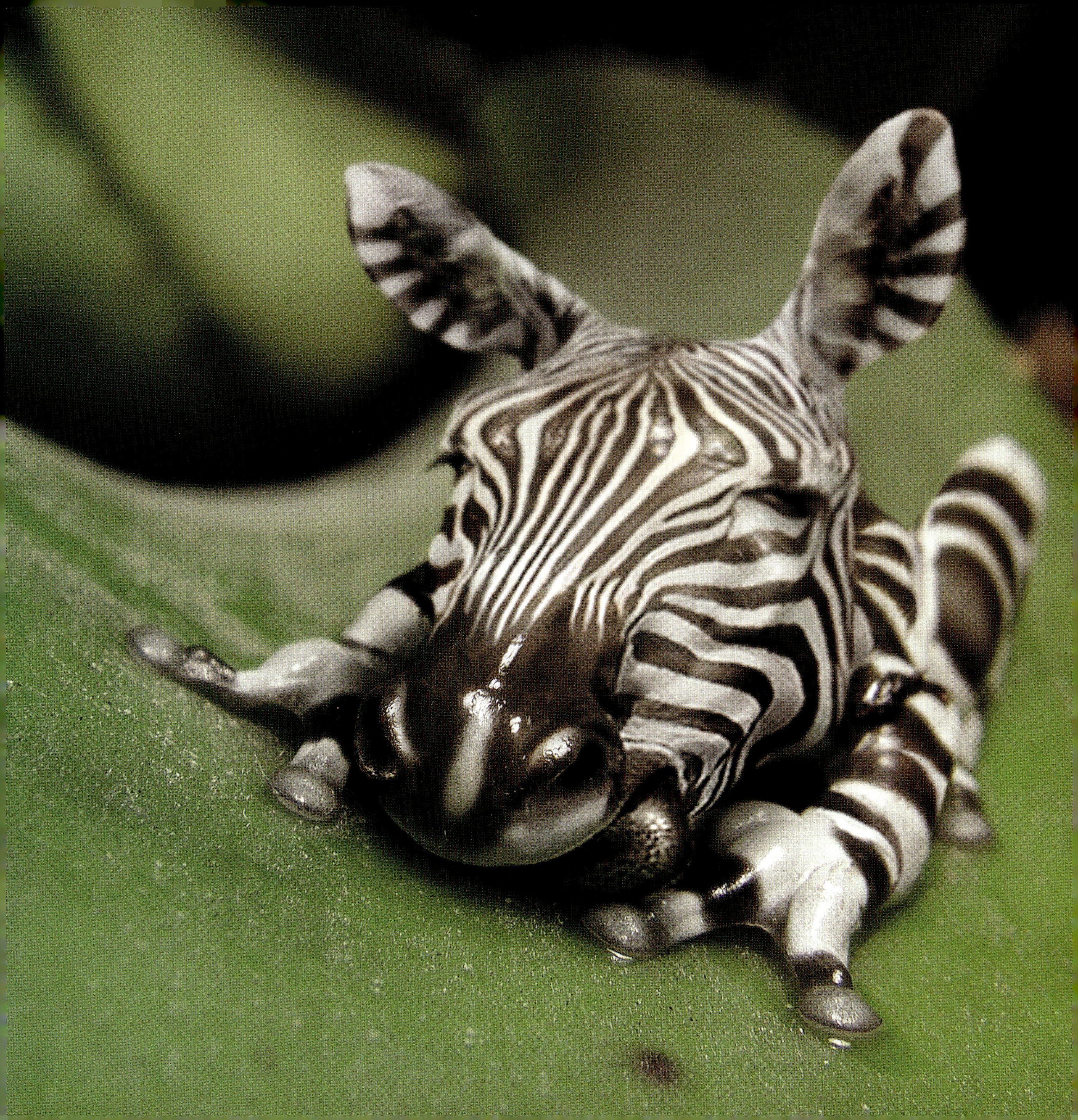

JONATHAN HOBIN

www.jhobin.com

Mock up a nightmarish contemporary event, such as the 9/11 attacks; add small children in costumes; and then stir slowly to await general outrage. Jonathan Hobin's photographs were always going to provoke a strong reaction. However, the Canadian photo-based artist is keen to stress that his prime intent is to explore the effects of media coverage on the young.

In the Playroom is an ongoing series of images. Alongside the aforementioned World Trade Center attacks, Hobin has recreated the murder of child beauty pageant queen JonBenet Ramsey, the abuse of Iraqi prisoners by American soldiers at Abu Grahib, the 2004 Boxing Day tsunami and eight other grimly iconic scenes. Previously, he has given fables and fairy tales a kitchen-sink twist, but turned his sights on the historic, tragic events of recent history for *In the Playroom*. Hobin has described such news stories as being 'modern fairy tales', drawing attention to the fact that, try as they might to protect them, parents can't completely shield their children from the images displayed in the world's media. Some of the children in the photographs are professional child models; others are family and the children of friends of the artist.

THE TWINS

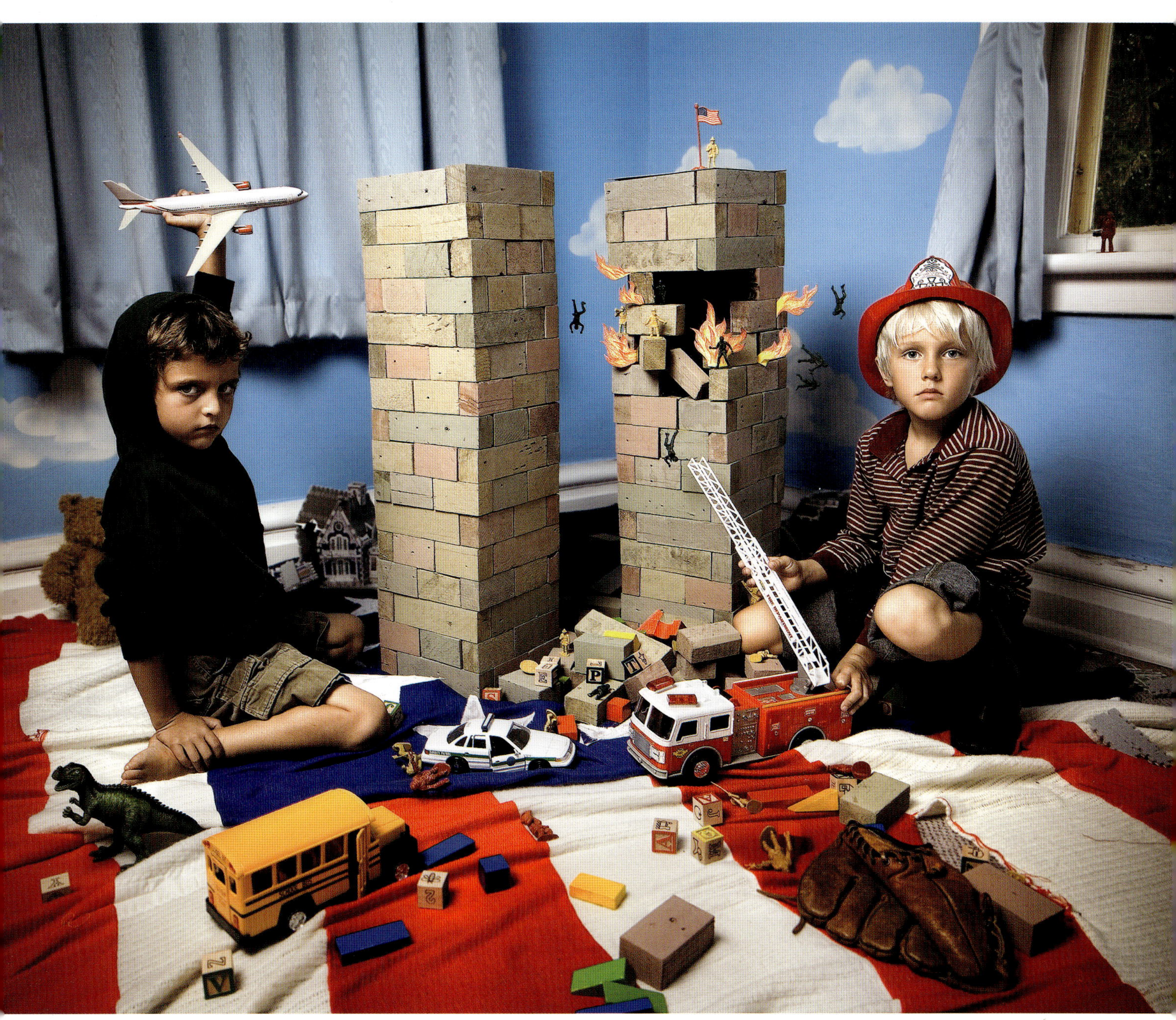

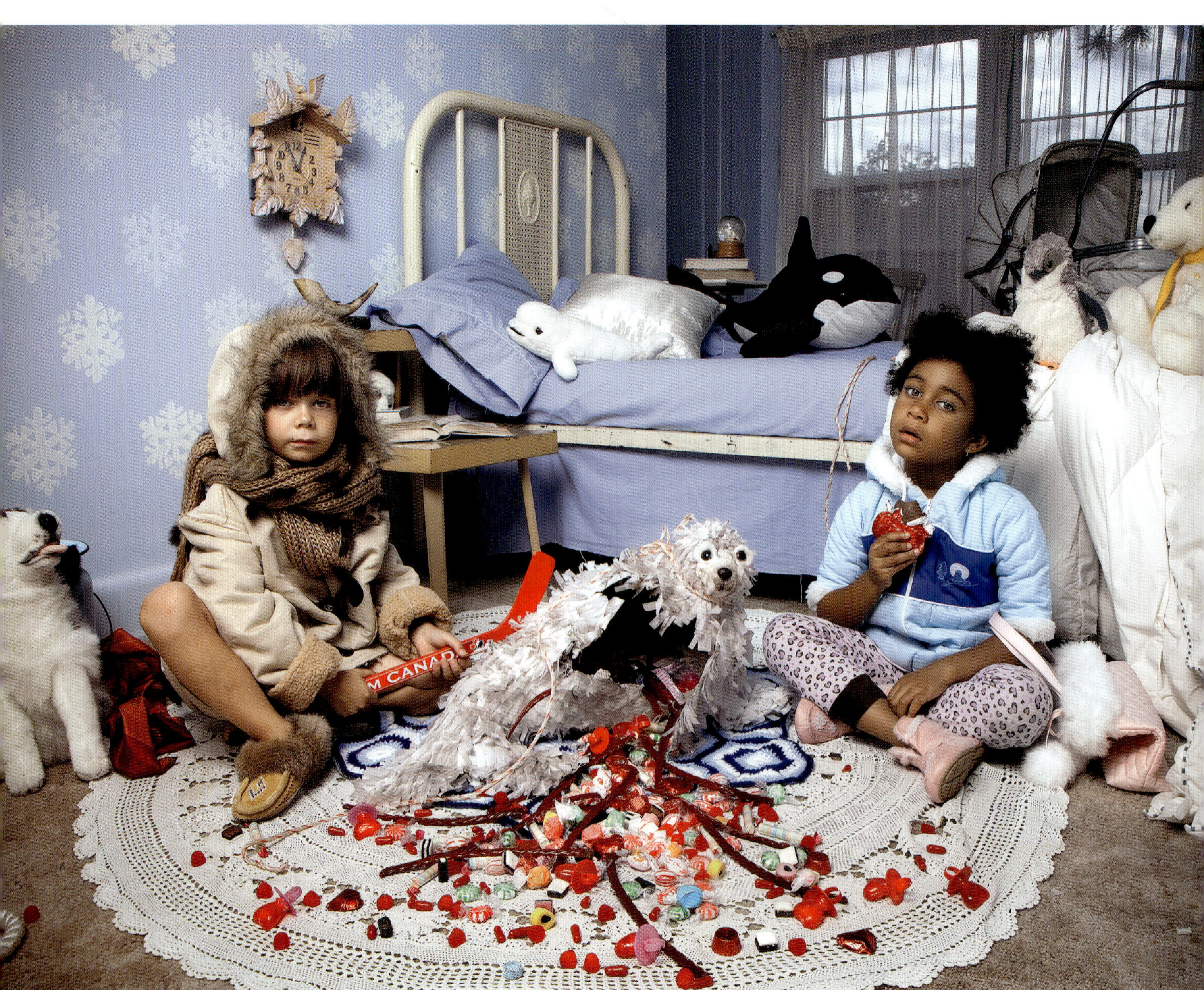

SEAL HEART

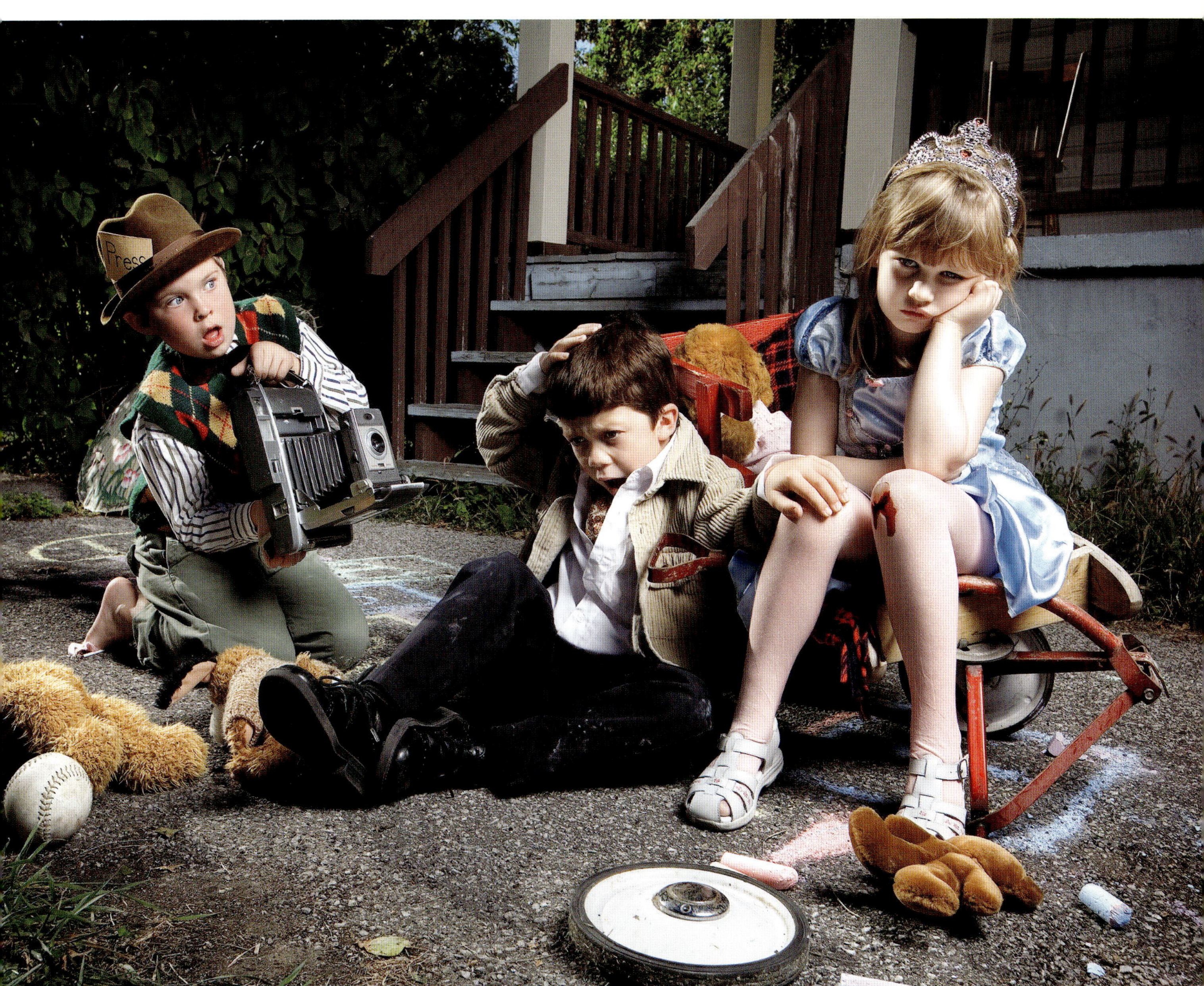

DIANA'S DEAD

LAURENCE DEMAISON

www.laurencedemaison.com

Blurred and dripping, the distorted figures in Laurence Demaison's photographs almost slide off the paper. They're self-portraits – tangled and tortured representations of an artist who reveals herself by disguise.

Perhaps the most remarkable thing about Demaison's work is the lack of digital manipulation involved. All of her photographs are analogue prints, developed and distorted in the studio and the darkroom. The self-taught French photographer and visual artist draws on what she describes as the disgust provoked by her own body to drive the creativity in her work. She manhandles her self-portraits, distorting the images in a bid to overcome this sense of disgust. The process involved is known as 'dissimulation', a technique in which back lighting, reflections and saturated whites conceal or disguise the subject's true form, creating a disturbing yet fascinating world. 'I entered into a process of camouflage to create someone else that I'd find more acceptable,' she explains. 'The only way out was to disappear, or at least to be something else, which amounts to the same thing.' By means of this disguise, Demaison hovers between prudery and indecency, or repulsion and attraction, leading us into a gentle yet brutal world of shadow and movement.

À TABLE
LA CHAISE ÉLECTRIQUE N°1
('The Electric Chair', overleaf, left)
LES BULLES N°1 - N°2 - N°3 - N°4
('Bubbles', overleaf, right)

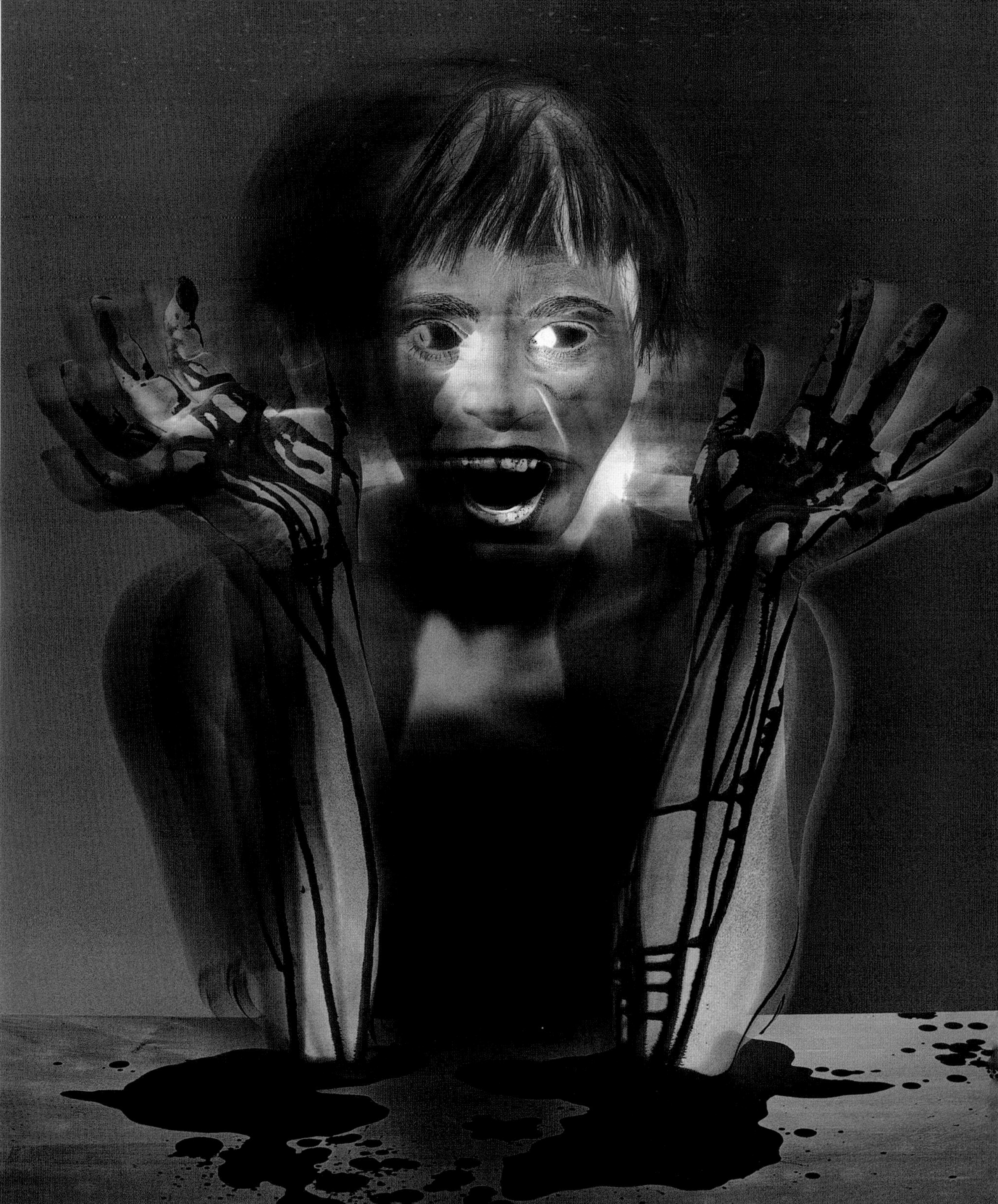

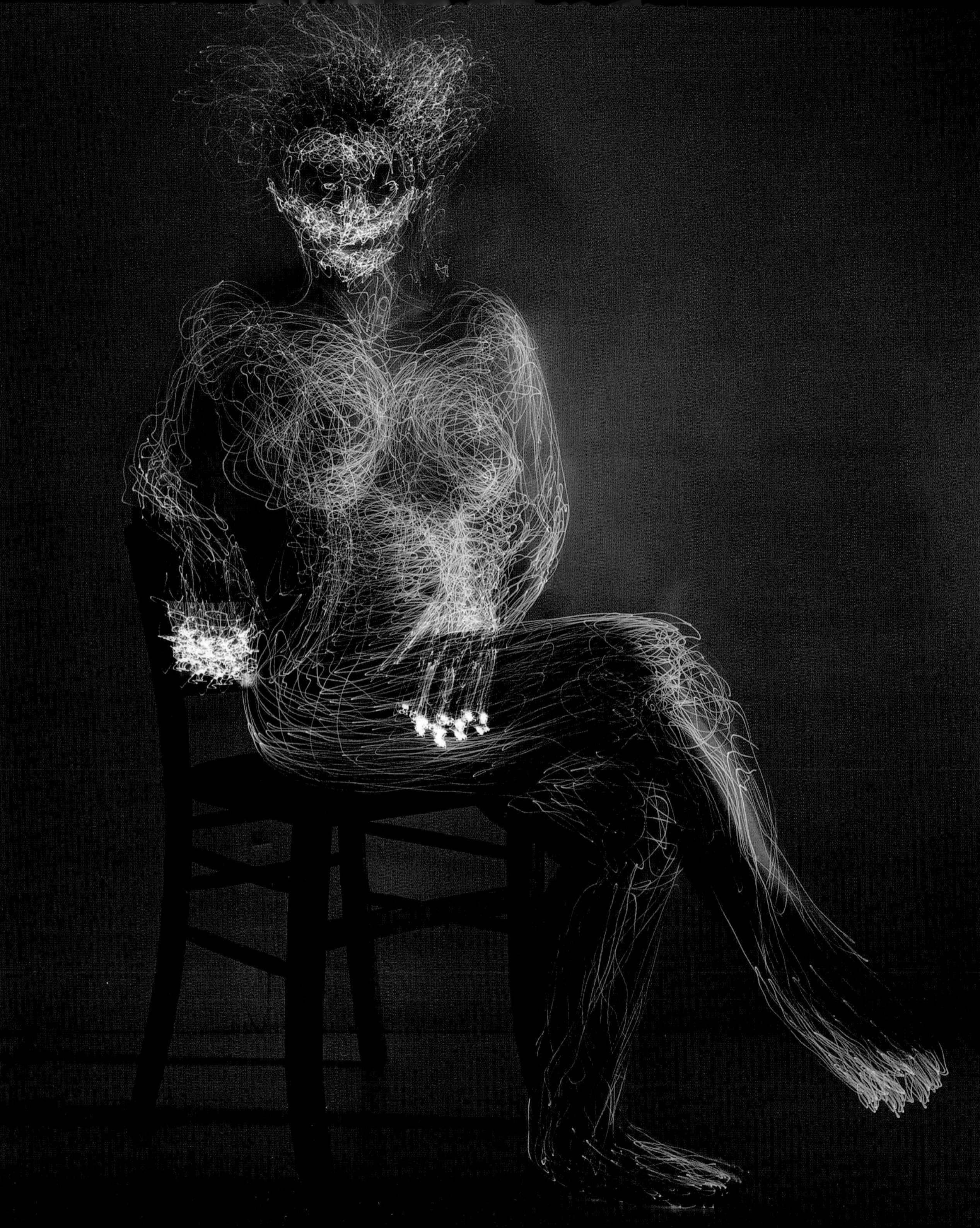

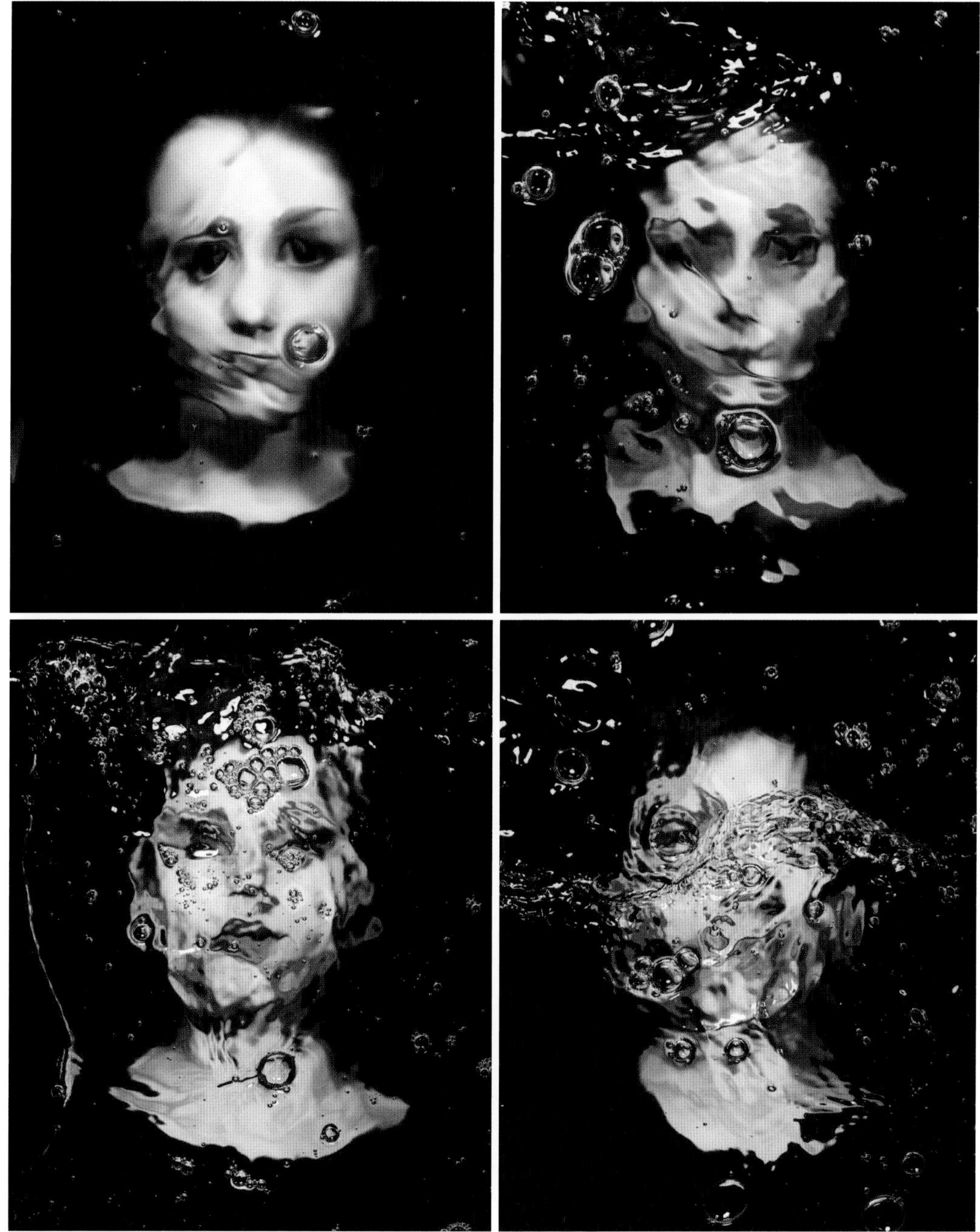

LIU DI

www.pekinfinearts.com

In Liu Di's China the animals are big. Really big. They impose themselves on the cities, static in the landscape with their faces set in a philosophical stare. For the viewer, the animals' presence forces a departure from the comfort and banality of everyday life.

The young Chinese photographer has exhibited his work in Beijing and Hong Kong as well as at the Musée de l'Élysée in Lausanne. In 2010 he won the Lacoste Élysée prize for his *Animal Regulation* series of manipulated photographs. The images present a reality-bending set of contradictory elements. The landscapes are familiar; their apartment buildings typical of many Asian cities, but the solitary creatures within are a huge distortion of what we're used to. Rhinos, pandas and toads are enlarged to an impossible scale; they sit or stand, oversized in the city, gazing out passively across the landscape. The animals' heads are out of proportion to their bodies, further testing the viewer's entrenched perceptions of nature. Liu Di asks us to break away from the conventional, monotonous ways in which we see the world. He wants us to deconstruct what we know, thereby enabling a re-examination of reality and, he hopes, the discovery of value in our trivial lives. The artist has given this approach a name: 'anti-common sense', a technique designed to attenuate the psychological numbness of our daily routines.

ANIMAL REGULATION NO. 4

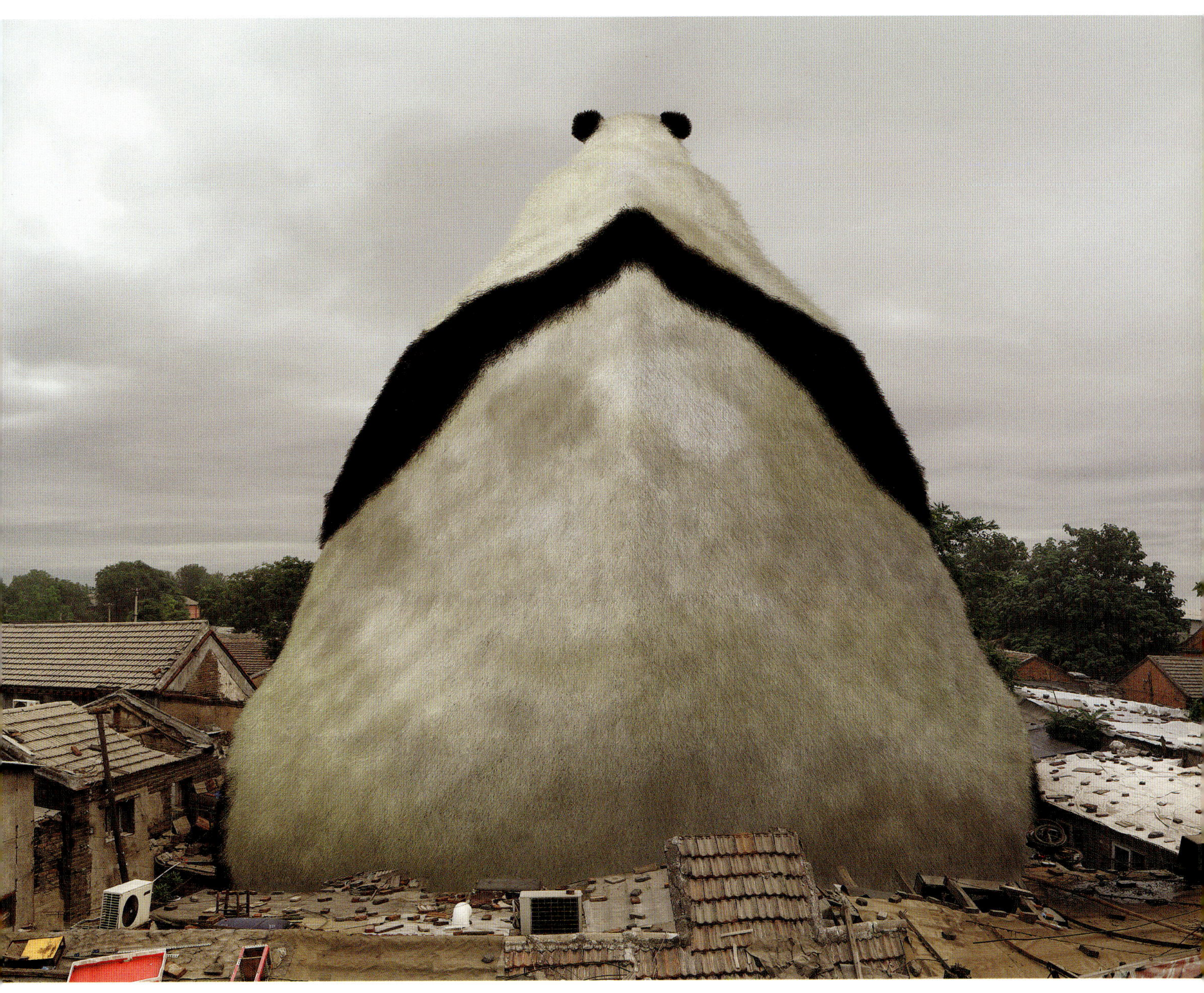

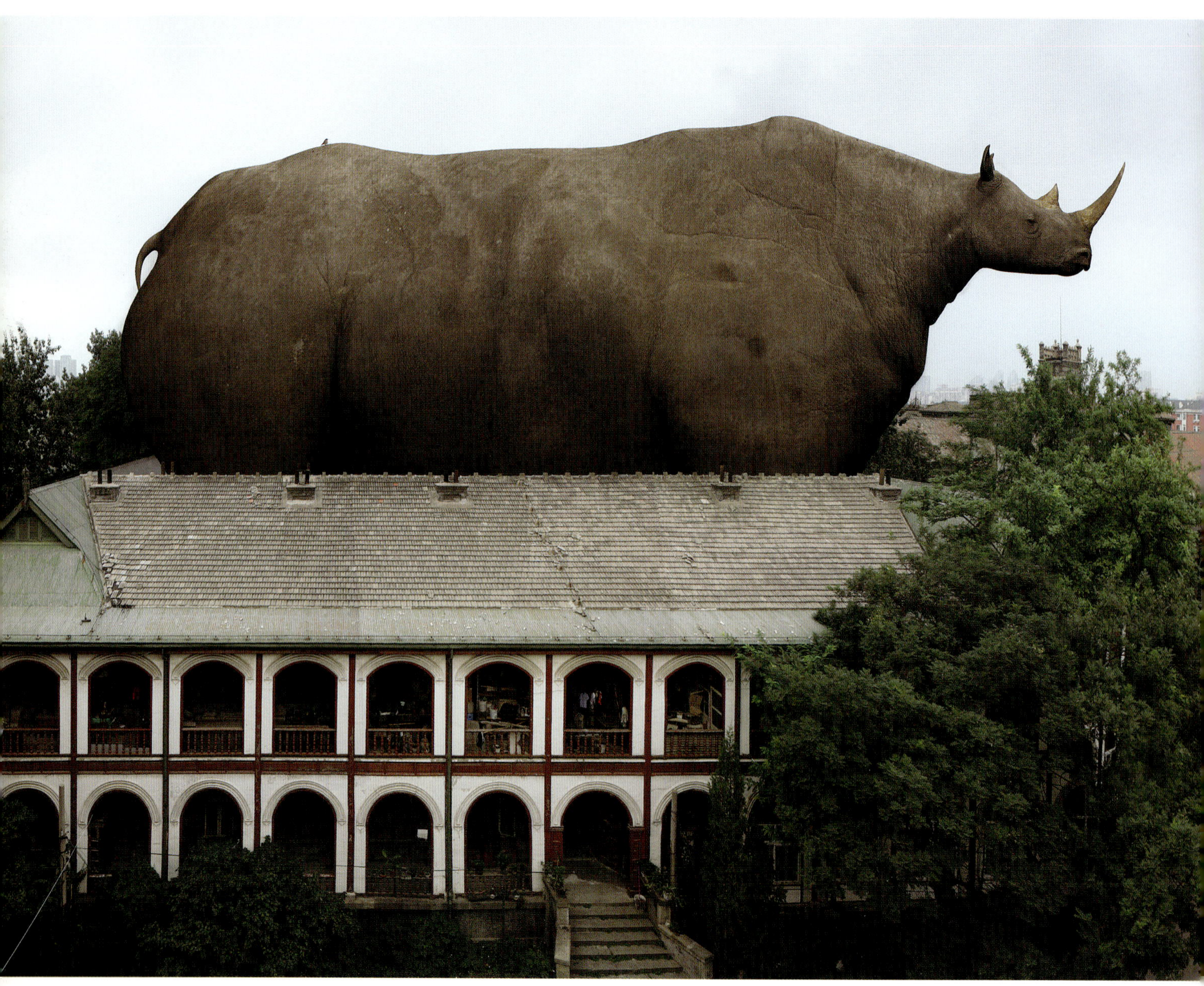

ANIMAL REGULATION NO. 6

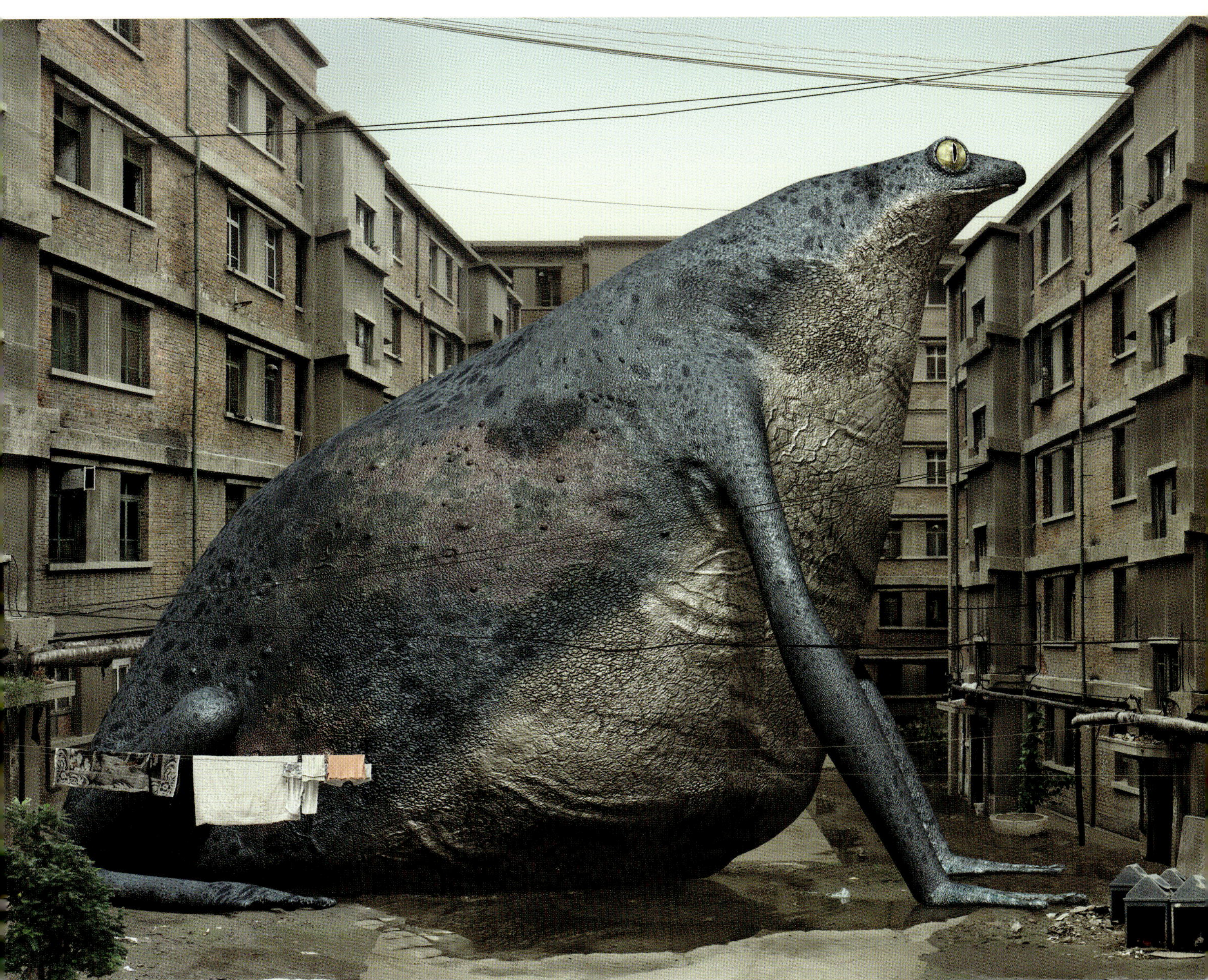

ANIMAL REGULATION NO. 2

LUCAS C. SIMÕES

www.lucassimoes.com.br

There has always been more to portraiture than aesthetics. A good portrait should also generate some insight into the sitter's character. Brazilian photographer Lucas C. Simões has carried this principle into the digital age with three-dimensional images led by the subjects' personalities.

The process behind the *Unportrait* series is fascinating. It begins when Lucas invites his friends to sit for a photograph. During the course of the shoot, he asks the subjects to reveal some secret about themselves, and then takes the image at the point of revelation. Lucas doesn't actually hear the secret – having requested that each sitter provide him with a song to listen to during the shoot, he's wearing headphones. Finally, he asks the subject if they have any colour preference for the final print. Each shoot generates between 200 and 300 images, from which the artist selects ten. The selected prints are then cut into recurring patterns in an interpretation of what the artist has learned about the sitter's character from their expression, music and choice of colour. Lucas uses AutoCAD software to split the images with heightened precision, and then cuts and pastes by hand. Each photo in the layered image represents a level, which builds into an impression of the subject rather like the contours of a map. The finished product bears little visual resemblance to the sitter but, Lucas hopes, does go some way toward reflecting their personality.

UNPORTRAIT (REQUIEM)

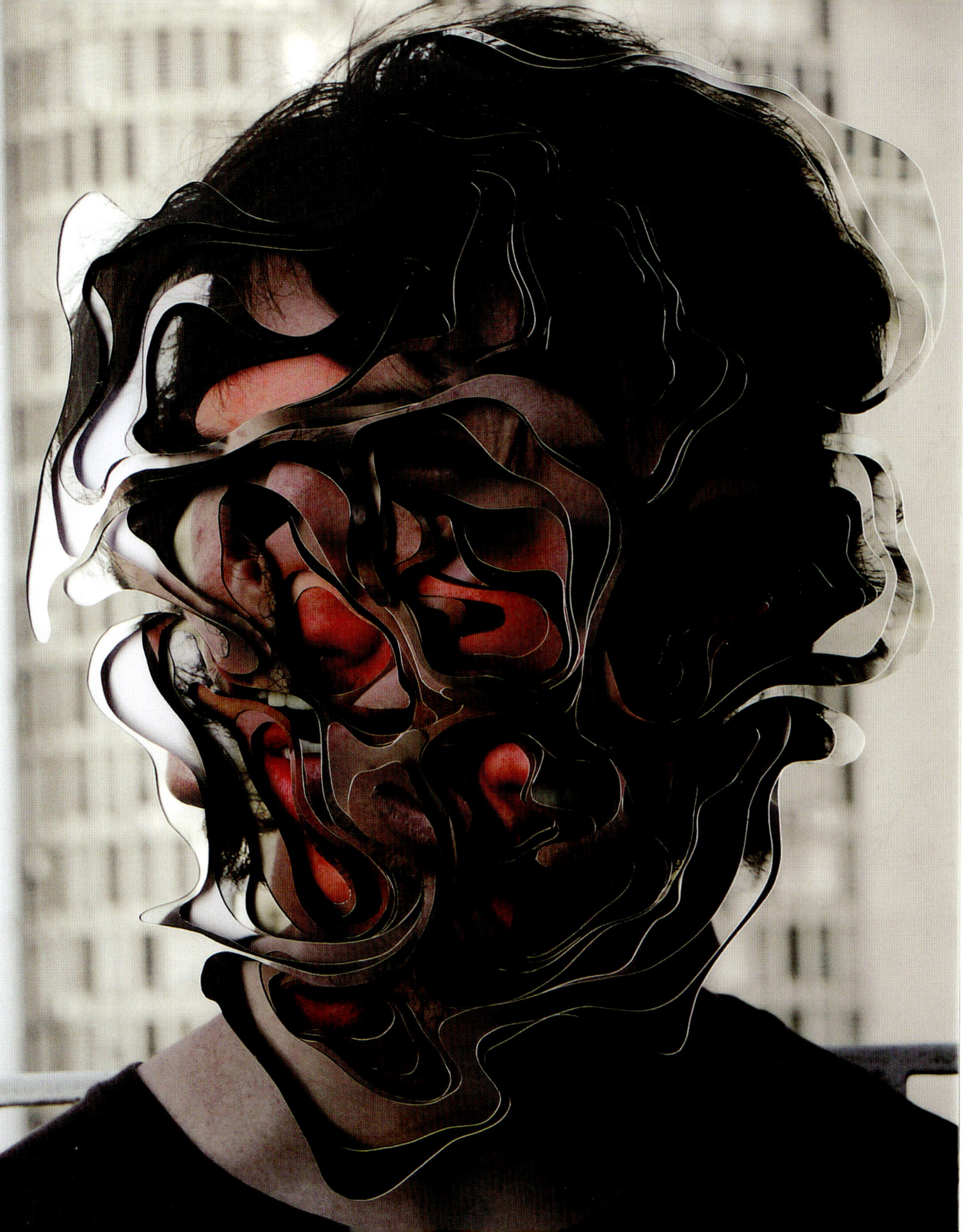

ANTON SEMENOV

http://gloom82.deviantart.com/

Anton Semenov's pseudonym, Gloom82, is well chosen. The young Russian artist, native to the remote city of Bratsk (once listed amongst the world's most polluted places), creates work that is dark and unsettling, depicting a world of fear and decay inhabited by sinewy beasts and mute, deathly figures.

Anton, a digital illustrator and designer for an advertising agency, began his artistic career as a painter but put down his pencils and paintbrushes in 2007, turning instead to the endless possibilities of digital art and, in particular, the tools of Photoshop and Genius WizardPen 4x3 with which he creates the haunting *City of Decay* series. The images reveal a post-apocalyptic world filled with gloom, where mutant animals snarl with aggression and the human figures shuffle in fear. Whilst Anton's work is reminiscent of the great fantasy artists, he uses real life as his prime inspiration and describes what he does as a 'visual interpretation of facts'. All of it produces an ambiguous response in the viewer – the initial horror and fear is soon tempered by a certain sympathy for the tortured souls that live in Anton's dingy digital world.

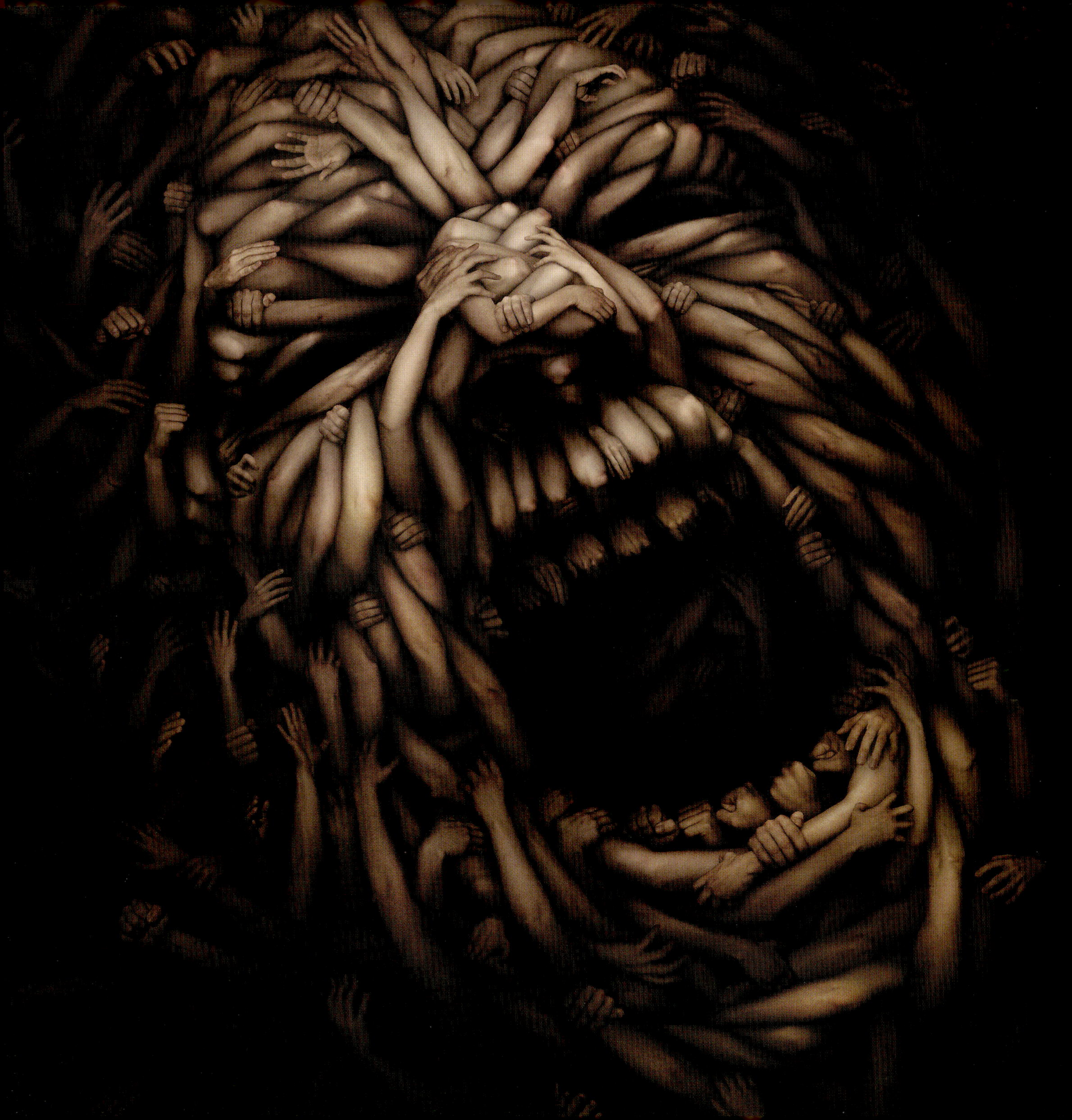

ANTHONY HIBBERT

www.anthony-hibbert.com

The landscape of New York lends itself well to scary monsters. Only a skyline as grandiose and iconic as Manhattan's could handle the attentions of King Kong and co. without being dwarfed or trampled underfoot.

English illustrator and designer Anthony Hibbert has played on the city's movie star looks to create *Hollidaying Horrors*, a series of light-hearted photographs in which the Big Apple is enveloped by sprawling tentacles. The black and white shots are reminiscent of all those disaster movies from the golden age of Hollywood. From the Brooklyn Bridge to the Chrysler Building, Central Park to Grand Central Station, the slithering black limbs are wrapping themselves around the city's best-loved landmarks. Anthony admits the influence of H.P. Lovecraft, the American fantasy and horror author of the early 20th century, who set parts of his literature in New York. However, where Lovecraft set out to unnerve, Anthony, it seems, is concerned primarily with having fun, commenting: 'The images are meant as a joke, even if I was the only one who laughed.' He also suggests that the monsters in those old movies meant no harm towards the buildings – in fact they were quite fond of them – but, unaware of their own strength, they couldn't avoid smashing them up.

HOLLIDAYING HORRORS
(Right and overleaf, left and right)

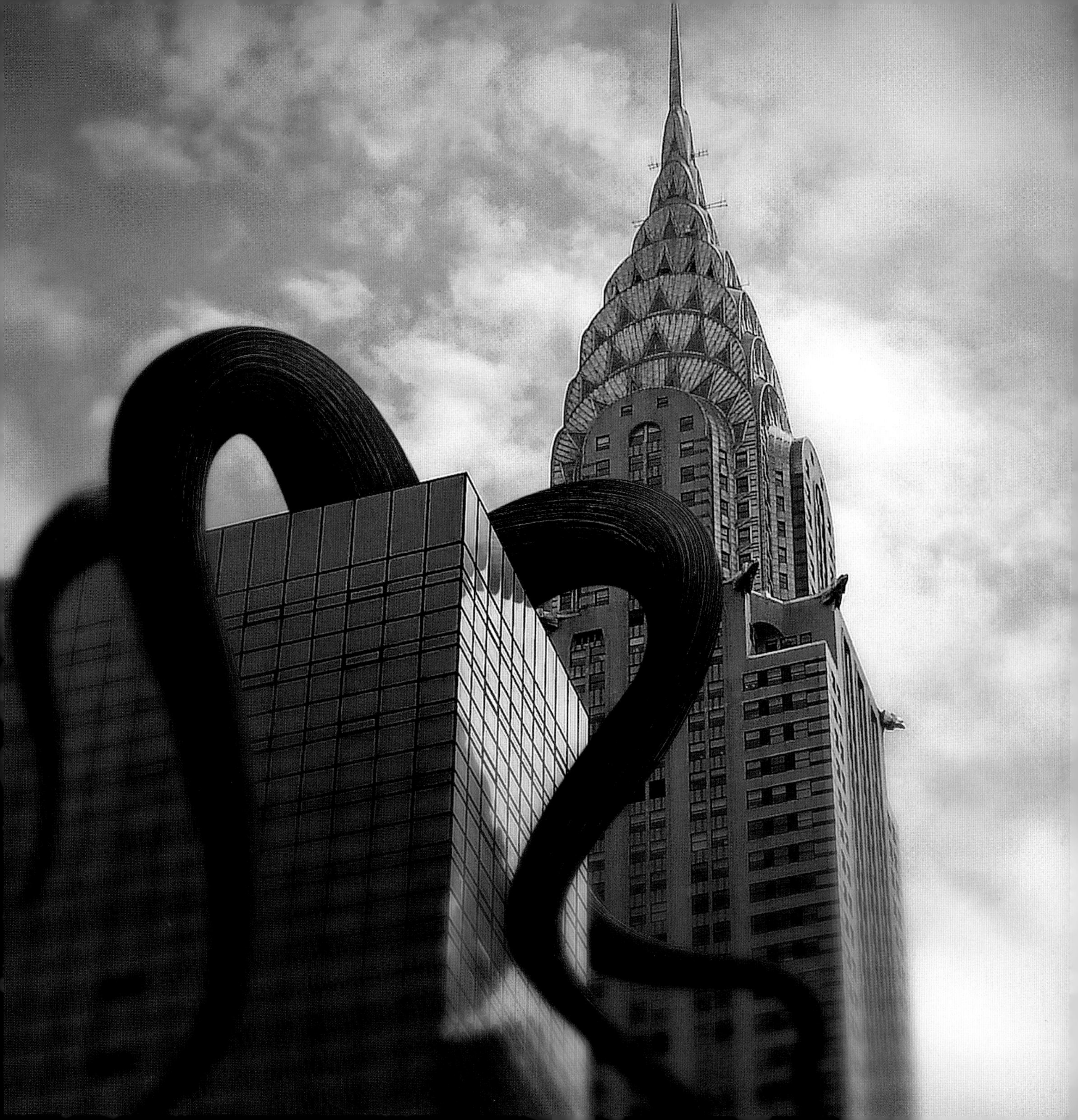

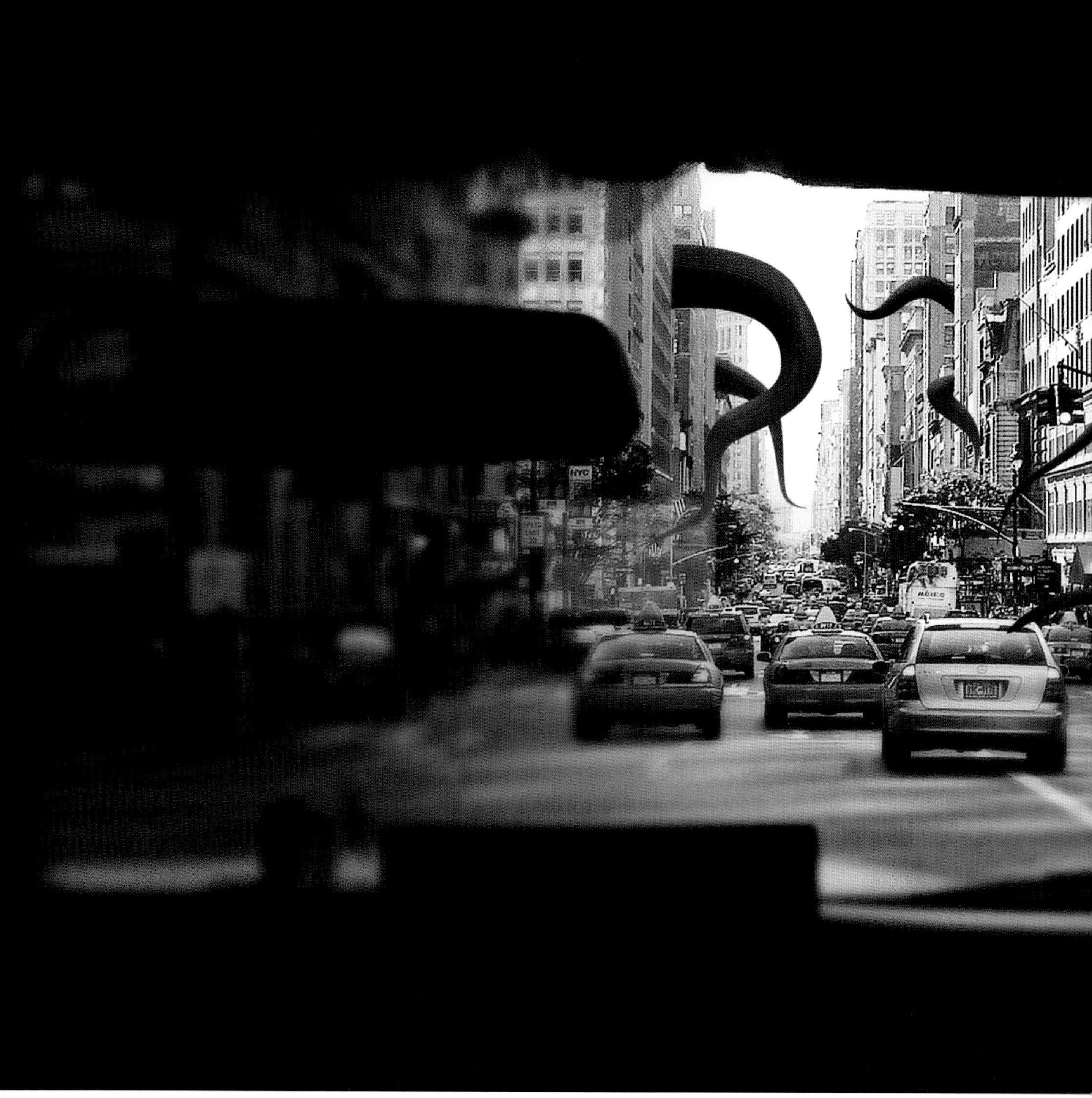
NYC

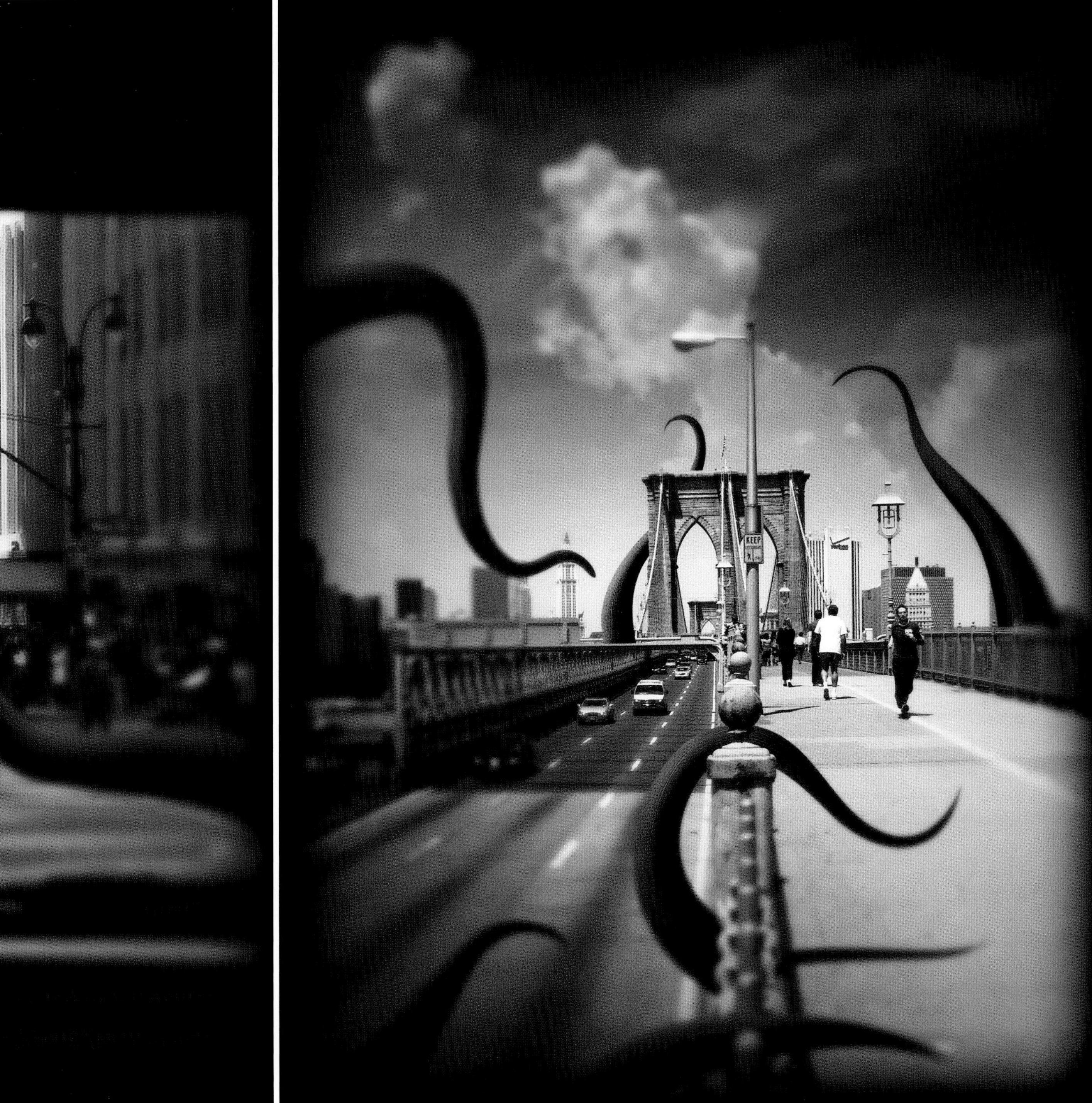
KEEP

TAYLOR JAMES

www.taylorjames.com

Computer generated images (CGI) were initially developed for industrial production, and as such struggled to recreate the complex nuances of skin and hair. However, in recent years creative agencies and production studios like Taylor James have pushed CGI to new levels, generating imagery that perfectly mirrors – and manipulates – the human form.

A pharmaceutical company commissioned the London-based studio to create a publicity campaign raising awareness of hereditary angioedema, a condition that causes sudden subcutaneous swellings. Taylor James adeptly captured the agony of the oedema with hands that clawed beneath the skin. The disturbing, lifelike images were created using Taylor James' unique RealWorld Rendering™ process to flawlessly integrate the photography and CGI. The campaign was an unqualified success, earning Taylor James a platinum gong at the Creativity Awards in New York, a Clio Healthcare Gold Award and a National Addy Award. Another commission found them manipulating flesh once again, with the ingenious depiction of a woman shedding her skin. Created for Invega, the image masterfully blends photography with photo-realistic CGI to bring to life the model detaching from her redundant skin.

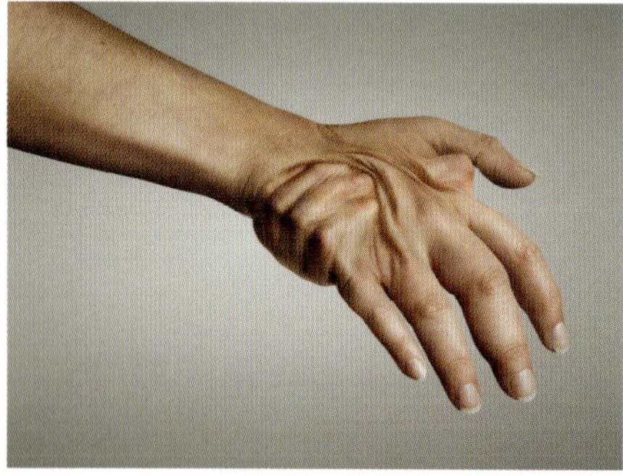

THE AGONY OF HEREDITARY ANGIOEDEMA (Left and right)
INVEGA SKIN (Overleaf)

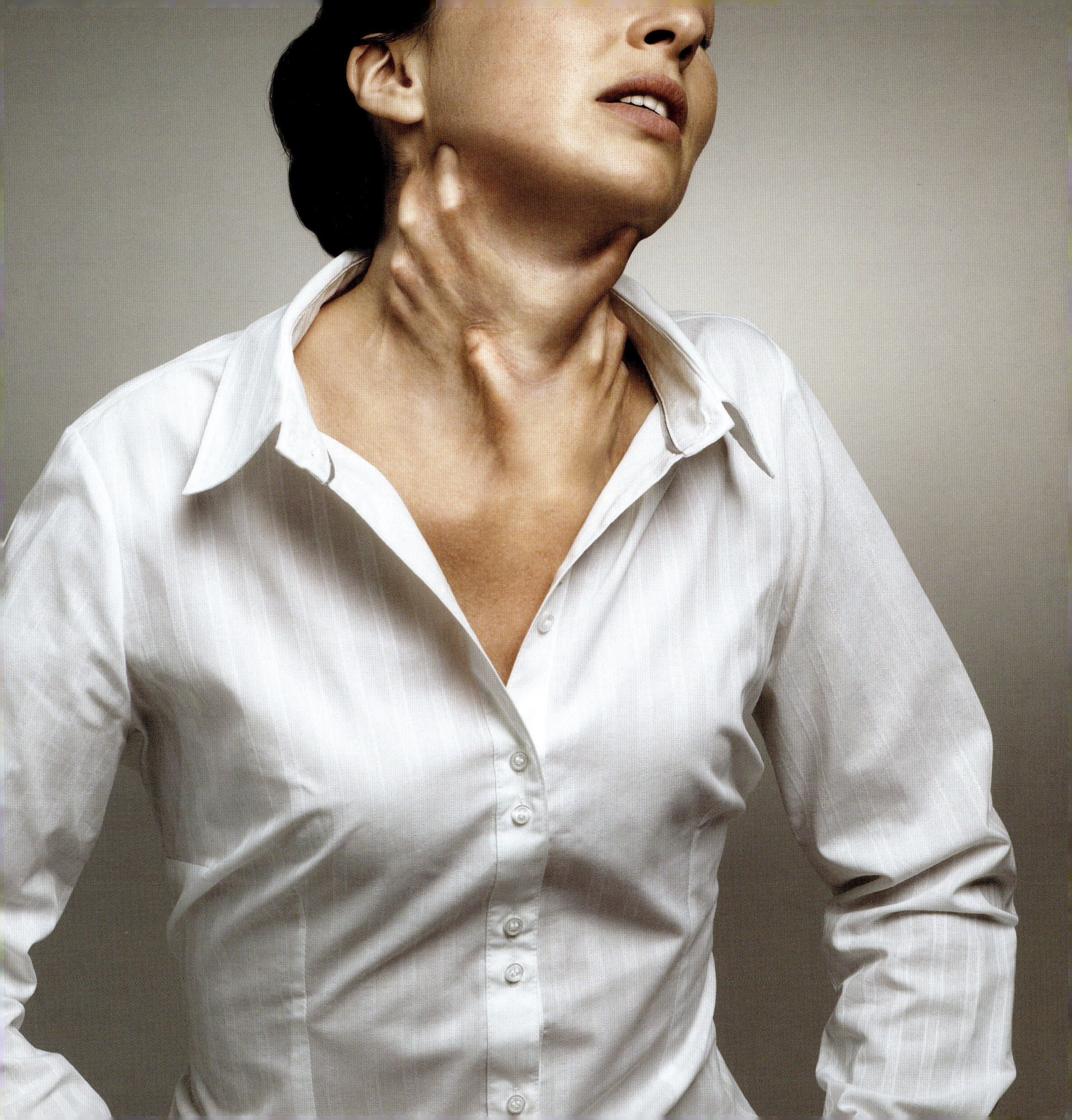

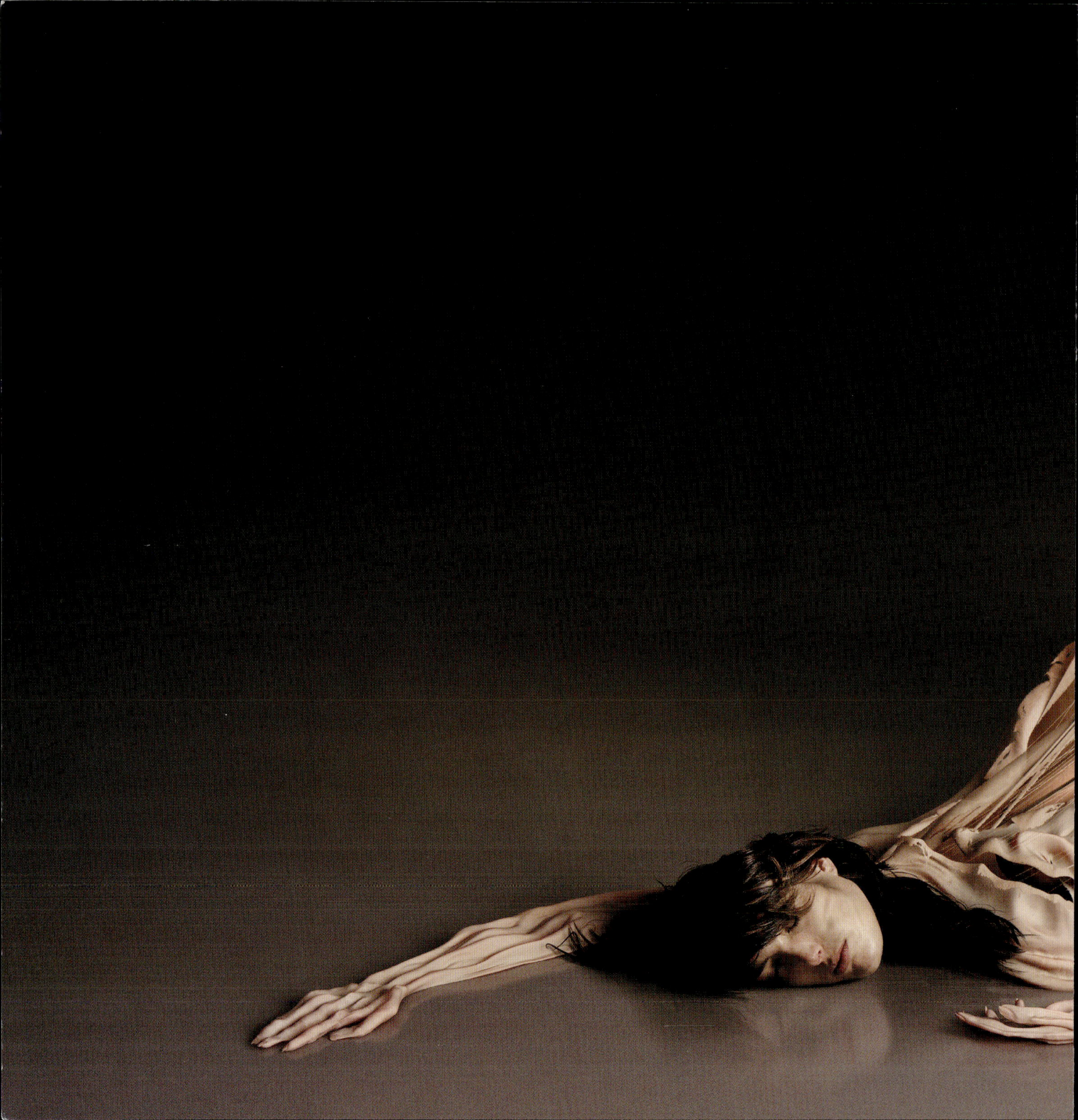

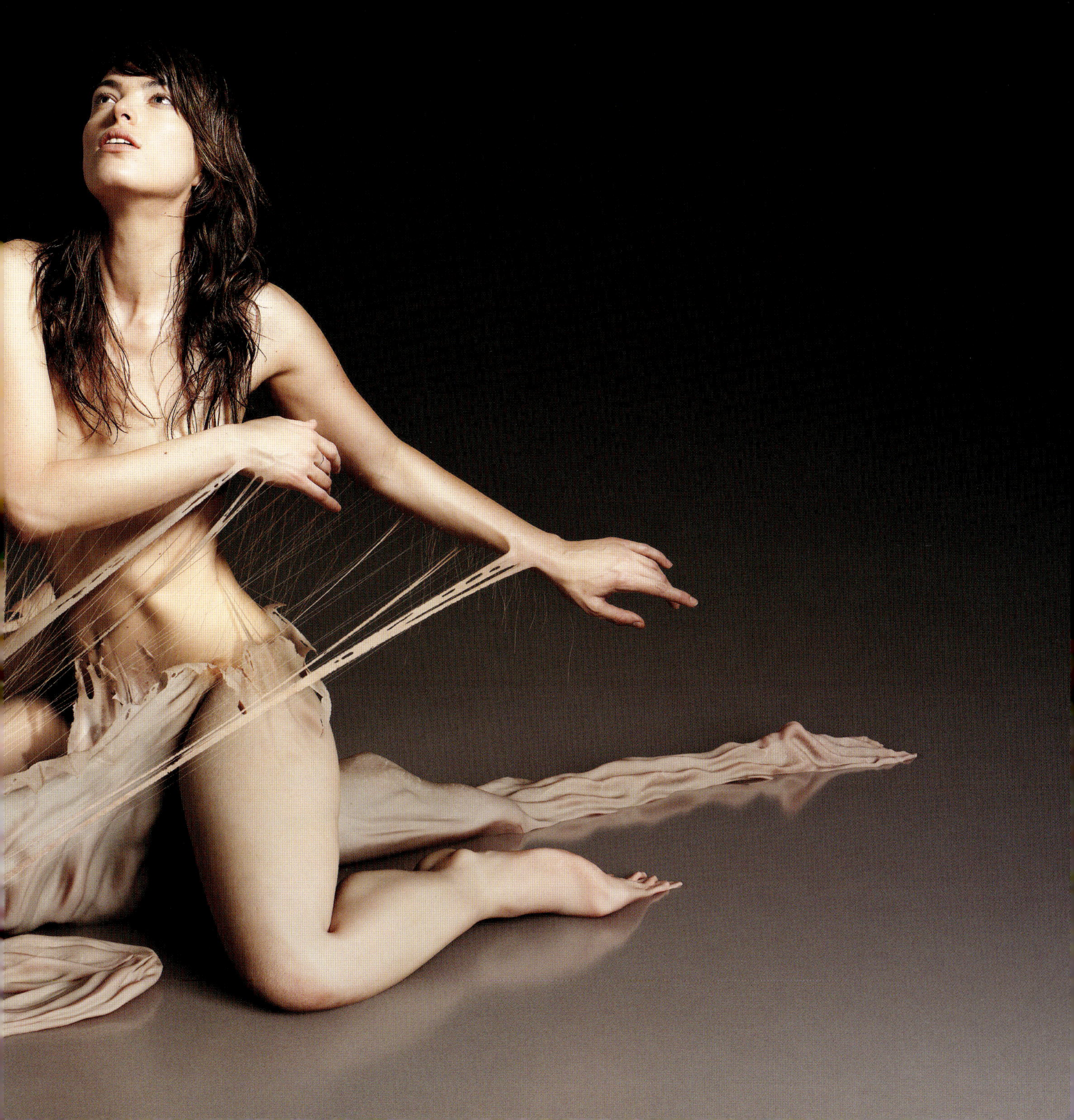

JÉRÔME ABRAMOVITCH

www.chapter9photography.com

Fascinated by tribal rituals, modern counter-culture, underground music and alternative sexuality, Montreal photographer Jérôme Abramovitch seeks to explore all that is different through his art. Blending traditional photograph montage techniques with the assistance of digital compositing, his *Mannequin* series is an investigation of perverse curiosities entwined with a dark sense of humor.

In a world where truth is stranger than fiction, his early career in the 90s as a performance artist included the amputation of his own finger, as well as his signature 'forehead injection' performance that gained him his second appearance in the *Guinness Book of World Records*, and spawned a strange cult following in Japan. His world spirals from the very real to the utterly imaginary, and through his photography, he documents and interprets the offbeat characters encountered as a part of his life travels. Moments captured and created, tangents to core desires and ideas, even his non-manipulated images cause viewers to doubt what is real and what is not. A personal inquiry into themes of duality and self-division, each piece from the *Mannequin* series is intended as a scene from a long-lost movie with no beginning and no end. Suspended in time, hybrid humans and plastic limbs, bare yet powerful in their state of vulnerability.

JENNIFER IN STUDIO

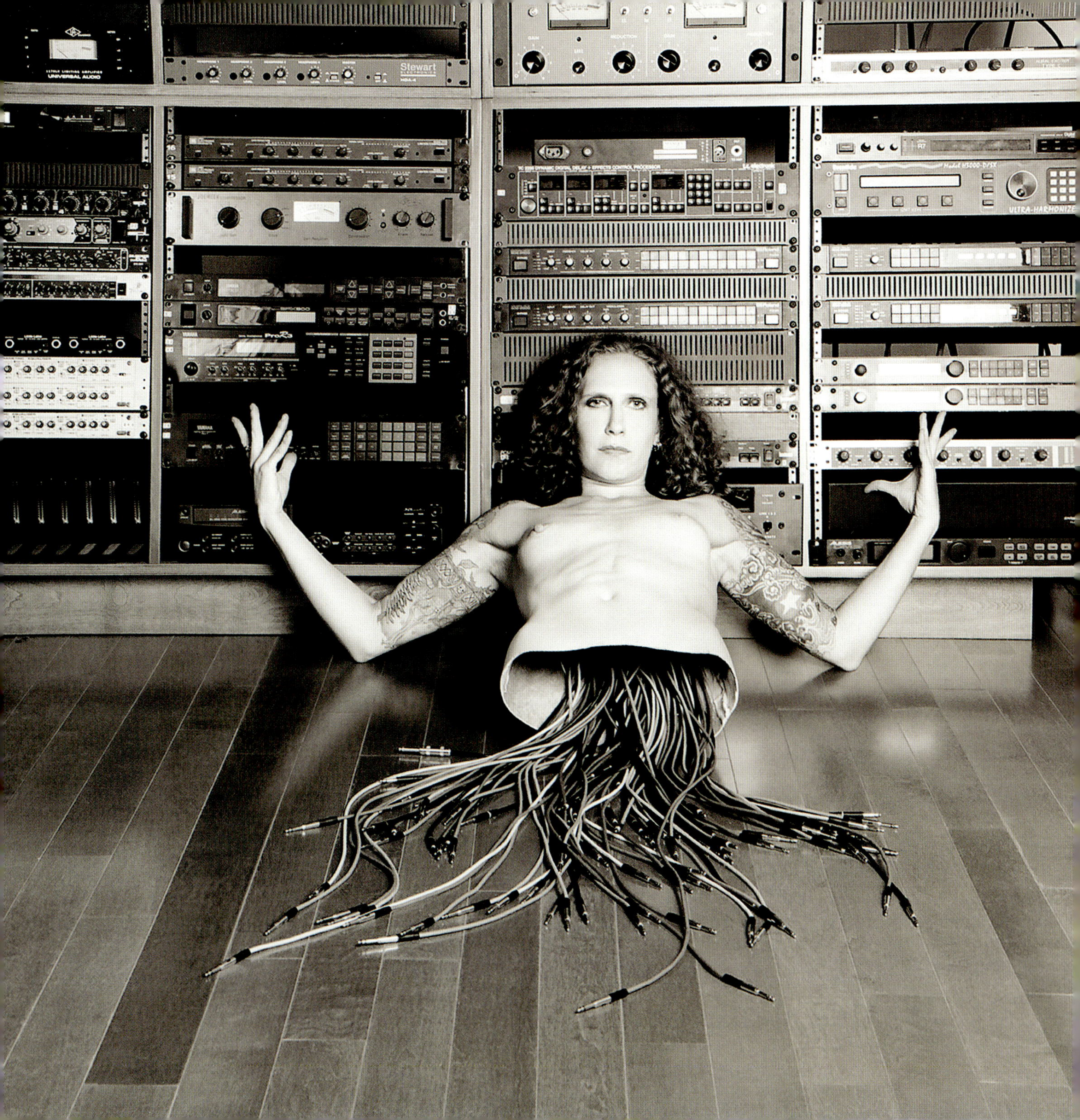
UNIVERSAL AUDIO
Stewart
Model H3000-D/SX
ULTRA-HARMONIZE

HILARY PECIS

www.hilarypecis.com

Hilary Pecis' collage photography captures the infinite and often overwhelming visual barrage thrown at us by the Internet, television and other media.

The San Francisco-based artist cuts images from magazines – from goats to helicopters – and then reassembles them in busy, surreal panoramas. She begins with the background landscape – the mountains, icebergs or cloudscapes – and then layers on the animals and objects that rush across the scene, creating a contrast between the ancient, serene backdrop and the chaotic contemporary cuttings. The abundance of images, crashing into one another, is disturbing. Pecis' use of wildly varying subject matter flags up our ability to either perceive or ignore the countless images that fly at us from magazines, TV adverts or web pages every day. The chaotic, often violent landscapes have a post-apocalyptic quality about them, although the artist feels they're rooted in the present.

MARLIN

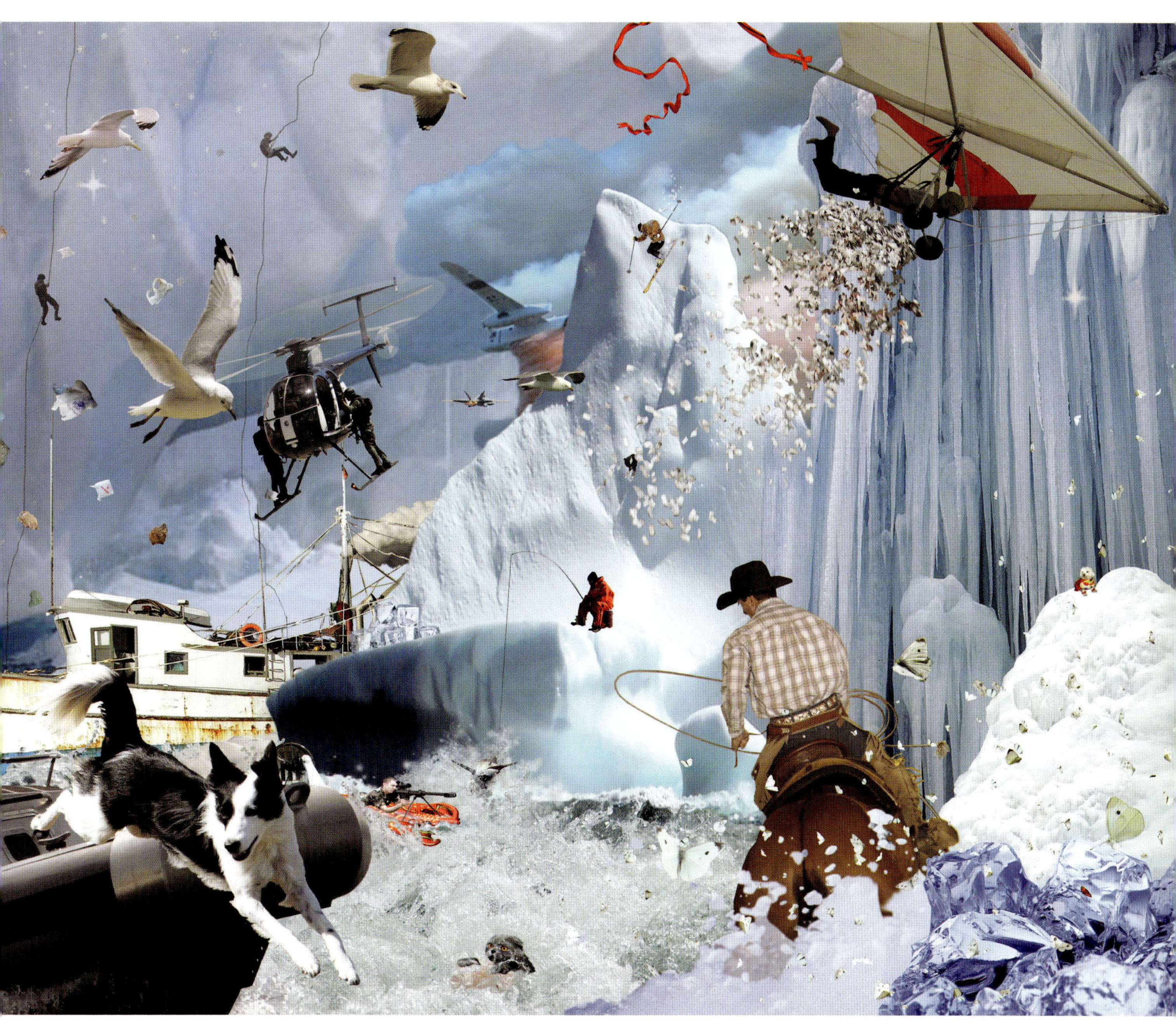

CRISTIAN CRISIS

www.flickr.com/photos/cristianadvertising

In the hands of Bogota-born photographer Cristian Rubio, aka Crisis, Barbie goes bad. She transforms from the model blonde in a long pink frock into a depraved wild child with a lust for guns, self-harm and group sex.

Crisis' *Barbie's Life* series places its eponymous plastic beauty in a series of highly compromising positions, dragging her well away from the supposed innocence of childhood play. He strips off her clothes and dignity, throwing her into a world of debauchery, where she and her friends (both male and female) experiment with firearms, sexual acts and even suicide. One image finds Barbie hanging from the ceiling by her neck, with one shoe off and her dress slipping down. Still, the red lipped smile remains. In another she lies back naked in a bath of bubbles, ready with a sword poised above her own wrist. A third has her being dragged around the room by a male action figure. The humour is undeniably depraved, but it's hard to take issue with Crisis' gift for aesthetic harmony. Indeed, composition is never left to chance – the wanton Barbies are enhanced with studio-style artificial lighting and posed with a genuine sense of drama.

BARBIES (Right and overleaf, left and right)

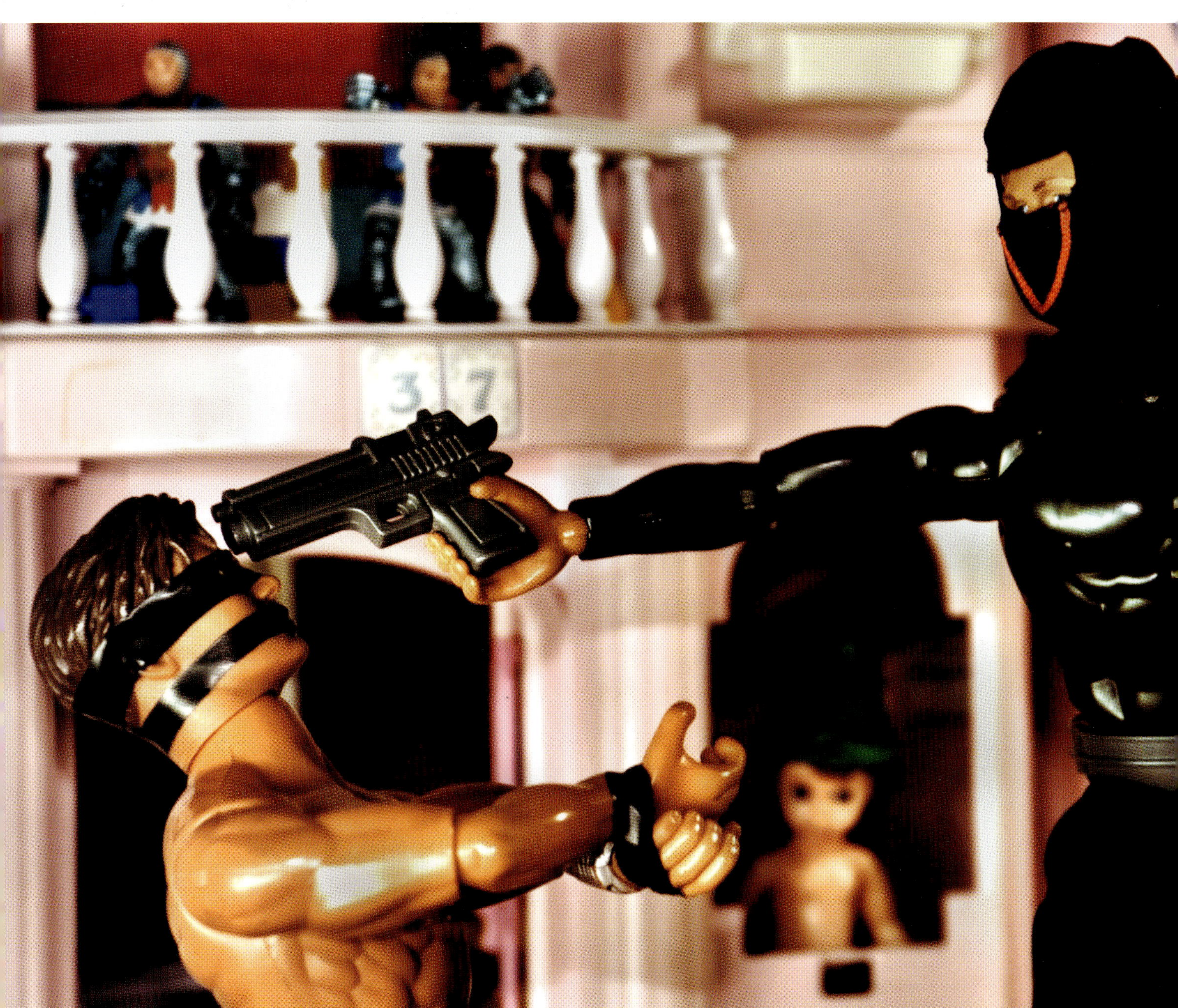
37

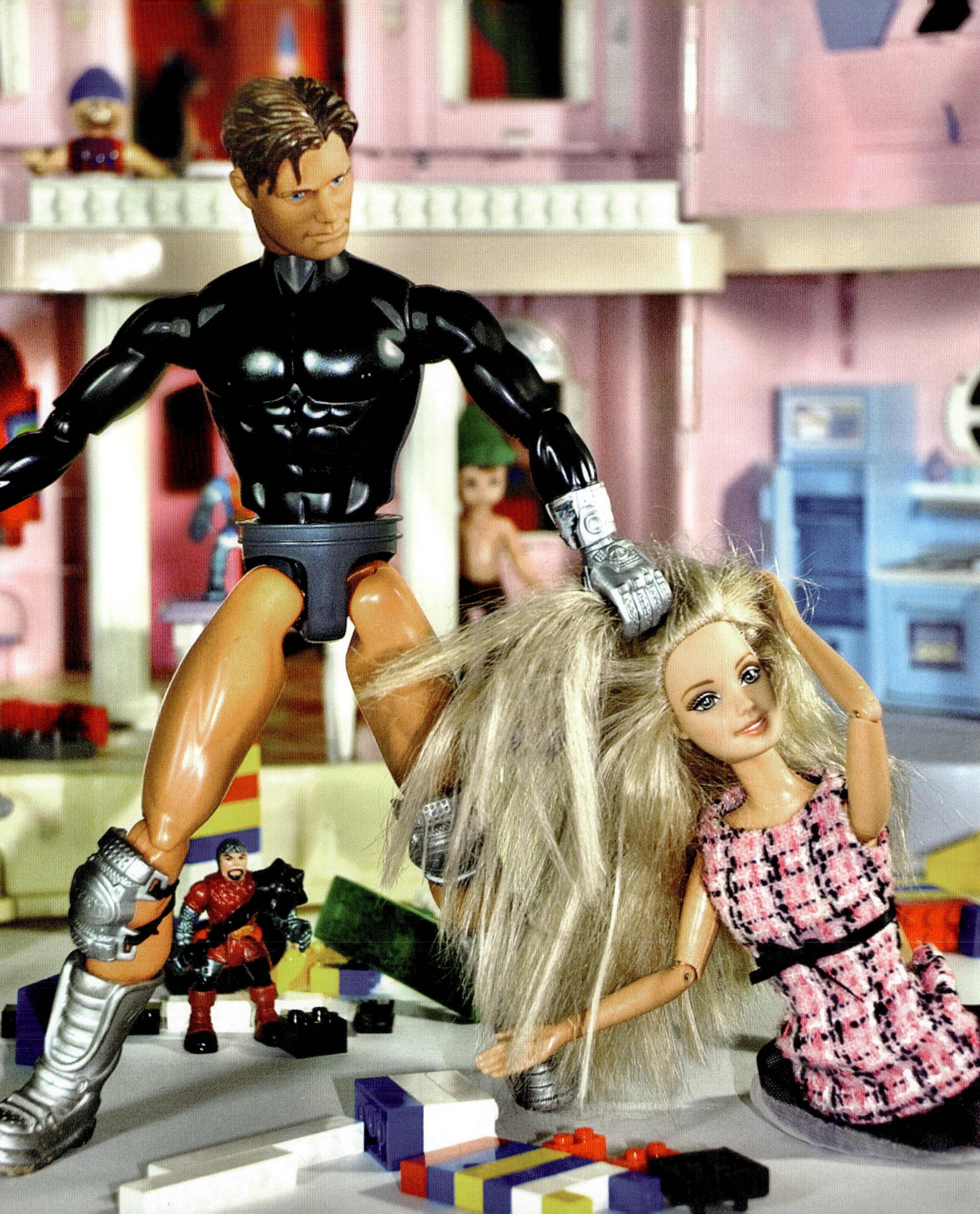

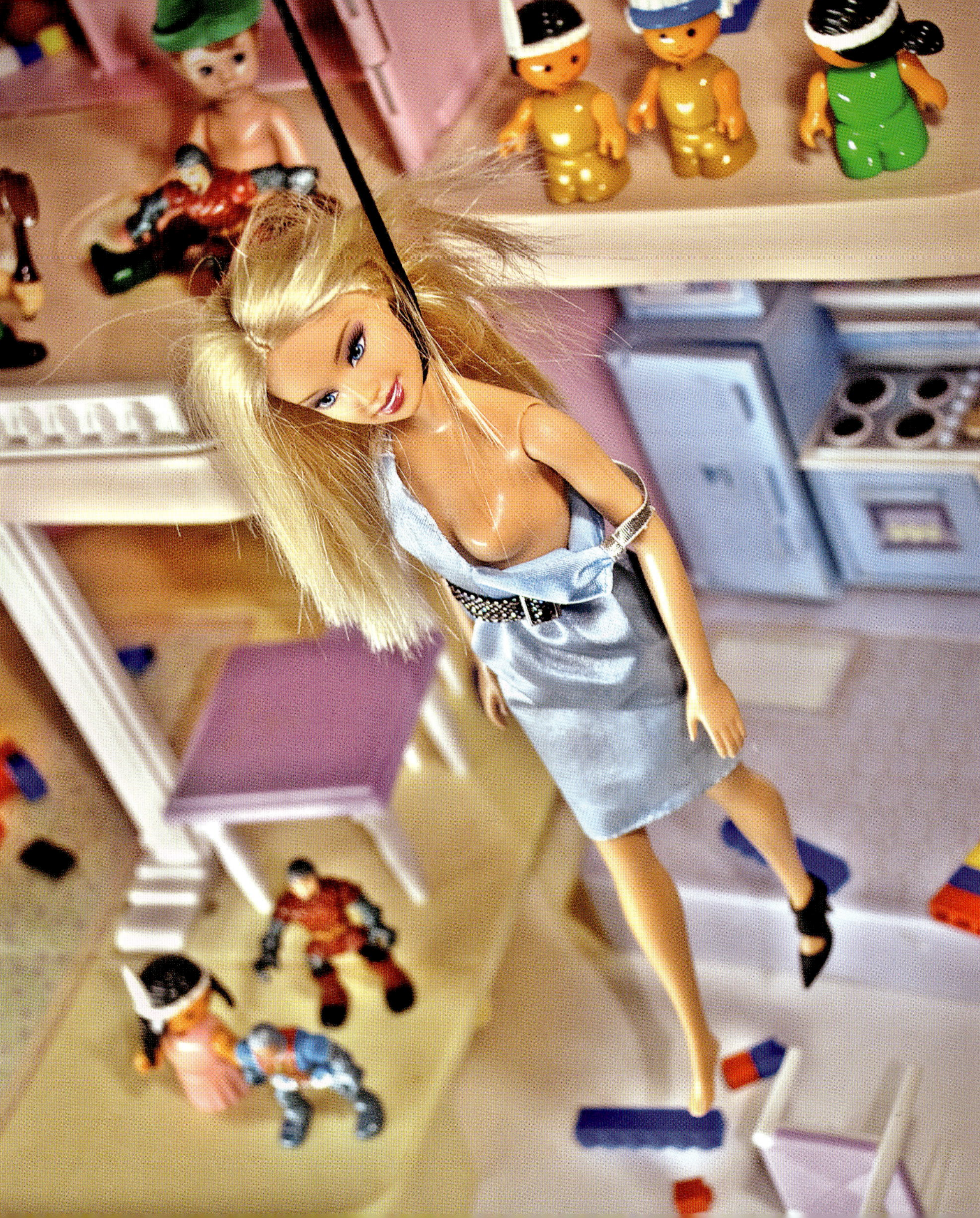

MARC DA CUNHA LOPES

www.marcdacunhalopes.com

Parisian photographer Marc Da Cunha Lopes' *Vertebrata* series has a remarkably melancholic quality about it. Despite the incongruity of large animal skeletons in the urban world, the photographs exude a very human sense of anguish and hopelessness.

The series benefits from the techniques of digital manipulation, the skeletons – from kangaroos to apes – implanted in the glumly empty surrounds of contemporary buildings. Marc was apparently inspired by his years spent studying biology. Some of the settings are domestic, such as a sparsely furnished bedroom; others are institutional, like an old school or hospital. The solitary skeletons depicted in each scene have been enlarged using Photoshop software. They appear to be waiting, but for what or for whom is unclear. By depicting the creatures in this solemn, unfulfilled environment, the artist successfully raises questions about loss and solitude.

VERTEBRATA 13

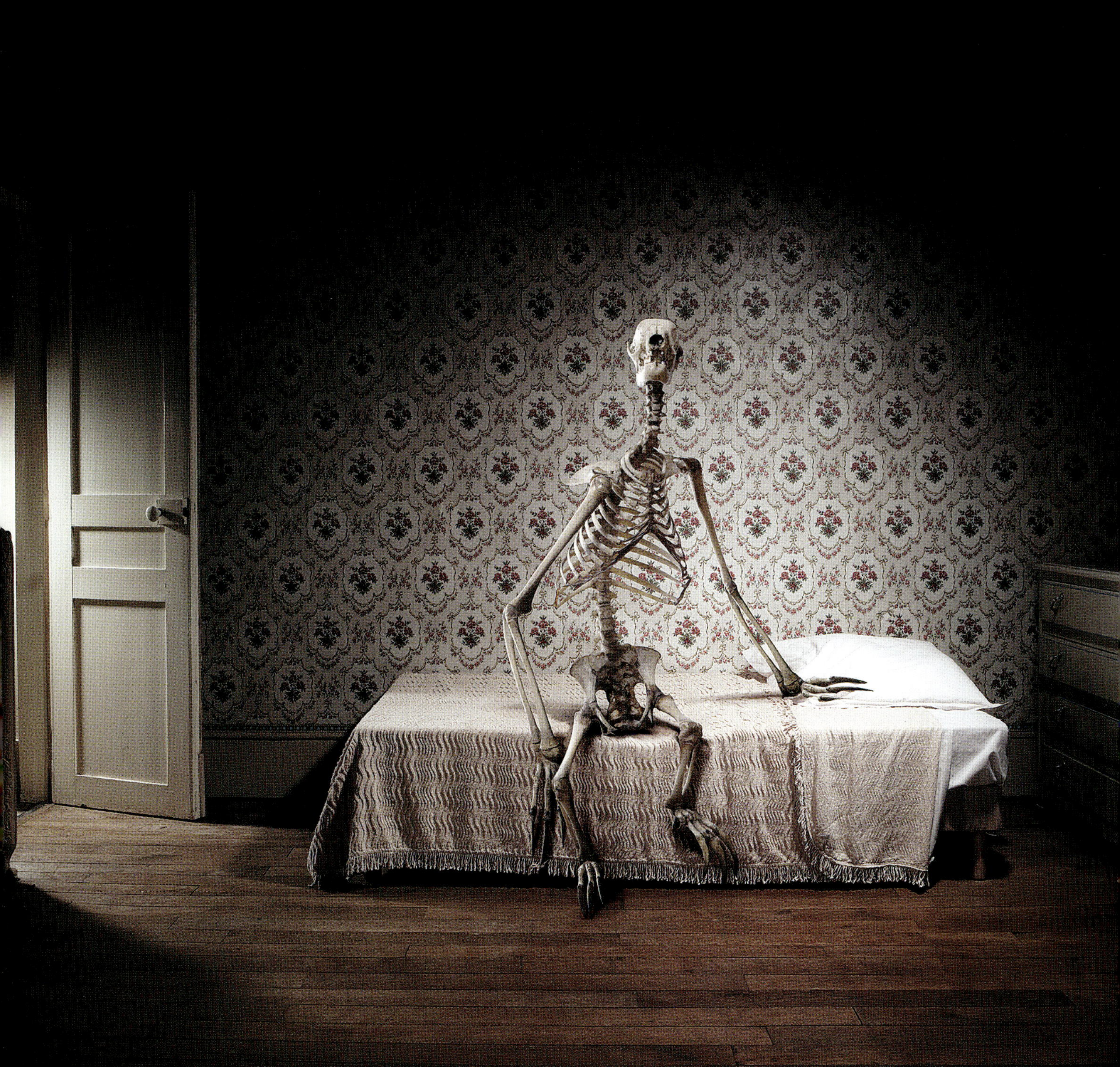

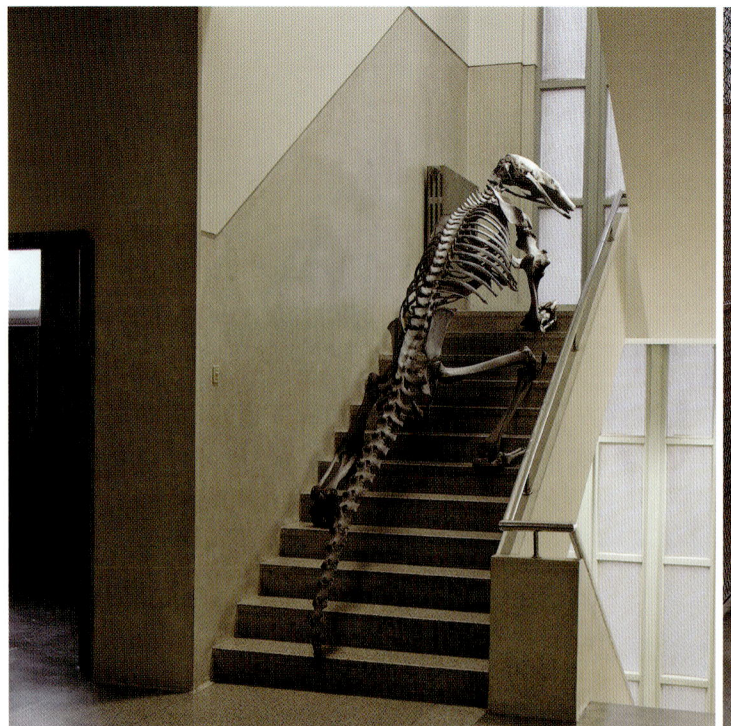

VERTEBRATA 05

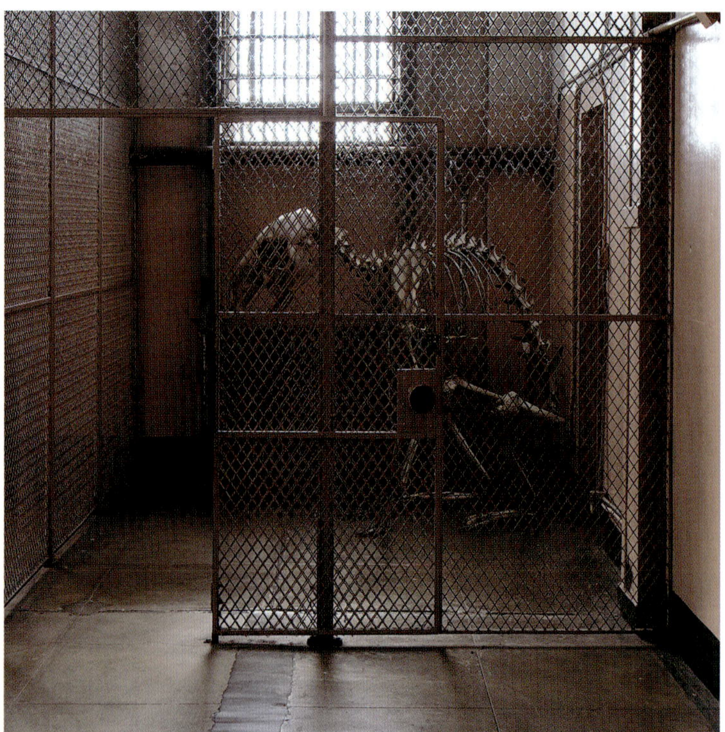

VERTEBRATA 03

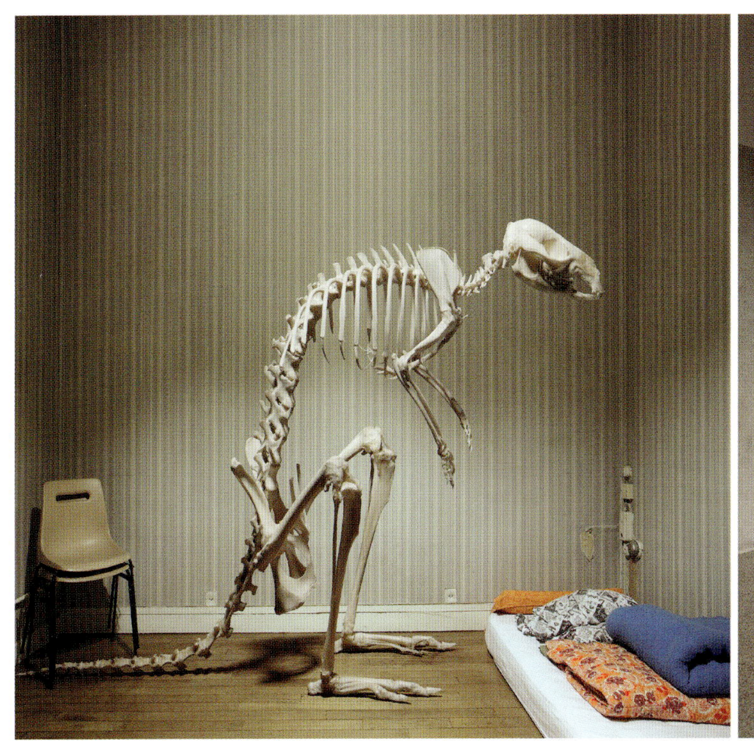

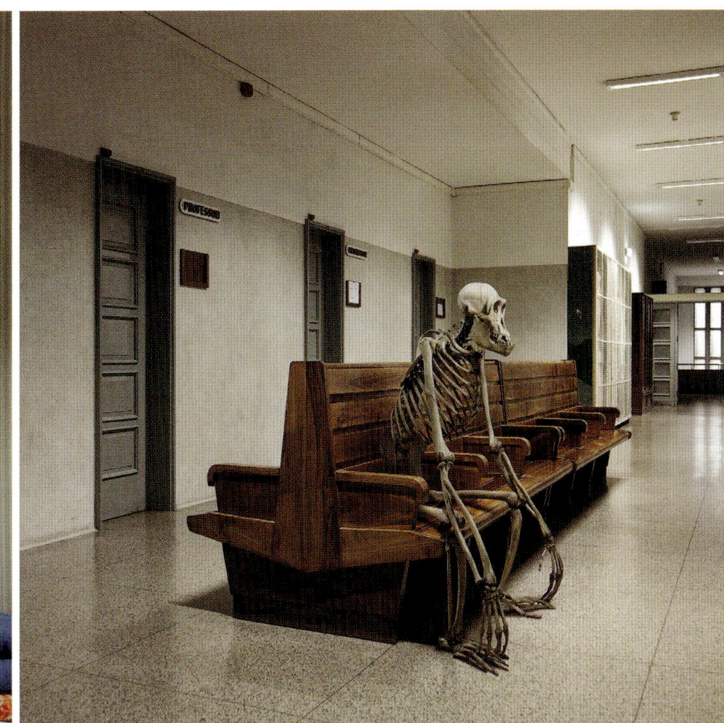

VERTEBRATA 01

VERTEBRATA 09

DREAMS

Photography, like all creative media, has the ability to spirit us away from reality. It gives us an excuse to indulge childlike fantasies, to roam into dream worlds where anything goes. Digital technology has pushed the boundaries of escapism further than ever before. Post-production trickery can place video game characters in the real world, or float ships in mid-air, high above the surface of the sea. Equally, it opens a portal into unseen worlds, enabling us to recreate ancient civilisations or to travel into the future, to a post-apocalyptic world where the plants are reclaiming the Earth.

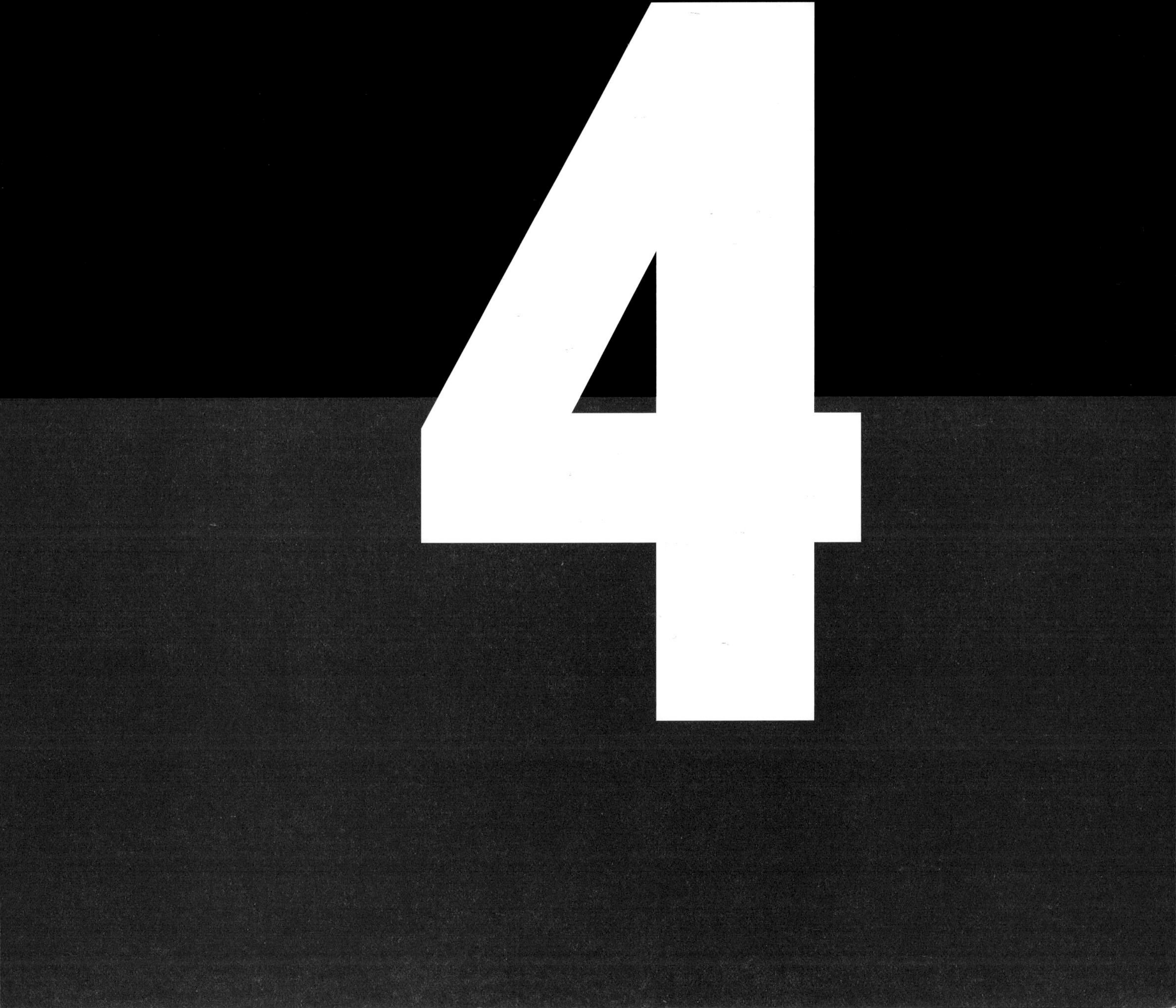
4

ANTON MARRAST

www.grape-frogg.com

Anton Marrast describes himself as a 'psychedelic surrealist'. He takes fictional, imaginary elements and places them in reality, creating bizarre and impossible scenes with unsettling yet visionary qualities.

Widely known as a painter who works under the pseudonym of Grape Frogg, Anton is based in Moscow. In his photographic work, boats are lifted from the water and suspended in the sky high above the ocean, or monstrous sea creatures curl menacingly over the buildings of an otherwise unremarkable Muscovite suburb. He describes his work as absurdist, and the processes that lead to its creation are suitably eccentric. Anton will concentrate on one image for several hours, awaiting inspiration. Eventually an idea will come and, with manipulation by dint of a digital pencil, a mirage-led blur between fantasy and reality will emerge. His inspiration comes from within, drawn from his own emotional state. As he explains: 'Good or bad, if I suffer an emotional shock, I'm pretty sure that this will be transformed into photography.'

QUEEN ELIZABETH 2

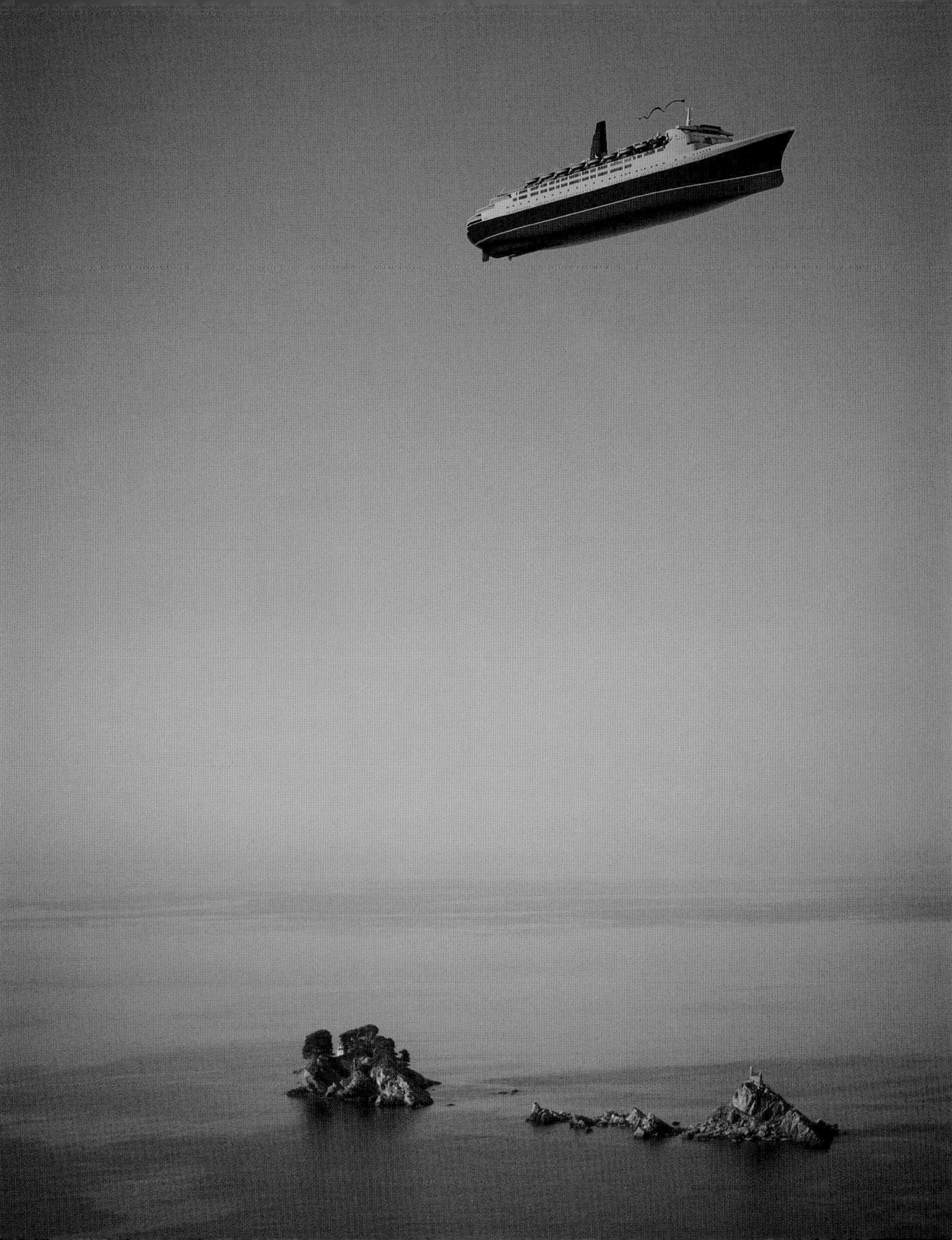

ALED LEWIS

www.aledlewis.com

The photographs of Aled Lewis recall the characters of early gaming. Funny, outdated and roughly pixelated, they bear little resemblance to the real world in which Aled now places them.

You could call Aled, a British illustrator and graphic designer, a 'nostalgeek'. His *Video Games vs Real Life* series of photographs finds the now middle-aged characters of early video gaming dolled up in their best pixels and out and about in the real world. The journey back to the nascent days of gaming is a nostalgic one. The once familiar heroes, the characters who slogged away on Sega Master Systems or the Super Nes, have been lovingly rescued from the museum and placed in suburbia, in the mountains or on a tropical beach. Donkey Kong turns up in the midst of a steaming jungle, whilst Hundred Hand Slap is captured administering brutal justice to a damaged car in a parking lot. Like much of Aled's work, which ranges from miniature animals with the power of speech (the *Toy Story* series) to grim dystopian worlds, the *Video Games vs Real Life* series is intelligent, kitsch and imbued with a sense of mischief. Aled reminds us of the place that such characters once held in popular culture.

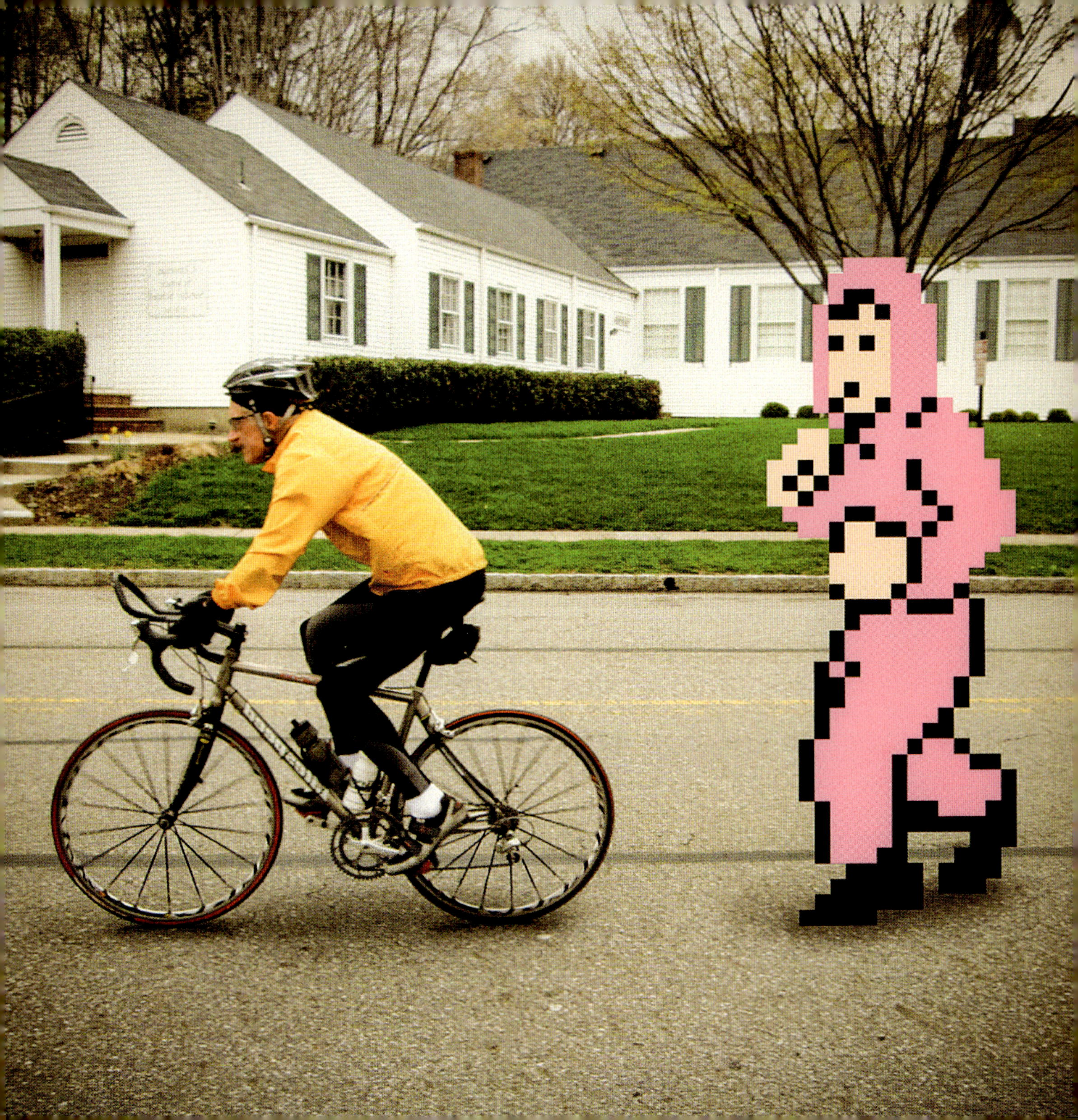

MICHAEL BOSANKO

www.michaelbosanko.com

Michael Bosanko describes his photography as light graffiti. He scrawls his designs in the air with a torch, in much the same way that a painter daubs a canvas, creating fleeting, other-worldly patterns in countryside and city.

Michael's first experiments with light art came by chance. He was in Greece in 2004, photographing the moonlight, when he discovered that unclipping the camera from the tripod and moving it around turned the moon into a pen that could be used to draw designs in light across the night sky. The Welsh artist soon progressed to static shots in which the light source rather than the camera moved around. Today, he travels the world, searching out inspiring locations in which to wave household torches, bulbs, LEDs, fire or anything else that emits light. The exposure time ranges from a few seconds to over an hour. The photos are printed as shot – nothing is retouched in the studio. 'I find enormous reward in creating a piece of work that only exists in that moment; the only evidence of its existence is what is recorded on camera,' Michael explains. 'The environment – my canvas – is all that's left behind, exactly as it was before my arrival.'

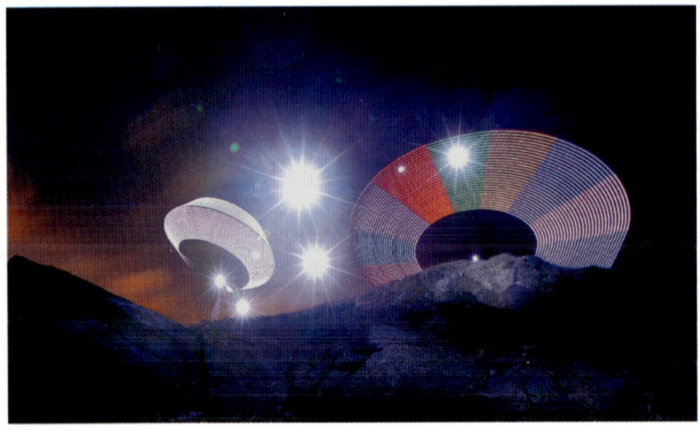

TAKEOVER
CONTACT (Left)
PASSING THROUGH (Overleaf)

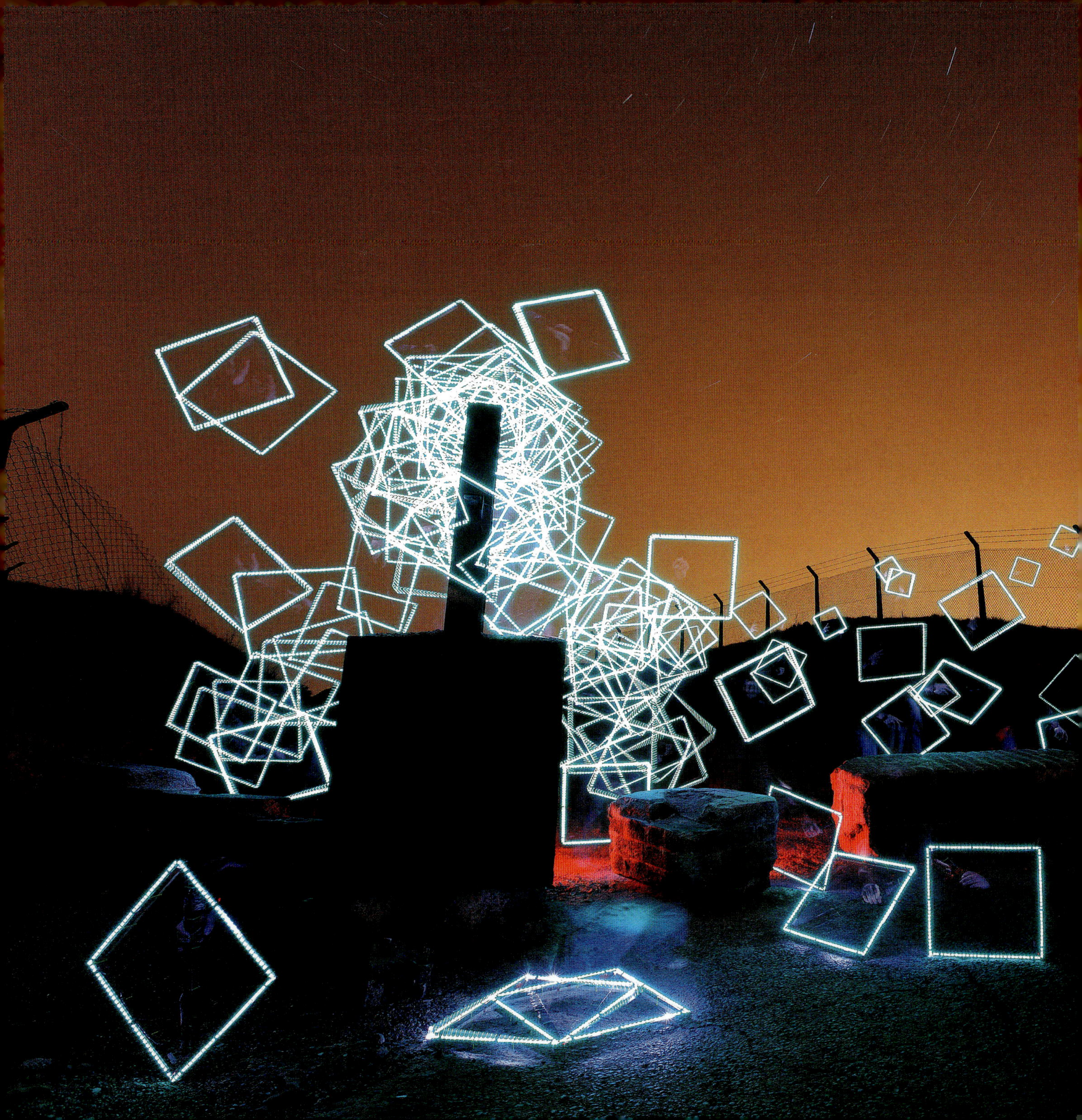

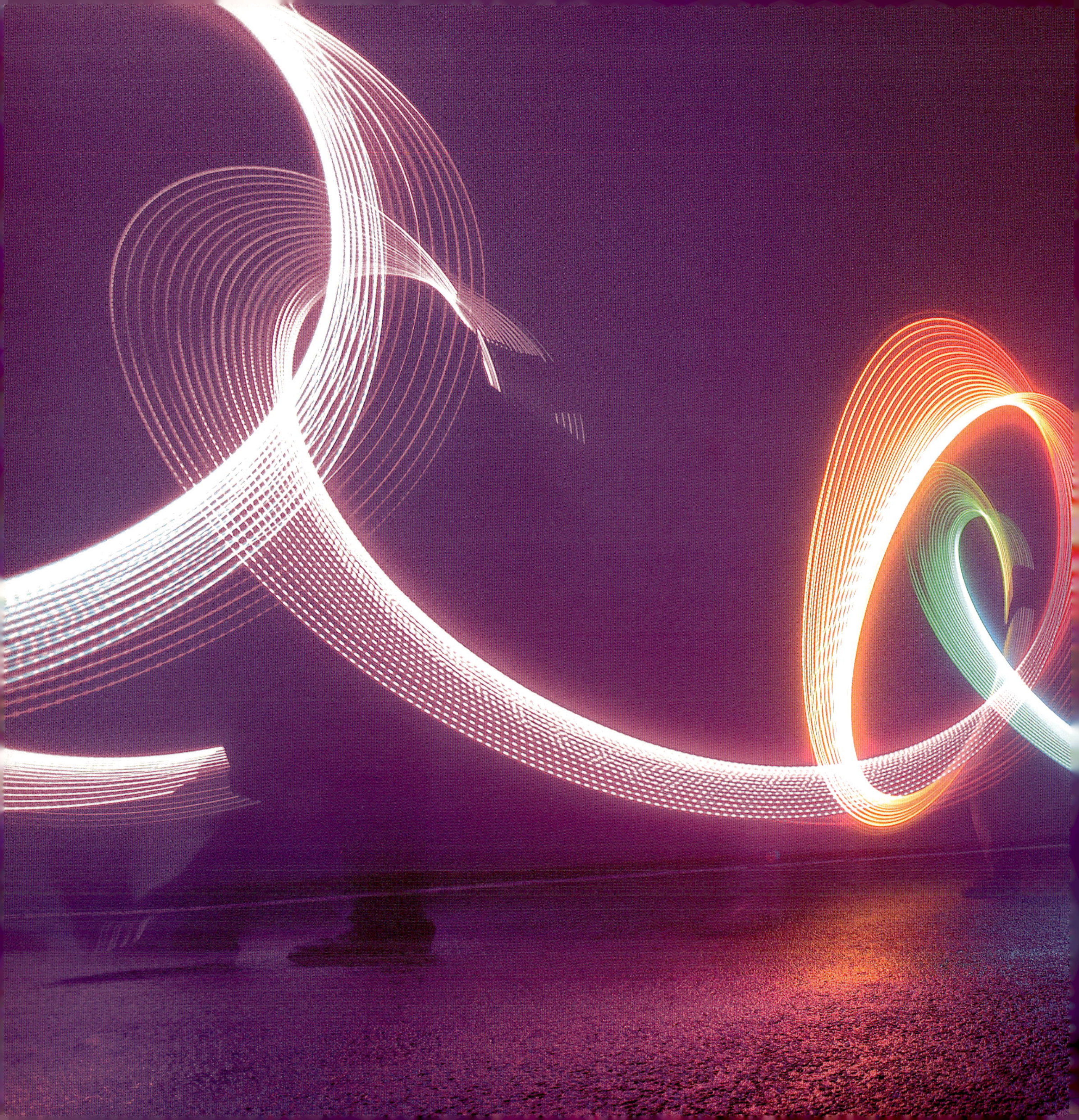

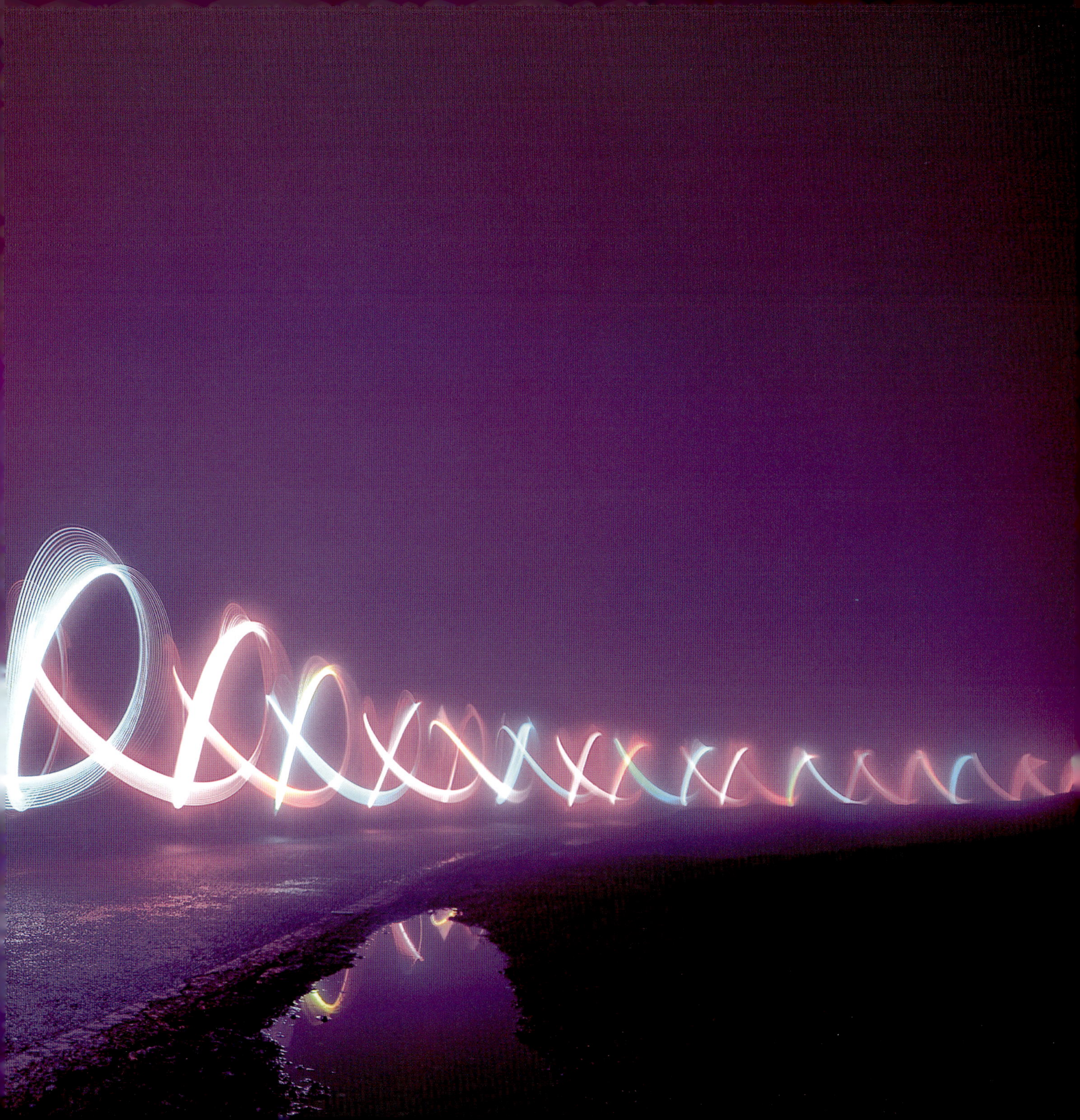

ROBERT OVERWEG

www.shotbyrobert.com

Video games aren't without their quirks. Programming glitches can generate buildings, figures or empty space in places where they don't belong. Sometimes the virtual world simply ends – the buildings stop and nothingness begins. Dutch artist Robert Overweg scours the outer reaches of the gaming world looking for these anomalies, documenting what he finds as works of art.

In the *Flying and Floating* series of images Robert takes us to the outer limits of Empire Bay, the vast fictional host city for *Mafia 2*, where 1950s American mobsters shoot it out for supremacy. But he ignores the guns and the gunslingers, searching out the dead space instead. He travels down dead ends and finds the buildings fragmenting or the roads disappearing into a foggy grey void. In Robert's images iron fire-escapes hang in the air and the rooflines of buildings levitate above absent walls. There is no editing work involved, no collage – everything photographed by Robert appears as it does on screen. The artist views himself as an explorer, trawling the virtual world in search of those places where things don't quite work, where the cracks appear and the natural order falls apart.

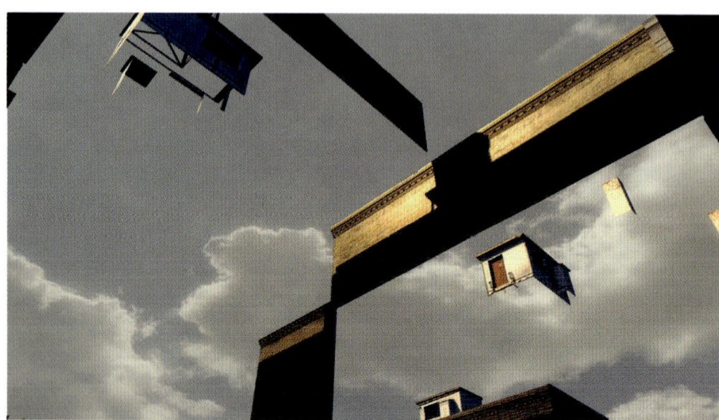

APARTMENT ONE, MAFIA 2
APARTMENT TWO, MAFIA 2 (Left)
HOTEL, MAFIA 2 (Overleaf)

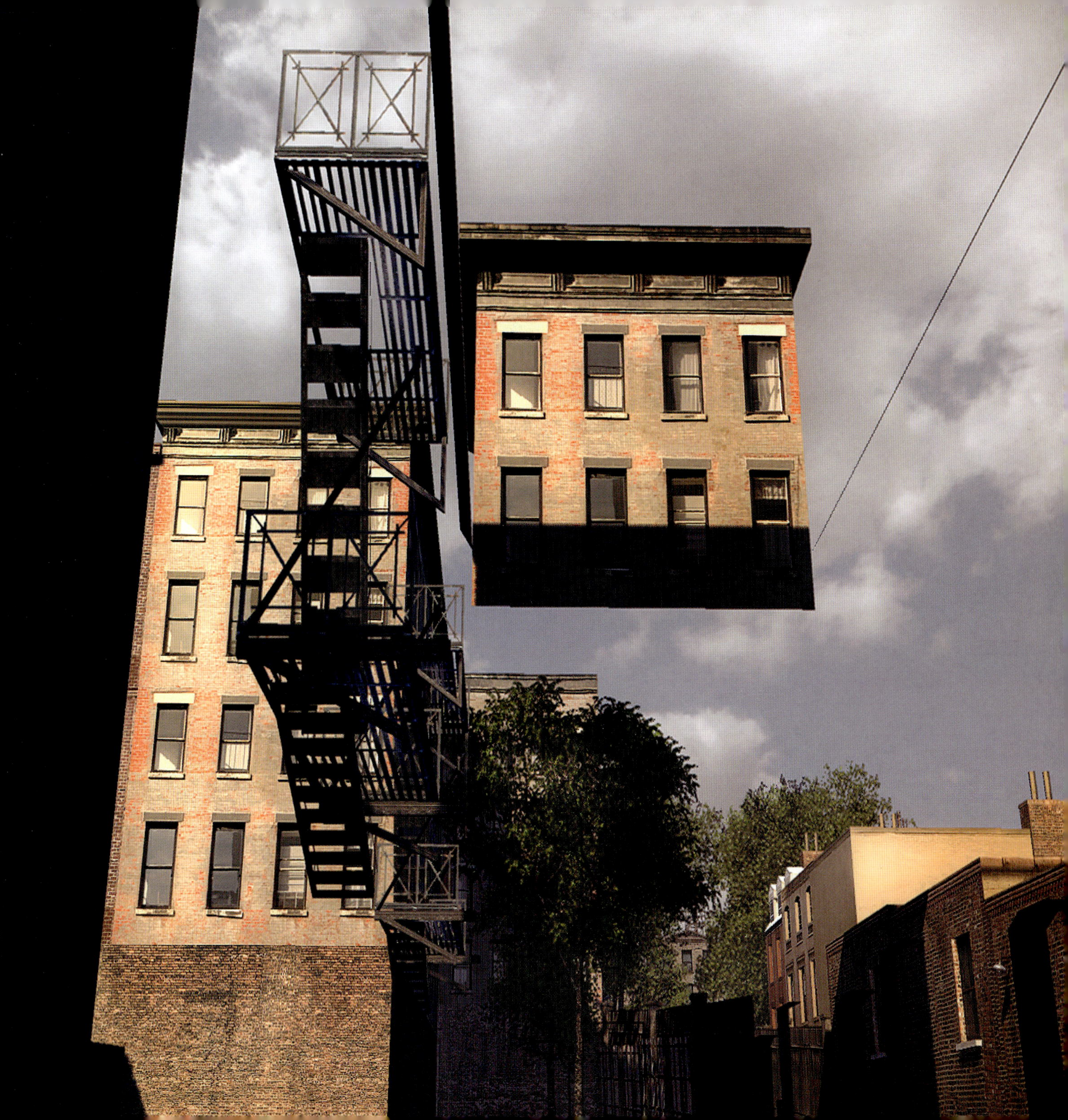

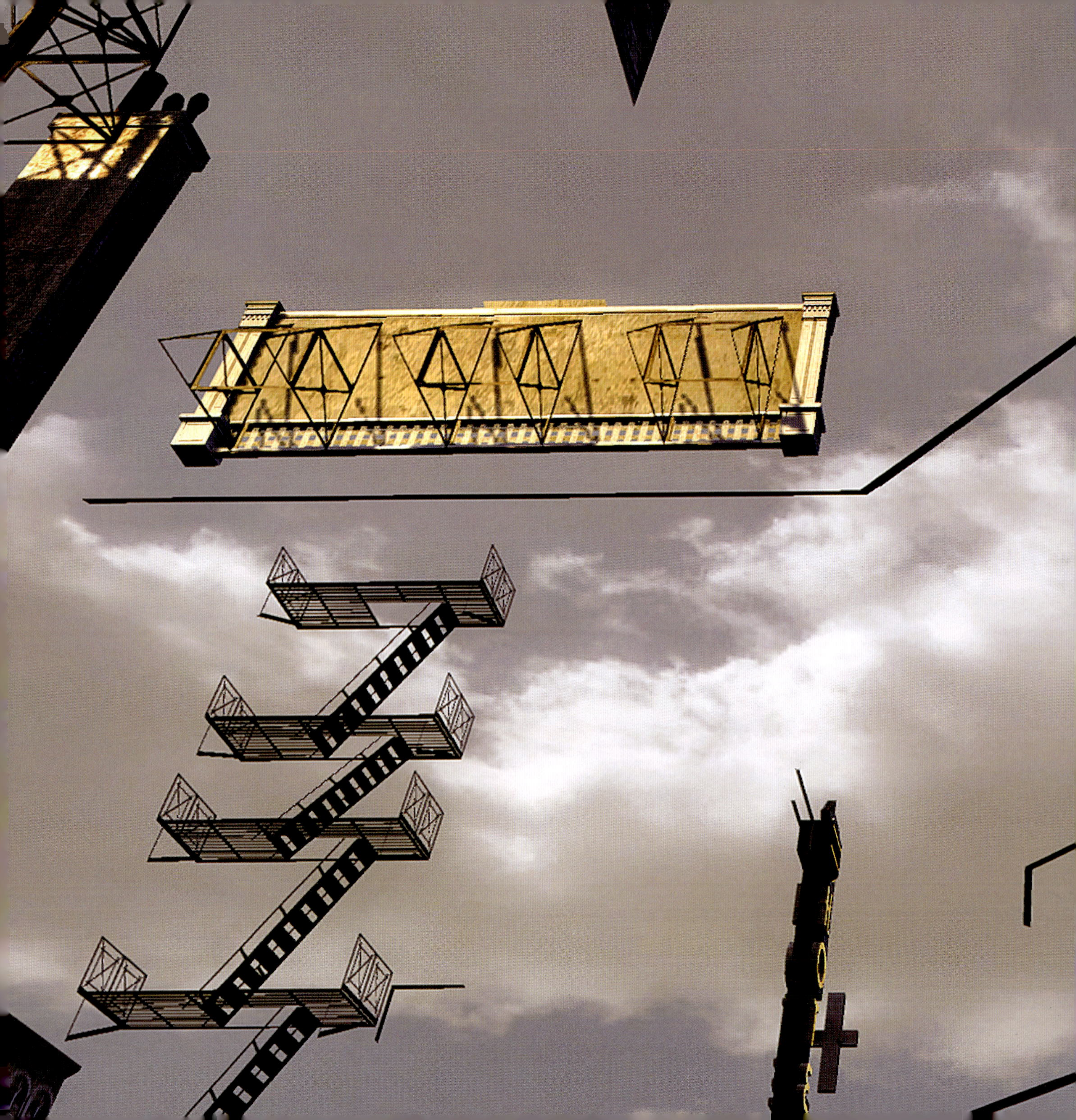

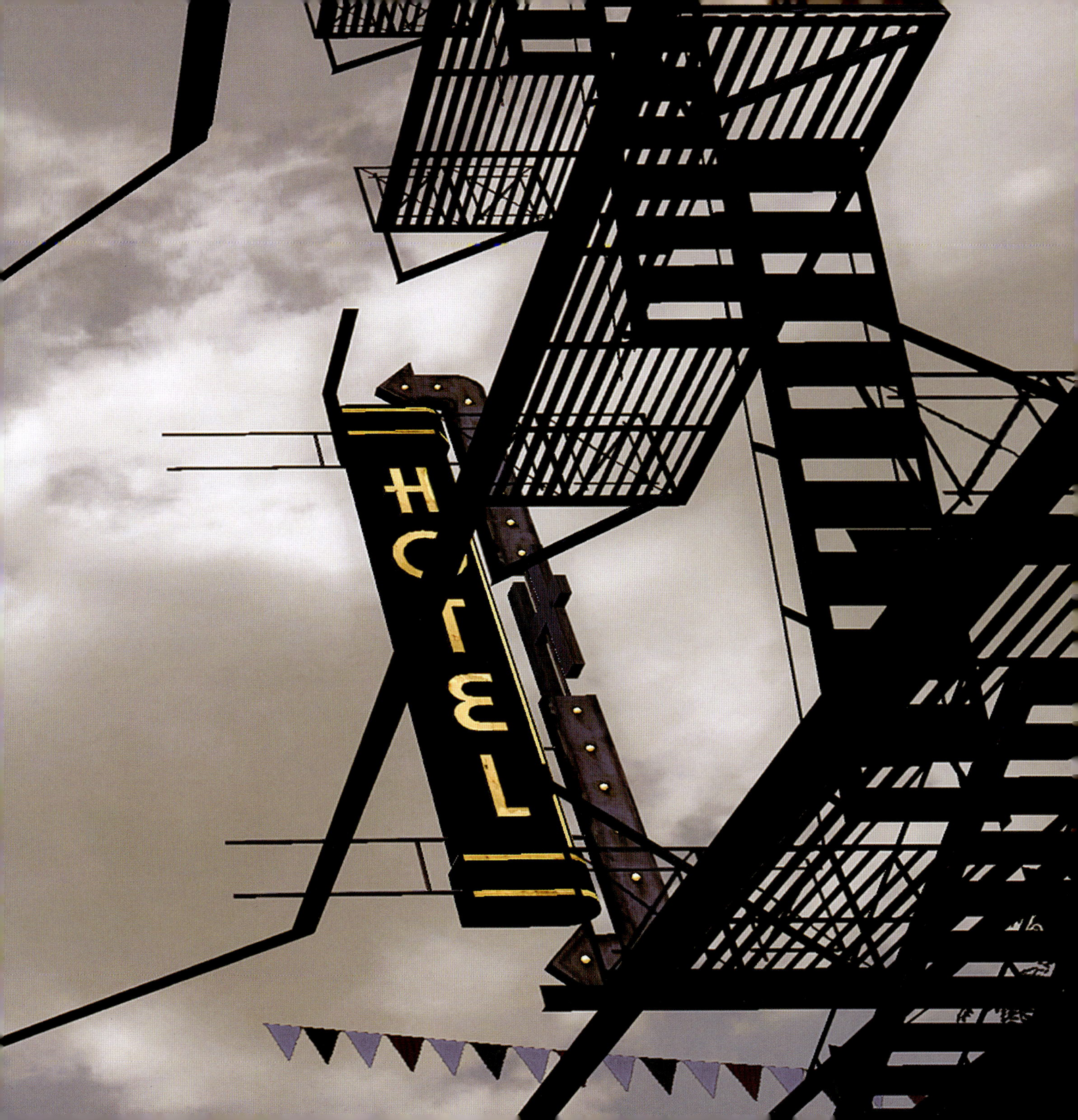

JAIME JASSO

www.jjassodigitalworks.com

The cigarette has long been an artist's prop, most often poised between the lips of a photographer's muse. However, in Jaime Hernández Jasso's cleverly manipulated photography, the cigarette itself becomes the work of art.

The Mexican artist, now working in California, is multi-talented, dividing his time between creating special effects for the cinema and video game industries, developing matte paintings (in which empty spaces are left, ready for the incorporation of filmed scenes) and producing digitally enhanced photographic images. Much of his time and talent is ploughed into creating futuristic cities reminiscent of Fritz Lang's *Metropolis*, but Jaime also devotes attention to smaller scale cityscapes, notably those in the *Cigarette City* series of images. The series depicts a number of smouldering cigarettes, each revealing an ashen city as the tobacco burns away. Look closely and you may well recognise the city, its identity revealed by the tiny grey monuments. For example, on the far left of one image you can see the Kingdom Centre Tower, and then the King Fahd international stadium – it can only be Riyadh, capital of Saudi Arabia. Jaime's work is one hundred per cent manipulated – everything you see is created in Photoshop.

CIGARETTE CITY

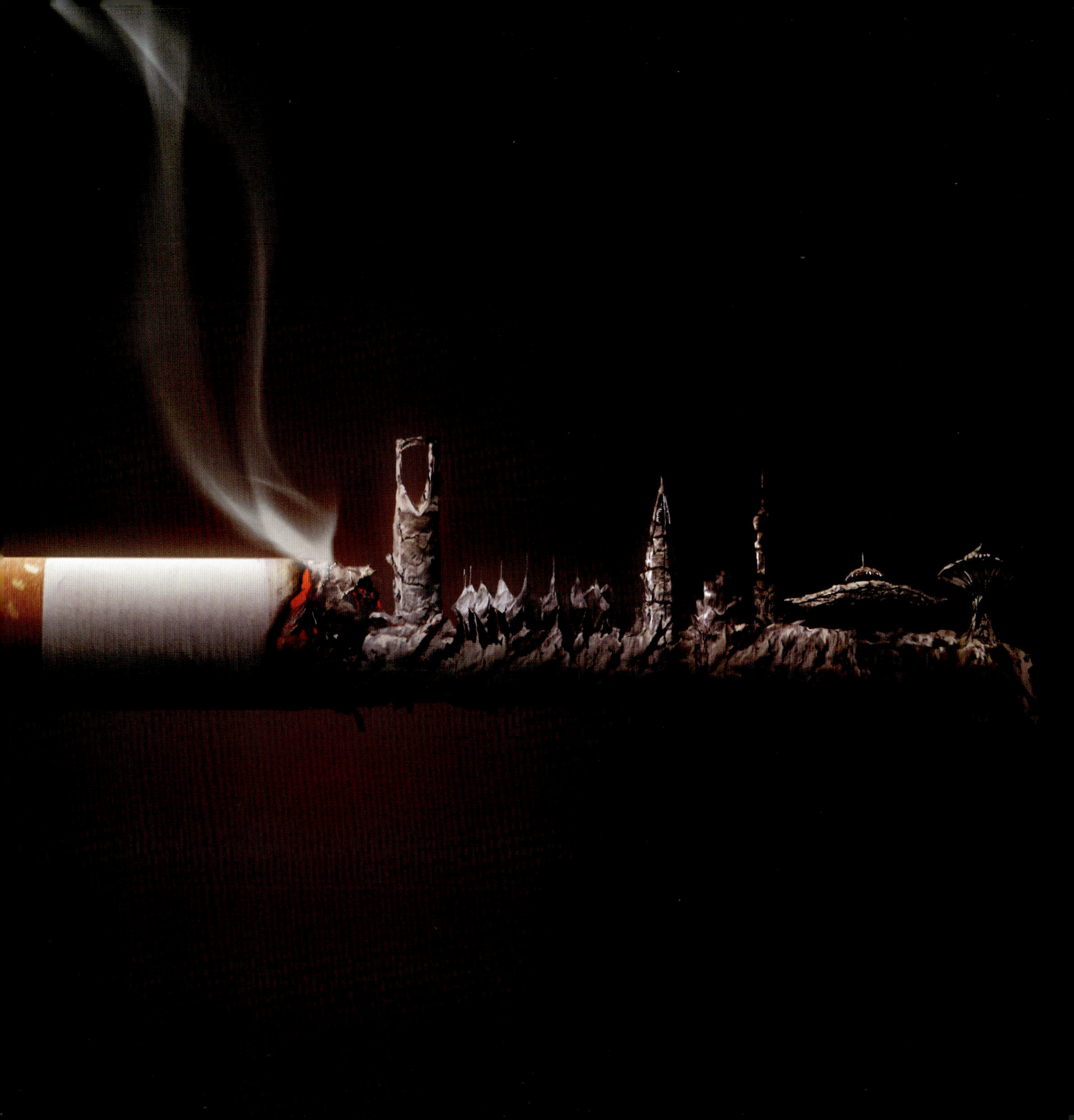

LI WEI

www.liweiart.com

Given the tools at his disposal in the digital age, we should marvel at the fact that Li Wei's absorbing photographs use none of them. Instead, he prefers the analogue-age charms of wires, mirrors, scaffolding and ladders.

The Chinese artist, endowed with the skills of a tightrope walker and gymnast, combines photography with performance art. In Li's world women fire off men from longbows and figures apparently hover in the trees or swing each other around at head height by the ankles whilst leaning out over vertiginous drops. Invariably, Li himself is the figure being flung skywards, buried head first in the ground or pushed off a tall building. It's unclear exactly how Li stages the images, but they're unfailingly powerful, created for more than mere curiosity. The artist questions the laws of gravity, but also draws the audience towards the themes of globalisation and, in particular, China's rapidly urbanising society. He reveals a certain scepticism about the future of his country, even whilst filling the photographs with a rich vein of humour.

ARROW OF LOVE

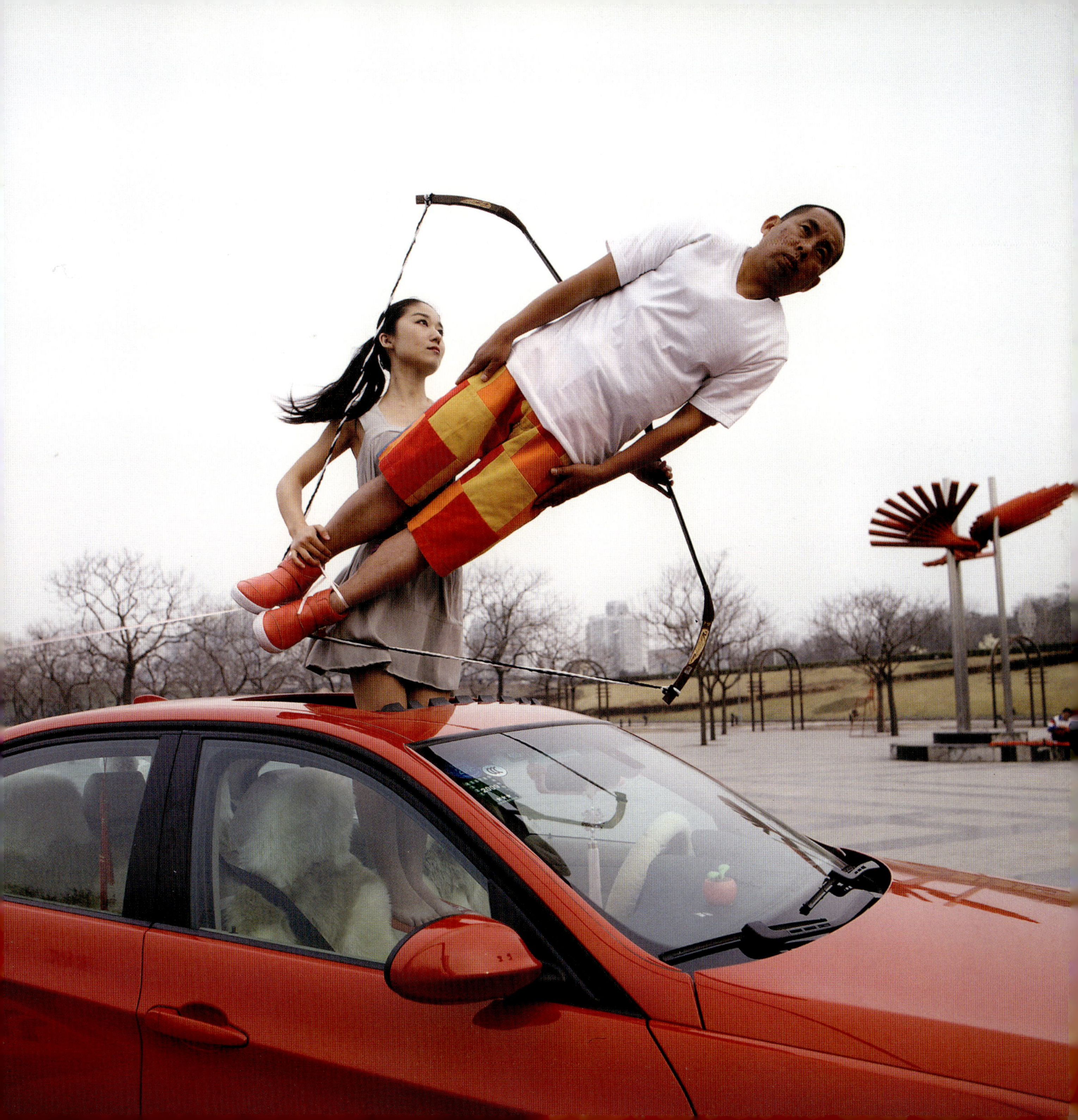

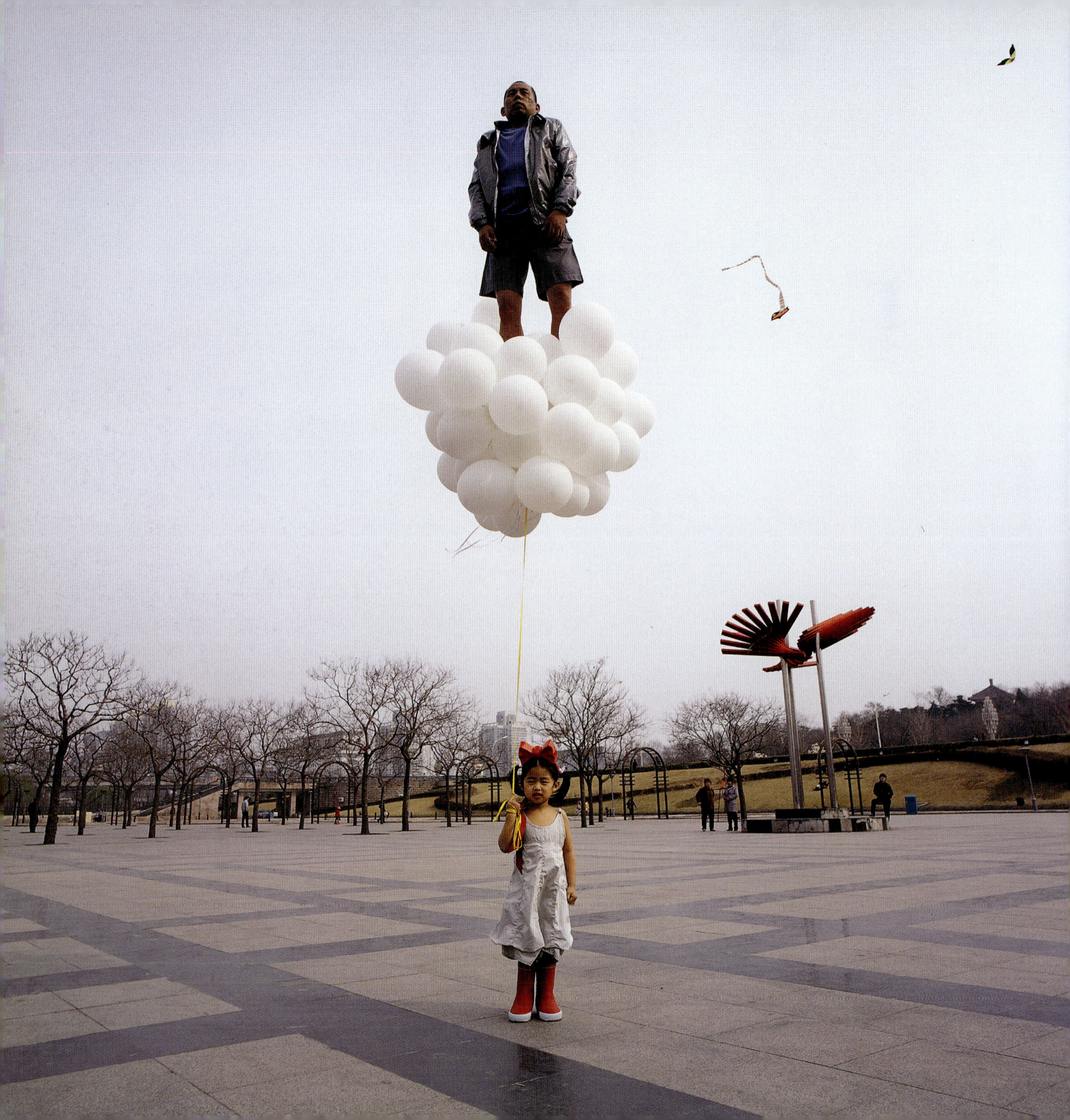

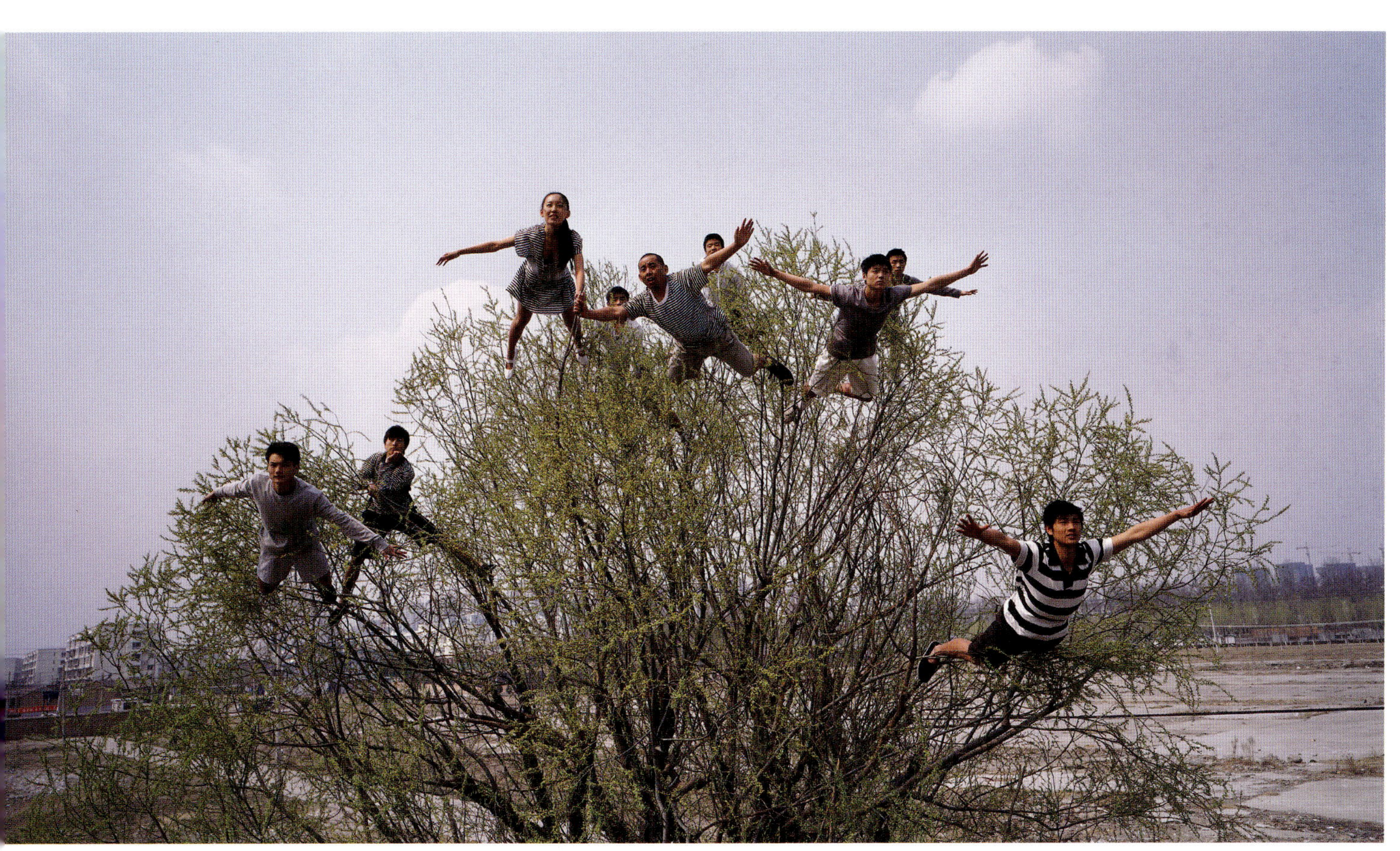

LIVE AT THE HIGH PLACE 7
BALLOONS 2 (Left)

ERIK JOHANSSON

www.alltelleringet.com

Erik Johansson is blessed with a vivid imagination. Where most of us see a rocky island sitting serenely in a Nordic harbour, Erik sees what lies beneath – a giant fish that carries the island on its back. Or where a digger gouges tarmac from the road, he imagines a giant game of noughts and crosses unfurling as the machine scours the dirt.

The twenty-four-year-old Swede works in the tradition of the illusionists; artists like M.C. Escher, who created famously infinite worlds using pencil and paper. Where Escher employed conventional materials, Erik uses the camera and Photoshop software. Having shot the required images, he spends around ten hours manipulating and retouching each one to achieve the desired effect. His work is both audacious and mischievous, drawing inspiration from everyday life but fusing the mundane with the absurd. 'For me photography is just a way to collect material to realise the ideas in my mind,' he explains. 'I get inspired by things around me in my daily life and all kinds of things that I see.'

ROADWORKERS' COFFEE BREAK

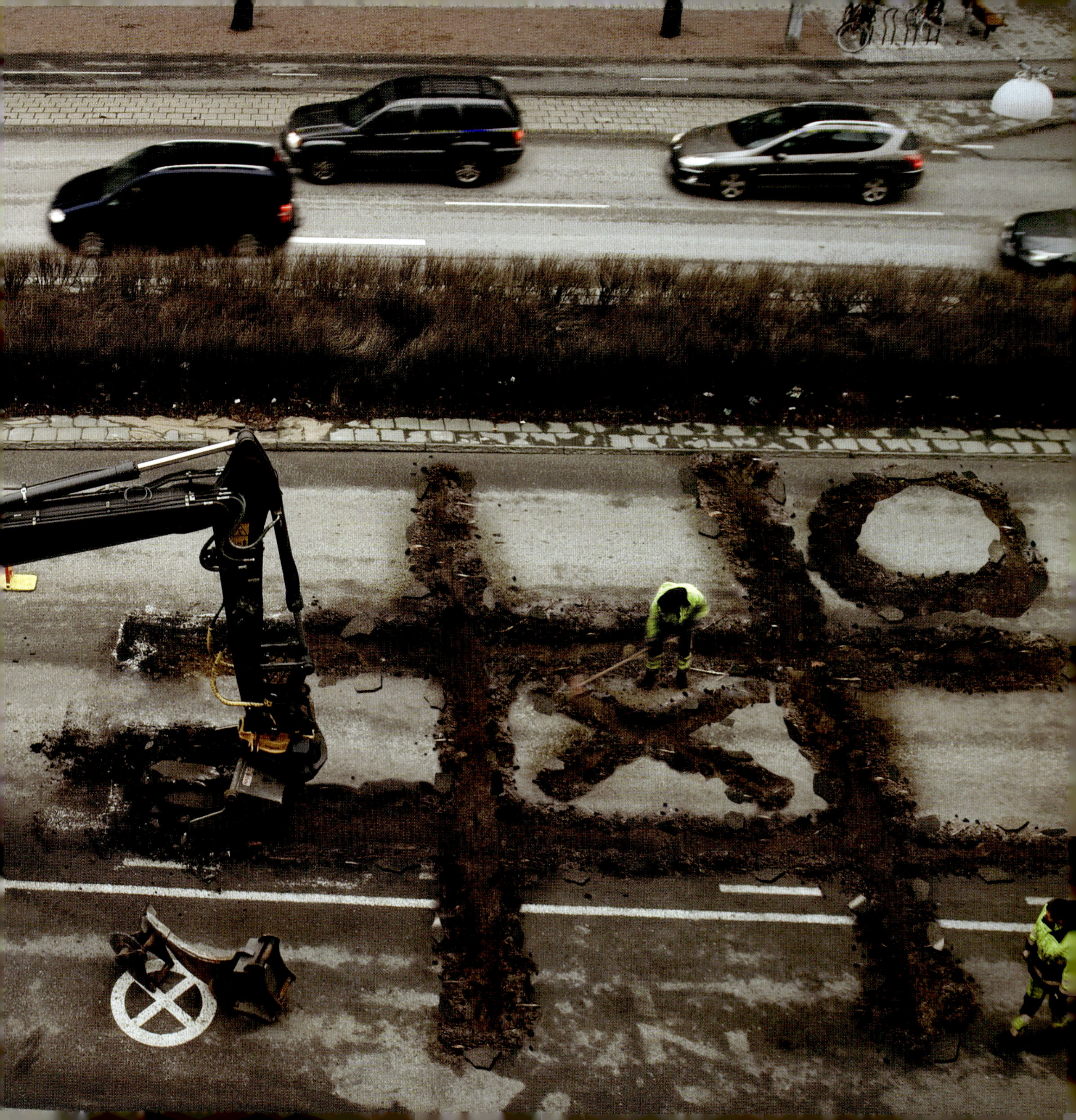

THOMAS EDWARDS

www.thomasedwards.com.au & www.ujinlee.com

The beguiling *Dust* series of images generates many more questions than it answers. The artists' intent is unclear. What exactly is that powder? And what are they hoping to convey through its release into the air?

The series was born of a collaboration between Sydney-based photographers Thomas Edwards and Ujin Lee. Each print depicts a cloud of white powder, suspended mid-scene rather like a swarm of tiny insects. Art galleries, roads, factories and waste ground all provide a setting for the palls of fine dust. The creative technique behind the series is unclear; the artists haven't revealed how they produce the photographs. One hypothesis has them exploding anti-smudge powder (of the sort used in printing) and then capturing the results on camera using a rapid shutter speed. Another suggests the photographs might be digitally manipulated. Whatever the processes involved, with their clouds of short-lived debris – the dust so redolent of decay – the images spotlight the ephemeral nature of life.

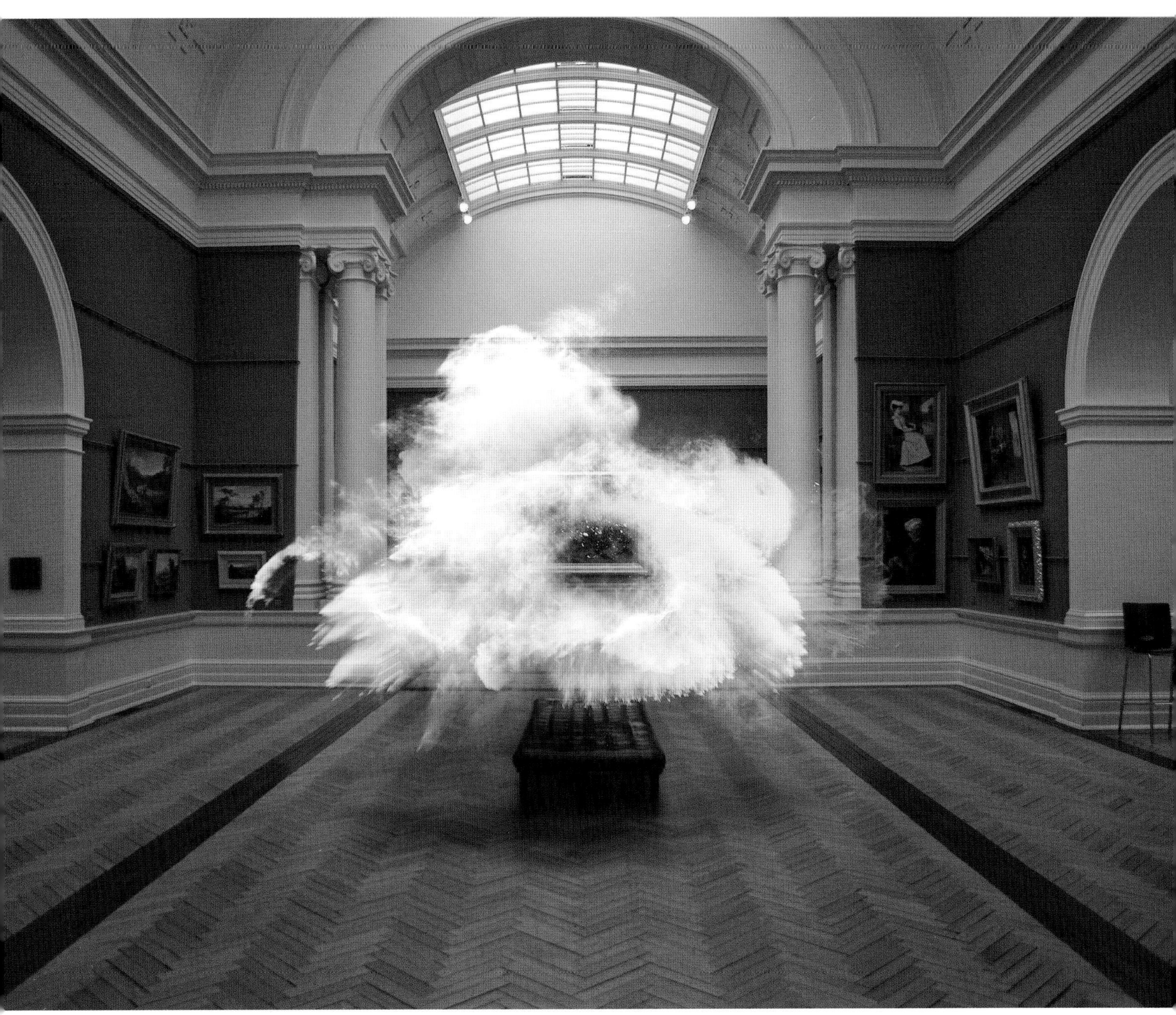

CECELIA WEBBER

www.ceceliawebber.com

It was in the course of taking a series of traditional nude photographs that Cecelia Webber noticed the uncanny similarity between the human back, with its contours and curves, and the natural shape of a flower petal.

She went on to create the *Flower* series, a collection of photographs in which the colourful, elegant flowers are composed entirely of multiple naked human forms. A recent graduate of the University of Southern California, Cecelia was a devotee of painting in acrylics before she began exploring the possibilities of digital photography. The *Flower* images begin life as a series of carefully posed individual photographs, which are then retouched, before being gathered together – sometimes in their hundreds – and shaped into the final photograph. Each print can take up to a month to produce. For Cecelia, the hardest part of the process lies in planning how each pose will relate to the next. Viewed from a distance, the component elements of the photographs aren't clear; only on closer inspection are the stems and petals revealed as human figures. Cecelia hopes the images will alter the traditional perceptions of nudity, helping us to consider the human body within the context of the natural world from which it comes.

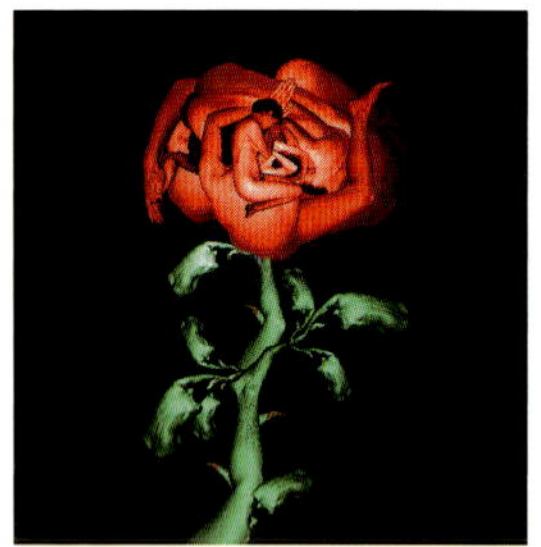

WHITE DANDELION
ROSE (Left)

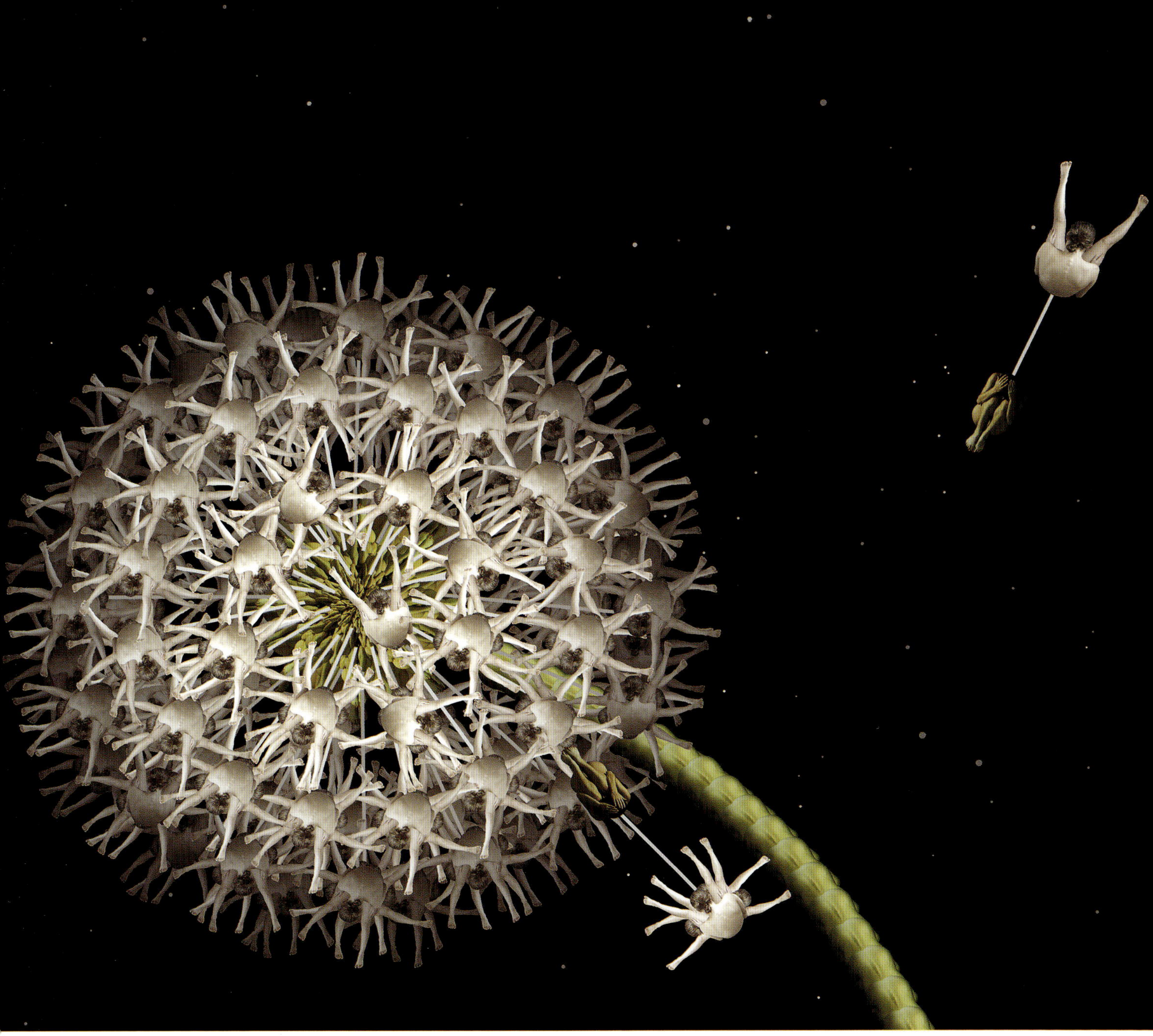

LORI NIX

www.lorinix.net

Everything that you see in Lori Nix's photographs exists – the images haven't been retouched. Each work in *The City* series features a miniature post-apocalyptic landscape, painstakingly crafted at tabletop scale by Lori over a period of several months.

The Brooklyn-based artist describes herself as a 'non-traditional' photographer, in so much as the subject matter is manufactured rather than 'found'. She depicts the decline of humanity, photographing a city devoid of inhabitants and in which the man-made structures decay – the museums, theatres and bars being reclaimed by Mother Nature. The influence of the great Romantic painters, so adept at rendering both horror and beauty, is clear. In Lori's work the danger and disaster is, however, tempered by a touch of humour, a manifestation, she says, of the sense of euphoria that a child might take from natural calamities such as a snowstorm, flood or insect infestation. In describing *The City* series, where the flora, fauna and insects reclaim the landscape that was theirs before man's encroachment, Lori comments: 'I am afraid of what the future holds if we do not change our ways regarding climate, but at the same time I am fascinated by what a changing world can bring.

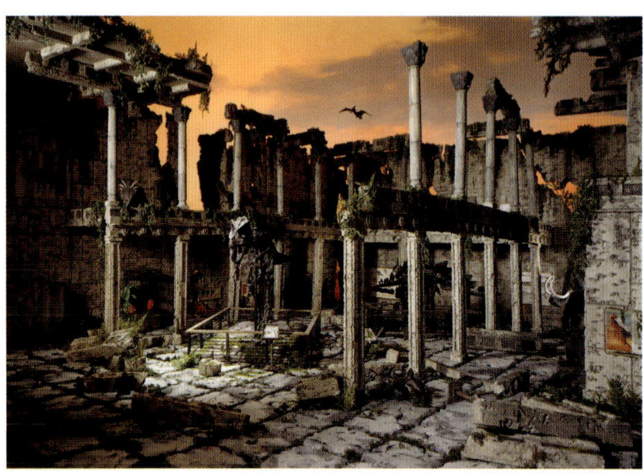

LIBRARY
GREAT HALL (Left)
MAP ROOM (Overleaf)

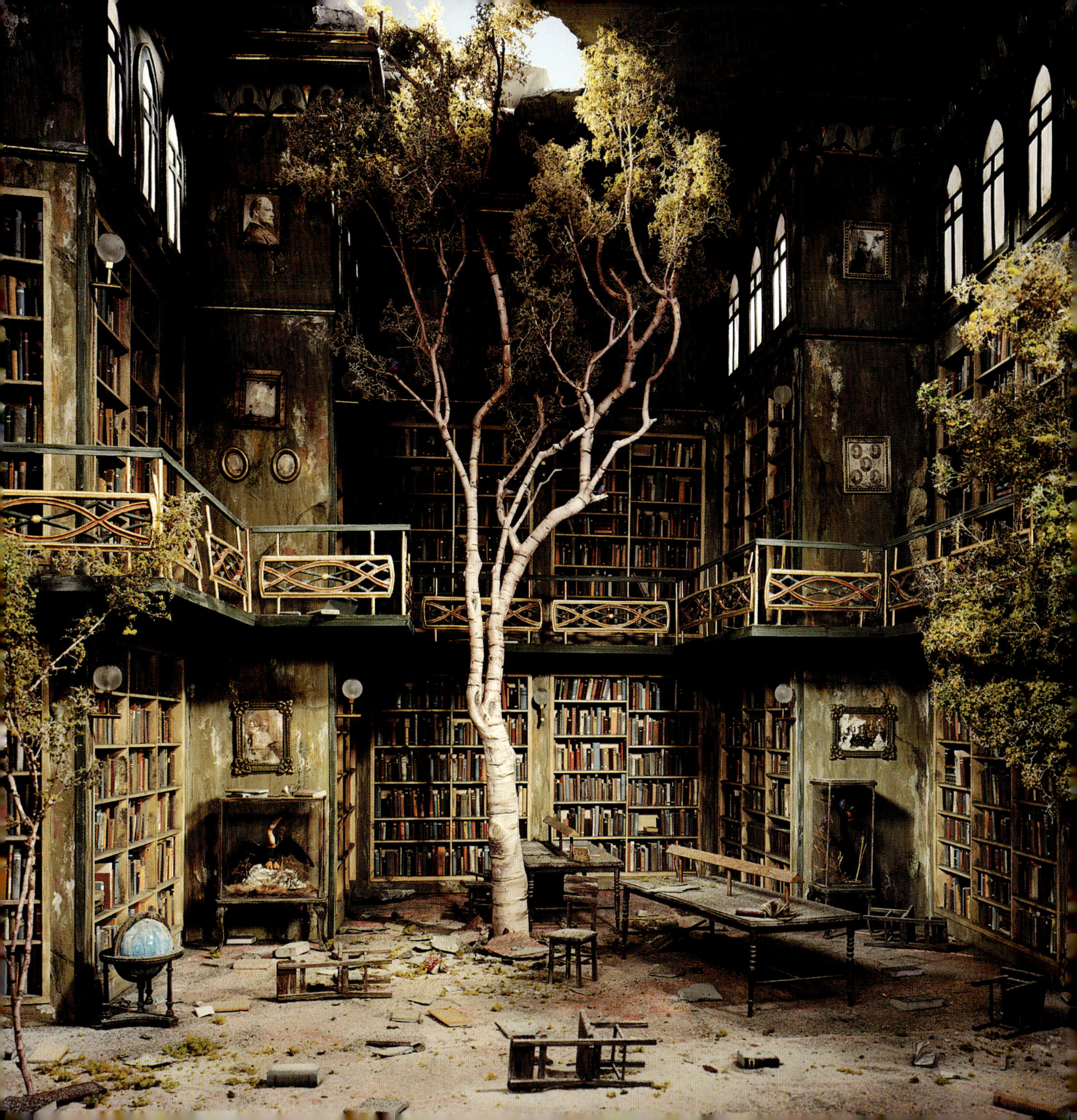

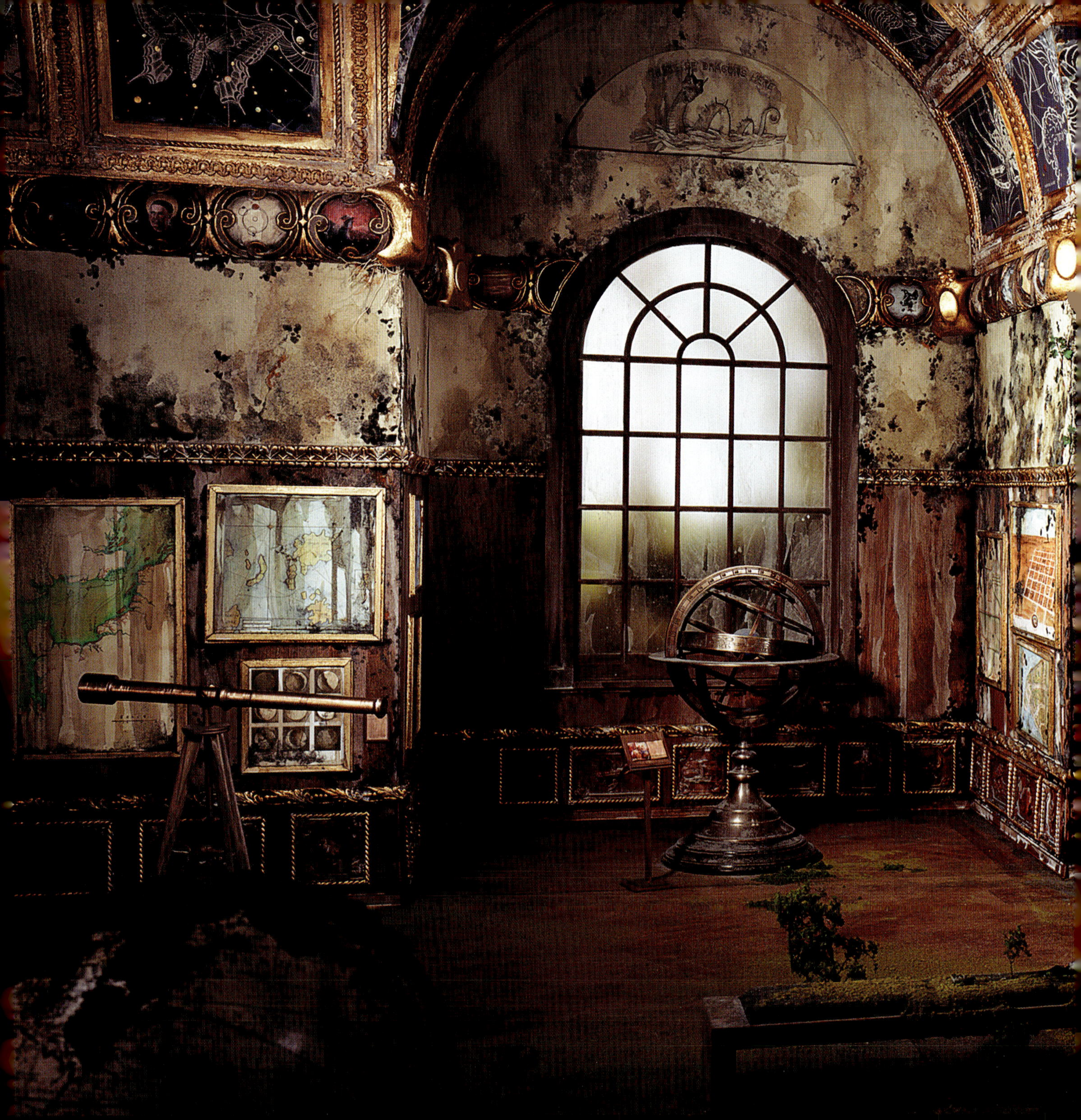

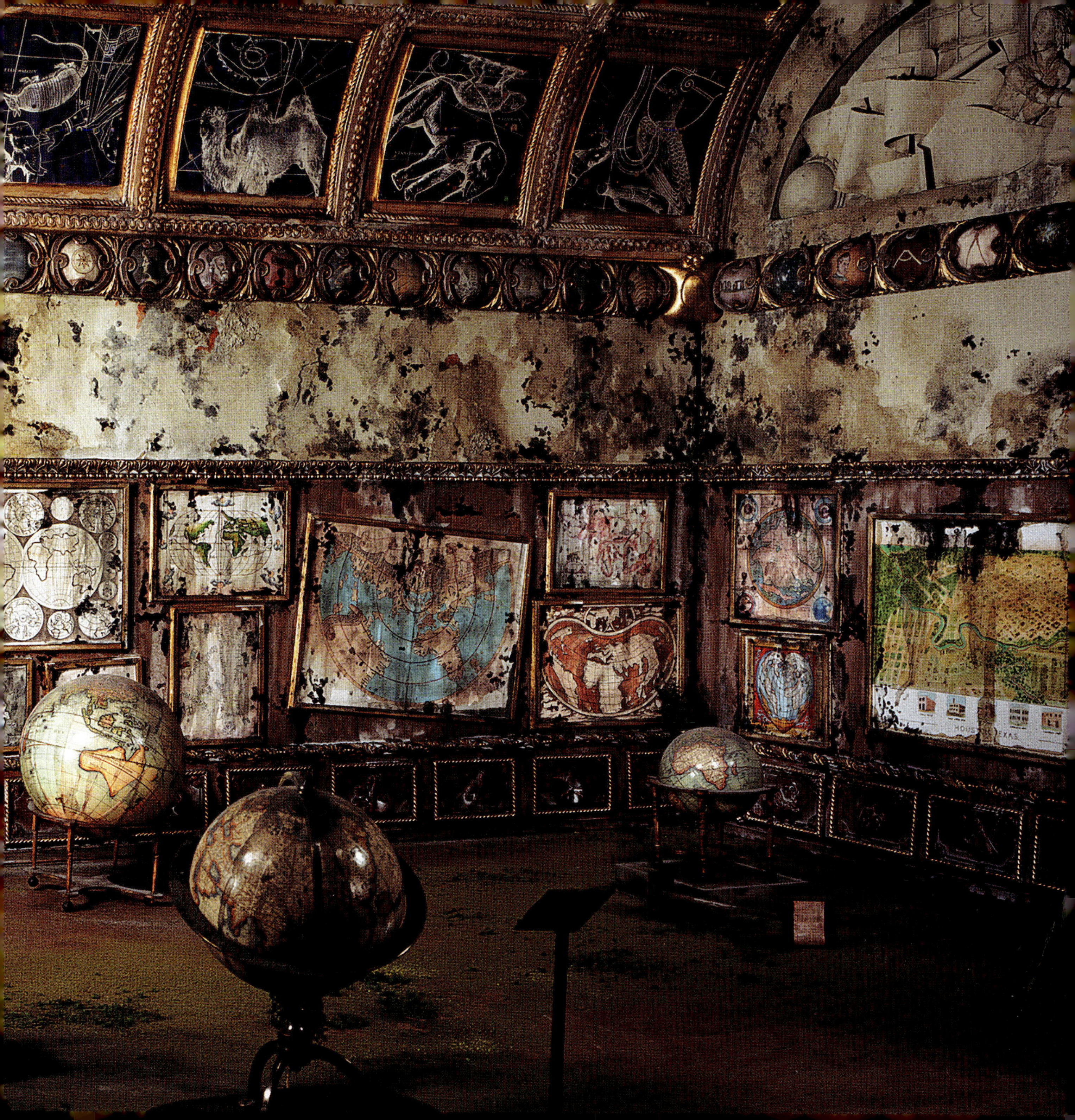

PHOTO CREDITS

4: ©Ari Mahardhika; 6: ©Levi van Veluw courtesy Ronmandos gallery; 6: ©Studio Parris Wakefield; 7: ©Jan Oliehoek; 7: ©Jaime Jasso; 11, 12, 13: ©Iain Crawford; 15: ©Ari Mahardhika; 17, 18, 19: ©Alex Castro; 21, 22, 23: ©Levi van Veluw courtesy Ronmandos gallery; 25: ©Alberto Seveso; 27: ©Bernard Demenge; 29, 30, 31: ©Phillip Toledano; 33, 34, 35: ©Giuseppe Mastromatteo of FabbricaEos Milan and Emmanuel Freming Gallery New York; 36, 37, 38-39: ©Romain Laurent; 41, 42, 43: ©Jens Sage; 45, 46, 47: ©Liu Bolin and Eli Klein Fine Art; 49: ©Mohammed Amine Nasseri; 53, 54-55: ©Carl Warner carlwarner.com; 57: ©Michael Hughes/ EUP&Images; 59, 60, 61: ©Studio Parris Wakefield; 62, 63: ©Todd McLellan; 65: ©Jack Ambridge; 67, 68, 69: ©Yang Yi; 71, 72, 73: ©Alexandre Orion; 75: ©Pep Ventosa; 77, 78, 79: ©Barry Underwood; 80, 81, 82-83: ©Michael Paul Smith; 84, 85, 86, 87: ©Pierre Javelle & Akiko Ida; 91, 92, 93: ©Jan Oliehoek; 95, 96, 97: ©Jonathan Hobin; 99, 100, 101: ©Laurence Demaison; 103, 104, 105: ©Liu Di, photo and text courtesy of the artist and Pékin Fine Arts; 107: ©Lucas C. Simões – unportraits; 109: ©Anton Semenov; 111, 112, 113: ©Anthony Hibbert; 114, 115, 116-117: ©Taylor James Studio; 119: ©Jérôme Abramovitch; 121: ©Hilary Pecis; 123, 124, 125: ©Cristian Crisis; 127, 128, 129: ©Marc Da Cunha Lopes; 133: ©Anton Marrast; 135: ©Aled Lewis; 136, 137, 138-139: ©Michael Bosanko; 140, 141, 142-143: ©Robert Overweg; 145: ©Jaime Jasso; 147, 148, 149: ©Li Wei; 151: ©Erik Johansson; 153: ©Thomas Edwards & Ujin Lee; 154, 155: ©2008-2011 Cecelia Webber; 156, 157, 158-159: ©Lori Nix.